ROMAN MOSAICS IN BRITAIN

AN INTRODUCTION TO THEIR SCHEMES AND A CATALOGUE OF PAINTINGS

ROMAN MOSAICS IN BRITAIN

AN INTRODUCTION TO THEIR SCHEMES AND A CATALOGUE OF PAINTINGS

BY

David S Neal

Central Excavation Unit, Department of the Environment

ALAN SUTTON
1981

Alan Sutton Publishing Limited
17a Brunswick Road
Gloucester GL1 1HG

Published by arrangement with
Society for the Promotion of Roman Studies

British Library Cataloguing in Publication Data

Typesetting & origination by
Alan Sutton Publishing Limited

Printed in Great Britain by
Redwood Burn Limited
Trowbridge & Esher

Microfiche produced by
Bell & Howell Limited
Micromedia Division

CONTENTS

LIST OF PLATES AND MOSAICS

NOTE: The plate number conforms to the mosaic number (except No 88 from Brantingham for which there is no description in the catalogue).

LIST OF FIGURES IN THE TEXT

ABBREVIATIONS

Antiq. Journ.	*Antiquaries Journal;*
Arch. Journ.	*Archaeological Journal*
B.A.R.	*British Archaeological Reports*
B.M.Q.	*British Museum Quarterly*
Bull.A.I.E.M.A.	*Bulletin de L'Association Internationale pour L'etude de la Mosaïque Antique*
Bull.B.C.S.	*Bulletin Board Celtic Studies*
Catalogue	*Catalogue.* Newsletter of the Colchester Archaeological Trust
C.A.	*Current Archaeology*
Dorset N.H. & A.F.C.	*Dorset Natural History and Archaeological Field Club*
Gents. Mag.	*Gentlemans Magazine*
Hants. Chron.	*Hampshire Chronicle*
JRS	*Journal of Roman Studies*
NPP.	Not previously published
Port.	Portfolio
P.D.A.E.S.	*Proceedings Devon Archaeological Exploration Society*
P.D.N.A.S.	*Proceedings Dorset Natural History and Archaeological Society*
Proc. Somerset A.N.H.S.	*Proceedings Somerset Archaeological and Natural History Society*
R.C.H.M.	Royal Commission on Historical Monuments
S.A.L.	Society of Antiquaries of London
Surrey A.C.	*Surrey Archaeological Collections*
Top. Coll.	Topographical Collections of the Society of Antiquaries of London
Trans.	Transactions
Trans. B.G.A.S.	*Transactions Bristol and Gloucestershire Archaeological Society*
Trans. E.R.A.S.	*Transactions East Riding Antiquarian Society*
Trans. E.A.S.	*Transactions Essex Archaeological Society*
Trans. Leics. A. & H.S.	*Transactions Leicestershire Archaeological and Historical Society*
Vet. Mon.	*Vetusta Monumenta*
VCH	*Victoria County History*
W.A.M.	*Wiltshire Archaeological Magazine*
Y.A.J.	*Yorkshire Archaeological Journal*

REFERENCES AND BIBLIOGRAPHY

Alexander and Ennaïfer 1975: M. Alexander and M. Ennaïfer. 'Quelques Précisions à propos de la Chronologie des Mosaïques d'Utique' in *La Mosaïque Greco-Romaine ii* (Centre Nationale de la Récherche Scientifique, Paris 1975), 31-39.

Anthony 1961: I. Anthony, 'A Roman Building at Gorhambury, St. Albans.' *Trans. St. Albans Architectural & Archaeological Society* 1961, 21-30.

Artis 1828: E.T. Artis, *The Durobrivae of Antoninus 1828*

Ashby *et al.*1902: T. Ashby, A.E. Hudd and A.T. Martin. 'Excavations at Caerwent, Monmouthshire, on the Site of the Romano-British City of Venta Silurum, in 1901.' *Archaeologia* 58, 1902, 119-52.

Ashby 1905: T. Ashby, 'Excavations at Caerwent, Monmouthshire, on the Site of the Romano-British City of Venta Silurum in the year 1904.' *Arch. Journ.* lix 1905, 289-310.

Barker 1900: W.R. Barker, 'Remains of a Roman Villa Discovered at Brislington, Bristol. 1899. *Trans. B.G.A.S.* 23, 1900, 289-308.

Bathurst 1879: W.H. Bathurst, *Roman Antiquities at Lydney Park, Gloucestershire,* 1879.

Becatti 1961: G. Becatti, *Scavi di Ostia iv, Mosaici e Pavimenti Marmorei.* Istituto Poligrafico Dello Stato (Rome), 1961.

Beesley 1841: A. Beesley, *History of Banbury* 1841.

Bidwell 1979: P.T. Bidwell, *The Legionary Bath House and Basilica and Forum at Exeter.* Exeter Arch. Reports i, 1979.

Boon 1950: G.C. Boon, 'The Roman Villa in Kingsweston Park . . . Gloucester'. *Trans. B.G.A.S.* lxix, 1950, 1-58.

Boon 1960-62: G.C. Boon 'The Mosaic Pavement from Backhall Street, Caerleon'. *Bull. B.C.S.* 19, 1960-62, 348-54.

Brakspear 1904: H. Brakspear, 'The Roman Villa at Box, Wiltshire.' *Arch. Journ.* 61, 1904, 1-32.

Brown *et al* 1969: P.D.C. Brown, A.D. McWhirr and D.J. Smith, 'Cirencester, 1967-8. Eighth Interim Report.' *Antiq. Journ.* xlix, 1969, 222-43.

Brown Port.: Brown Portfolios in the Library of the Society of Antiquaries of London.

Buckman and Newmarch 1850: J. Buckman and C.H. Newmarch, *Remains of Roman Art. The Site of Ancient Corinium,* 1850.

Bulleid and Horne 1924-6:
A. Bulleid and E.E. Horne, 'The Roman House at Keynsham, Somerset.' *Archaeologia* 75, 1924-26, 109-38.

Butcher 1955:
S.A. Butcher, 'Interim Report on Excavations in St. George's Street, Winchester 1954', *Proc. Hants. Field Club* xix pt. I, 1955, 2-12.

Clark 1935:
M.K. Clark, *Gazetteer of Roman Remains in E. Yorks,* 1935

Clifford 1933:
E.M. Clifford, 'The Roman Villa, Hucclecote near Gloucester.' *Trans. B.G.A.S.* 55, 1933, 323-76.

Clifford 1946-8:
E.M. Clifford, 'Mosaic Floor at Cirencester.' *Trans. B.G.A.S.* 67, 1946-8, 381-95.

Colebrooke Reade 1885:
R. Colebrooke Reade, 'The Roman Villa at Great Wemberham in Yatton.' *Proc. Somerset A.N.H.S.* 31, 1885, 64-73.

Colley March 1900:
Hy Colley March, 'On some Roman Pavements . . .' *Dorset N.H. & A.F.C.* 21, 1900

Collier 1906:
C.V. Collier, 'The Roman Remains at Harpham'. *Trans. E.R.A.S.* xiii, 1906, 141-52.

Corder 1951-1961:
P. Corder, *The Roman Town and Villa at Great Casterton, Rutland.* First Interim Report 1951; Second Interim Report for the years 1951-1953, 1954; Third Report for the years 1954-1958, 1961. University of Nottingham

Cunliffe 1969:
B.W. Cunliffe, *Roman Bath,* Reports of the Research Committee of the Society of Antiquaries of London, No. XXIV, 1969.

Cunliffe 1971:
B.W. Cunliffe, *Excavation at Fishbourne 1961-1969,* Vol i. Reports of the Research Committee of the Society of Antiquaries of London. No. XXVI, 1971

Daniels 1966:
C.M. Daniels, 'Excavations on the site of the Roman Villa at Southwell', *Trans. Thoroton Soc. of Nottinghamshire* lxx, 1966, 33-40.

Dent 1877:
E. Dent, *Annals of Winchcombe and Sudeley,* 1877.

Dorigo 1971:
Wladimiro Dorigo, *Late Roman Painting,* 1971

Down and Rule 1971:
A. Down and M. Rule, *Chichester Excavations* Vol. i, 1971.

Down 1979:
A. Down, *Chichester Excavations 4: The Roman Villas at Chilgrove and Upmarden,* 1979.

Dunnett 1965:
B.R.K. Dunnett, 'Excavations on North Hill, Colchester, 1965', *Arch. Journ.* cxxiii, 1967, 27-61.

Fennelly 1969:
L.R. Fennelly, 'Excavations of the Roman Villa at Combley, Arreton. I.O.W., 1968-1969'. *Proc. Isle of Wight Nat. Hist. and Arch. Soc.* vi, pt. IV, 1969, 271-82.

Fowler Coll.:
Fowler Collection. Collection of drawings by William Fowler in the Library of the Society of Antiquaries of London. Vol. i, ii and iii.

Fowler 1907:
J.T. Fowler ed., *The Correspondence of William Fowler,* 1907.

Fox 1897:
G.E. Fox, 'Uriconium', *Arch. Journ.* liv, 1897, 123-73.

Fox and Hope 1901:
G.E. Fox and W.H. St. J. Hope, 'Excavations on the site of the Roman city at Silchester, Hants. in 1900', *Archaeologia* lvii, 1901.

Fox Coll.:
Fox Collection. Collection of drawings by G.E. Fox in the Library of the Society of Antiquaries of London.

Franklin 1967:   P.M. Franklin, 'A Roman Villa on the North Side of the Vale of Pickering', *The Rydale Historian* No. 3, April 1967.

Frere 1957:   S.S. Frere, 'Excavations at Verulamium 1956; Second Interim Report', *Antiq. Journ.* xxxvii, 1957, 1-15.

Frere 1958:   S.S. Frere, 'Excavations at Verulamium 1957. Third Interim Report', *Antiq. Journ.* xxxviii, 1958, 1-14

Frere 1959:   S.S. Frere, 'Excavations at Verulamium 1958. Fourth Interim Report', *Antiq. Journ.* xxxix, 1959, 1-18.

Frere 1960:   S.S. Frere, 'Excavations at Verulamium 1959. Fifth Interim Report', *Antiq. Journ.* xl, 1960, 1-24.

Frere 1972:   S.S. Frere, *Verulamium Excavations* Vol. i. Reports of the Research Committee of the Society of Antiquaries of London No. XXVIII, 1972.

Goodburn 1972:   R. Goodburn, *The Roman Villa, Chedworth*. The National Trust Guide, 1972.

Goodburn 1978:   R. Goodburn, 'Winterton: some villa problems', in *Studies in the Romano-British Villa* ed. by M. Todd, 1978, 93-101.

Green 1975:   M.J. Green, *The Bradwell Roman Villa*. First Interim Report. Occasional Papers in Archaeology No. i, 1975. Milton Keynes Development Corporation.

Gurney Benham 1884:   W. Gurney Benham, *Essex Arch. Soc.* (N.S.) 2, 1884.

Gurney Benham 1923:   W. Gurney Benham, 'Two Roman Pavements at Colchester', *Essex Arch. Soc.* (N.S.) 16, 1923, 294-6.

Hakewill 1826:   H. Hakewill, *An Account of the Roman Villa discovered at Northleigh, Oxfordshire in the years 1813-16*, 1826.

Hamilton 1959:   A. Hamilton, 'Woolstone Roman Villa' *Berks Arch. J.* 57, 1959, 83-5.

Hanworth 1968:   R. Hanworth, 'The Roman Villa at Rapsley, Ewhurst'. *Surrey A.C.* lxv, 1968, 1-70.

Hassall and Rhodes 1974:   M. Hassall and J. Rhodes, 'Excavations at the new Market Hall, Gloucester, 1966-7'. *Trans. B.G.A.S.* xciii, 1974, 15-100.

Haverfield 1905:   F. Haverfield, *The Athenaeum* No. 4035, 25 Feb, 1905.

Hav. Coll.:   Haverfield Collection in Ashmolean Museum, Oxford.

Hayward 1952:   L.C. Hayward, 'The Roman Villa at Lufton near Yeovil', *Proc. Somerset A.N.H.S.* xcvii, 1952, 91-112.

Hayward 1974:   L.C. Hayward, 'Ilchester Mead Roman Villa. Part I: The Western Building.' *Notes and Queries for Somerset and Dorset*, March 1974, 299.

Hewitt 1971:   M. Hewitt, *Roman Villa, West Park, Fordingbridge*, 1971 ed. (Guidebook).

Hinks 1933:   R.P. Hinks, *Catalogue of the Greek, Etruscan and Roman Paintings and Mosaics in the British Museum*, 1933.

Hoare 1821:   R.C. Hoare, *The History of Ancient Wiltshire* ii (Roman Aera), 1821.

Hope and Fox 1896:   W.H. St. John Hope and G.E. Fox, 'Excavations on the site of the Roman city at Silchester, Hants, in 1895', *Archaeologia* lv part I, 1896, 215-56.

Hull 1958:   M.R. Hull, Roman Colchester. Reports of the Research Committee of the Society of Antiquaries of London No. XX, 1958.

Hurst 1972:   H. Hurst, 'Excavations at Gloucester, 1968-1971: First Interim Report'. *Antiq. Journ.* lii, 1972, 24-69.

Hurst 1974:   H. Hurst, 'Excavations at Gloucester 1971-1973: Second Interim Report'. *Antiq. Journ.* liv, 1974, 8-52.

Hutchins 1863:   J. Hutchins, *The History and Antiquities of the County of Dorset,* 1863.

Illingworth 1808:   C. Illingworth, *A Topographical Account of the Parish of Scampton in the County of Lincoln . . .,* 1808.

Ingram 1849:   J. Ingram, 'Notices of the Mosaic Pavement discovered at Thruxton, Hants in 1823.' *Proc. Royal Archaeological Institute,* Vol. for the Wilts and Salisbury meeting 1849, 241-45.

Jack 1916:   G.H. Jack, *The Romano-British Town of Magna (Kenchester),* Hereford, 1916.

Johnston 1972:   D.E. Johnston, *The Sparsholt Roman Villa: Summary of Excavations 1965-72* (tract).

L'Orange & Nordhagen 1966: H.P. L'Orange and P.J. Nordhagen. *Mosaics from Antiquity to the early Middle Ages,* 1966.

Lysons 1797:   S. Lysons, *An Account of Roman Antiquities Discovered at Woodchester in the County of Gloucester,* 1797.

Lysons 1813:   S. Lysons, *Reliquiae Britannico-Romanae,* Vol i, 1813.

Lysons 1817:   S. Lysons, *Reliquiae Britannico-Romanae,* Vols ii and iii, 1817.

MacLean 1887-8:   Sir J. MacLean, 'Manor of Tockington, Co. Gloucester, and The Roman Villa', *Trans. B.G.A.S.* 12, 1887-8, 123-69.

McWhirr 1973:   A.D. McWhirr, 'Cirencester, 1969-1972: Ninth Interim Report.' *Antiq. Journ.* liii, 1973, 191-218.

McWhirr 1978:   A.D. McWhirr, 'Cirencester, 1973-6: Tenth Interim Report.' *Antiq. Journ.* lviii, 1978, 161-80.

Meates 1955:   G.W. Meates, *Lullingstone Roman Villa,* 1955.

Meyer 1888:   F.S. Meyer, *Handbook of Ornament.* For an unabridged and unaltered republication of the English translation, see Dover Publications reprint 1957.

Michelson 1963-6:   N. Michelson, 'Roman Malton: The Civilian Settlement. Excavations in Orchard Field, 1949-1952.' *Y.A.J.* 41, 1963-66, 209-61.

Morgan 1855:   O. Morgan. 'Excavations prosecuted by the Caerleon Arch. Ass. within the Walls of Caerwent in the Summer of 1855'. *Archaeologia* xxxvi, 1855, 418-37.

Morgan 1866:   O. Morgan, *Notice of a Tessellated Pavement Discovered in the Churchyard, Caerleon.* Monmouthshire and Caerleon Ant. Soc. 1866.

Morgan 1882:   O. Morgan, *Goldcliff and the Ancient Roman Inscribed Stone . . . together with other Papers.* Monmouthshire and Caerleon Ant. Soc. 1882.

Morgan 1886:   T. Morgan, *Romano-British Mosaic Pavements,* 1886.

Neal 1967:   D.S. Neal, 'The Roman Mosaic in the Church of St. Oswald, Widford', *Antiq. Journ.* xlvii, 1967, 110.

Neal 1974:   D.S. Neal, *The Excavation of the Roman Villa in Gadebridge Park, Hemel Hempstead 1963-8.* Reports of the Research Committee of the Society of Antiquaries of London, No. XXXI, 1974.

Neal 1974–6:	D.S. Neal, *Northchurch, Boxmoor, Hemel Hempstead Station: The Excavations of Three Roman Buildings in the Bulbourne Valley.* Reprinted from *Hertfordshire Archaeology* 4, 1974–76, 1–135.
Neal 1976:	D.S. Neal, 'Floor Mosaics', Chapter 19 in *Roman Crafts,* ed. by D. Strong and D. Brown, 1976, 241–52.
Neal 1976:	D.S. Neal, 'A new drawing of the Woodchester mosaic pavement', *Antiq. Journ.* lvi, 1976, 244.
Oakeshott 1967:	W. Oakeshott, *The Mosaics of Rome,* 1967.
O'Neil 1952:	H.H. O'Neil, 'Whittington Court Roman Villa, Whittington, Gloucestershire — a report of the Excavations undertaken from 1948 to 1951', *Trans. B.G.A.S.* 71, 1952, 18–87.
Painter 1967:	K.S. Painter, 'The Roman Site at Hinton St. Mary Dorset', *B.M.Q.* xxxii, Nos. 1–2, 1967, 15–31.
Pollard 1974:	S. Pollard, 'A Late Iron Age Settlement and a Romano-British Villa at Holcombe, near Uplyme, Devon', *P.D.A.E.S.* 32, 1973–74, 59–161.
Price and Price 1881:	J.E. Price and F.G. Hilton Price, 'Remains of Roman Buildings at Morton, Isle of Wight', *Trans. Institute of British Architects* 1880–81, 125–60.
Putnam and Rainey 1975:	W.G. Putnam and A. Rainey, 'Seventh Interim Report on Excavations at Dewlish Roman Villa, 1975', *P.D.N.A.S.* 97, 1975, 54–7.
Rahtz 1963:	P.A. Rahtz, 'A Roman Villa at Downton', *W.A.M.* lviii, No. 211, 1963, 303–41.
Rainey 1971:	A. Rainey, 'The Mosaics of the Halstock Villa, Dorset', *Dorset N.H. & A.F.C.* 93, 1971, 146–51.
Rainey 1973:	A. Rainey, *Mosaics in Roman Britain,* 1973.
Rennie 1971:	D.M. Rennie, 'Excavations in the Parsonage Field, Cirencester, 1958', *Trans. B.G.A.S.* 90, 1971, 64–94.
Reid Moir and Maynard 1931–33:	J. Reid Moir and G. Maynard, 'The Roman Villa at Castle Hill, Whitton, Ipswich', *Suffolk Institute of Arch. Proc.* 21, 1931–33, 240–62.
Richmond 1963:	I.A. Richmond, *The Roman Pavements from Rudston, East Riding,* Hull Museums Publication No. 215, 1963.
Roach Smith 1868:	C. Roach Smith, *Collectanea Antiqua,* vi, 1868.
R.C.H.M. *Dorset:*	*An Inventory of Historical Monuments in the County of Dorset,* Vol. ii, *South-East,* Pt. 3. R.C.H.M., 1970.
R.C.H.M. *Glos.* i:	*Ancient and Historical Monuments in the County of Gloucester,* Vol. i, *Iron Age and Romano-British Monuments in the Gloucestershire Cotswolds.* R.C.H.M., 1976.
R.C.H.M. *Roman London:*	*An Inventory of the Historical Monuments in London,* Vol. iii, *Roman London.* R.C.H.M., 1928.
R.C.H.M. *Roman York:*	*An Inventory of the Historical Monuments in the City of York,* Vol.i, *Eburacum, Roman York.* R.C.H.M., 1962.
Scarth 1864:	H.M. Scarth, *Aquae Solis or Notices of Roman Bath.* 1864.
Slack 1948–51:	P.E. Slack, 'Report on a Roman Villa at Brantingham, E. Yorks.' *Y.A.J.* 37, 1948–51, 514–20.
Smith 1852:	H.E. Smith, *Reliquiae Isurianae,* 1852.

Smith 1958-60:   D.J. Smith, 'The Labyrinth Mosaic at Caerleon', *Bull. B.C.S.* 18, pt. 3, 1959, 304-10.

Smith 1964:   J.T. Smith, 'The Roman Villa at Denton.' *Lincolnshire Architectural and Arch. Soc. Reports & Papers,* x, 1964, 75-104.

Smith 1965:   D.J. Smith, 'Three fourth-century Schools of Mosaic in Roman Britain', in *La Mosaïque Gréco-Romaine* (Centre Nationale de la Recherche Scientifique, Paris, 1965), 95, 116.

Smith 1969:   D.J. Smith, 'The Mosaic Pavements', in *The Roman Villa in Britain,* ed. by A.L.F. Rivet, 1969, 75-125.

Smith 1973:   D.J. Smith, *The Great Pavement and Roman Villa at Woodchester, Gloucestershire.* Guide published by the Woodchester Roman Pavement Committee, 1973.

Smith 1975:   D.J. Smith, 'Roman Mosaics in Britain before the Fourth Century', in *La Mosaïque Gréco-Romaine* ii (Centre Nationale de la Recherche Scientifique, Paris 1975), 269-90.

Smith 1976:   D.J. Smith, *The Roman Mosaics from Rudston, Brantingham, and Horkstow.* City of Kingston upon Hull Museums & Art Galleries, 1976.

Smith 1977:   D.J. Smith, 'Mythological Figures and Scenes in Romano-British Mosaics', in *Roman Life and Art in Britain* pt. i, B.A.R. 41(i), 1977, ed. by J. Munby and M. Henig

Stead *et al.* 1973:   I.M. Stead, Joan Liversidge and D.J. Smith, 'Brantingham Roman Villa: Discoveries in 1962', *Britannia* iv, 1973, 84-106.

Stead 1976:   I.M. Stead, *Excavations at Winterton Roman Villa and other Roman Sites in North Lincolnshire 1958-1967.* D.O.E. Archaeological reports No. 9.

Stern 1957:   H. Stern, *Recueil Général des Mosaïques de la Gaule* i, Province de Belgique; 1. Partie Ouest, Xe Supplement à *Gallia*, Paris, 1957.

Stern 1963:   H. Stern, *Recueil Général des Mosaïques de la Gaule,* i, Province de Belgique; 3, Partie Sud, Xe Supplement à *Gallia*, 1963.

Stone 1929:   P.G. Stone, 'The Roman Villa at Newport, Isle of Wight', *Antiq. Journ.* ix, 1929, 141-51.

Strange 1779:   J. Strange, 'An Account of some Remains of Roman and other Antiquities in Monmouthshire', *Archaeologia* v, 1779, 33-80.

Swain 1978:   E.J. Swain (ed.), *Excavations: The Chessals, Kingscote.* Kingscote Archaeological Association, 1978.

Taylor 1941:   M.V. Taylor, 'The Roman Tessellated Pavement at Stonesfield, Oxon.' *Oxoniensia* vi, 1941, 1-8

Toynbee 1962:   J.M.C. Toynbee, *Art in Roman Britain,* 1962.

Toynbee 1964:   J.M.C. Toynbee, *Art in Britain Under the Romans,* 1964.

Toynbee 1964 b: J.M.C. Toynbee, 'A New Roman Mosaic Pavement Found in Dorset'. *JRS* liv, 1964, 7-14.

V.C.H.:   Victoria County History (Romano-British Chapters).

Wacher 1964:   J.S. Wacher, 'Cirencester 1963, Fourth Interim Report' *Antiq. Journ.* xliv, 1964, 9-18.

Watkin 1886:   W.T. Watkin, *Roman Cheshire,* 1886.

Wheeler & Wheeler 1932:   R.E.M. Wheeler & T.V. Wheeler, *Report on the Excavation of the Prehistoric, Roman and Post-Roman Site in Lydney Park, Gloucestershire.* Reports of the Research Committee of the Society of Antiquaries of London No. IX, 1932.

Wheeler & Wheeler 1936:   R.E.M. Wheeler & T.V. Wheeler, *Verulamium: A Belgic and two Roman Cities.* Reports of the Research Committee of the Society of Antiquaries of London, No. XI, 1936.

Whitwell 1970:   J.B. Whitwell, *Roman Lincolnshire* ii, 1970.

Wright and Hassall 1973:   R.P. Wright and M.W.C. Hassall, 'Roman Britain in 1972. II. Inscriptions', *Britannia* iv, 1973, 324–37.

ACKNOWLEDGEMENTS

The writer would like to record his debt of gratitude to Professor S.S. Frere, not only for editing his monograph, but for many years of encouragement to this and other projects. Had it not been for his stimulus during the Verulamium excavations the collection would never have grown, nor would the writer have moved from a career in advertising into archaeological illustration. Dr. David Smith, the master of Romano-British mosaic studies, has also given the writer much advice and encouragement; he has devoted much time to reading the manuscript and has made many valuable suggestions which are embodied in the text. Needless to say, however, the writer alone is responsible for any errors of any kind.

Many colleagues in the Ancient Monuments Inspectorate have also given encouragement — among them particularly the former Chief Inspector, Arnold Taylor, and Sarnia Butcher, John Hamilton, and the late Gerald Dunning. I am also indebted to a large number of excavators who have informed me of, and invited me to record, their discoveries and have thereby assisted in the formation of the collection. They are J. Barnbrook, P. Crummy, Professor B. Cunliffe, A. Detsicas, Miss R. Dunnett, L.R. Fennelly, Professor S.S. Frere, E. Greenfield, Viscountess Hanworth, M. Hassall, H. Hurst, D. Johnston, A.D. McWhirr, D. Mynard, T. Pacitto, B. Phillips, Mrs. M. Rule, J. Rhodes, Dr. I.M. Stead, and E.J. Swain.

The production of this volume has also been greatly assisted by the staff of the Royal Commission on Historic Monuments. Mrs. P. Drummond has provided liaison in the preparation of many of the photographs which have been ably produced by D. Kendall of the Photographic Section under the auspices of R. Parsons, Chief Photographer. Other photographs have been supplied by the Department of the Environment.

INTRODUCTION

In 1978 it was suggested to the author that his collection of paintings of Romano-British mosaics should be published as a monograph. This was an incentive to complete as many unfinished drawings as possible; but since the start of the task the number of mosaics discovered on excavations has continued unabated and now the backlog of unfinished work remains almost the same as before. Such is the pace of new discoveries found either during the development of our ancient city-centres, or during road-construction, quarrying or farming.

So often accidental discoveries of mosaics have caused damage to them, and lack of time and money has prevented the opportunity for preservation. It is a sad reflection that of the 88 mosaics illustrated in this volume 35 are lost or only small areas of them survive. It is an even sadder fact that of about 1,000 mosaics recorded since the seventeenth century most are destroyed. Journals report depressingly on the ravages of winter upon mosaics left exposed, on souvenir-hunters removing handfuls of tesserae, or, as in the case at Brantingham, of a mosaic (Pl. 88) being stolen overnight!

Antiquarian interest in villas was of course frequently aroused by the presence of mosaics, and fortunately in the late eighteenth and early nineteenth centuries many discoveries were recorded by such well-known antiquaries as Samuel Lysons (b. 1763 — d. 1819) or William Fowler (b. 1761 — d. 1832). These produced lavish hand-tinted engravings which today are often the only record of the mosaics. It is ironic that with the introduction of photography and half-tone reproduction the standard of much recording fell. An oblique photograph was often all that was published. Notable exceptions are the chromolithographs of G.E. Fox's water-colours of the Silchester mosaics — drawings perhaps influenced by the work of Lysons and showing every detail, including discolouration. The tradition of water-coloured illustrations was continued by the publication of N. Davey's and T.V. Wheeler's excellent drawings of several of the Verulamium pavements found in the early 1930s (Wheeler and Wheeler 1936): these water-colours are on view in Verulamium Museum and they were possibly the inspiration for the first drawings undertaken by the writer, then a student of graphic design at Watford School of Art and a frequent visitor to the museum.

The first painting and the origin of this collection was the Verulamium Bacchus mosaic (No. 74) discovered in 1959. Its fragmentary condition stimulated the preparation of a reconstruction, published in the interim report the following year (Frere 1960, pl. v). The second painting was made in 1960 and was of the Lion mosaic (No. 75), also from Verulamium. From 1961 the collection rapidly expanded with the appointment of the writer as an archaeological illustrator to the Ancient Monuments Inspectorate of the Ministry of Works (now the Department of the Environment). One of his duties was to record mosaics discovered on excavations sponsored directly or indirectly by the department. Soon after his appointment mosaics were being excavated at Rudston (East Yorks), Winterton (S. Humberside), Colchester (Essex), and Fullerton (Hants.). Now, after 20 years, the collection totals over 100 drawings, 87 of which are illustrated here and the remainder (site-drawings awaiting completion) listed in an appendix (p. 123).

17

Although the collection is mainly concerned with mosaics discovered from 1959 onwards, it is not a complete record. In 1961, for example, so many new mosaics were found at Fishbourne (Sussex) that it was impossible for the writer to keep pace recording discoveries. Elsewhere some mosaics were found and destroyed before the artist was informed. Nor are all the paintings of new discoveries. Some, such as the pavements from Winterton and from Woodchester, are new surveys of mosaics already recorded by William Fowler or Samuel Lysons. Comparisons between their drawings and the new surveys provides not only a guide to the accuracy of their work, but also to the extent of damage since the original surveys were made. In the case of Winterton and Woodchester ploughing and gravedigging respectively have been responsible for such damage. Many of the drawings are the only surviving record, or the only record of the pavement in totality. In some cases vertical photography was impossible, or fragments of the same floors may have been excavated in different seasons.

The drawings are not merely records of mosaics as surviving, but are also reconstructions which attempt to show the basic schemes. It has been possible in many examples to interpret the appearance of the original design from very small fragments, which emphasises the need for detailed site-drawings in addition to a photographic record. It is often asked of the writer why is it not sufficient merely to photograph the pavements? The answer is that frequently the pavements are found in a very dirty state and no amount of conventional cleaning will remove a lime concretion covering the pavement's surface. Small isolated fragments sometimes go unrecorded, but it may be these very fragments which are the key to reconstructions; on several of the drawings it is the presence of only a few critical tesserae which has enabled a reconstruction to be made. Considerable mutilation often occurs on the periphery of fragments, and interpretation of and correction of displaced tesserae may be necessary. To draw these pieces in their actual position might confuse a reconstruction. An example is No. 41 from Colchester, which had slumped into a pit. Another aim of the collection is to record the mosaics to the same $1/10$ scale. This has been achieved with all the drawings except Nos. 83–85 from Winterton, which are at $1/12$ scale because the writer worked from field-drawings not prepared by himself.

Apart from a few mosaics which have been drawn entirely from photographs or from excavators' field-drawings, the majority have been recorded *in situ* using either a portable or a fixed drawing-grid. The early drawings were made on graph-paper, but now drawing film is used. The field-drawings are much simplified, repeating patterns being recorded in a 'short-hand' form; e.g. guilloche with only the central 'eye' between braids indicated together with details of intersections and anomalies. The field-drawings record the number of tesserae across the *width* of a band, but no attempt is made on either the field-sketches or the final paintings to show the exact number of tesserae in the *length* of a band. Colours are indicated in crayon with marginal notes describing tonal values.

The first drawings made, Nos 66–7 and 74–5, were completed on site with poster-colours painted directly onto graph-paper, with the result that the lines of the graph-paper remain apparent. This practice, however, was soon discarded in favour of tracing the field-drawings and paintings onto Whatman water-colour paper in the cleaner and warmer environment of a studio, aided by photographs and colour-slides. First the area of the surviving mosaic is painted with a yellow–ochre background wash (so that white tesserae show up) over the pencilled tracing, followed by the various coloured tesserae. Unlike the construction of a mosaic, which is 'completed' as it progresses across the floor, the drawings are painted in stages. The grey tesserae forming the structure of the pattern are painted first, followed by white, red and yellow. Figured subjects will be completed last. Because mosaics are invariably stained, the paintings attempt to show the colours in a restored condition. Therefore, with a few except-ions, the backround tesserae are painted white, showing up against the yellow–ochre wash, and the remaining colours as though the tesserae are damp and consequently brighter.

SCHOOLS OF MOSAIC

It is not the intention of this Introduction to give a history of mosaic, but it would be negligent not to refer to the important work undertaken over the past 30 years by Dr. David Smith in the identification of schools of mosaic or *officinae*. His work is based on stylistic comparisons between groups of mosaic in various regions. Papers by him on the subject are well known (Smith 1965; Smith 1969) as are his specialist reports on mosaics, particularly those of Cirencester (McWhirr 1973; McWhirr 1978) which broaden discussion on the Corinian *officina*. Four schools of mosaicists, all attributed to the late third and four centuries have been identified; they were based at or practised in the region of Dorchester, Dorset (the Durnovarian school), Cirencester, Glos (the Corinian school), Water Newton, Hunts. (the Durobrivan school) and possibly Brough on Humber, N. Humberside (the Petuarian school). Evidence has also emerged for other groups in the south of England for instance in Somerset, based at Ilchester (Smith 1965, 112); and it is possible to detect regional similarities in pavements from Colchester and Verulamium dated to the second century A.D.

That schools of mosaicists practising in the second century continued during the third century is unlikely. At present only a very few pavements can be attributed with confidence to that period (but see Rapsley, No 65), and it is unlikely there would have been the demand to sustain more than a few jobbing contractors. However, increased prosperity in the later third or early fourth centuries saw a major programme of reconstruction and building of villas especially in the Cotswolds, Somerset and Dorset. A possible reason suggested for this is an influx of capital from the continent following the German incursions of 260-75, for neither in northern Gaul nor the Rhineland is there comparable evidence for rural prosperity. Wealthy provincial farmers from these regions may have emigrated to Britain and purchased estates, and perhaps they took up previously uncultivated land. In the wake of this possible emigration artisans may have followed and, to put it baldly, cashed in on the boom.

The Cotswolds saw many new villas in this period. From the evidence of a coin of Allectus (293-6) in mint condition possibly once sealed by the Orpheus pavement at Barton Farm, Cirencester, the Corinian *officina* may have been one of the first to be established. The palatial villa at Woodchester near Stroud, Glos., with the same subject but grander, was surely the inspiration not just for the Orpheus pavements at Barton Farm and Dyer Street, Cirencester, but for other inferior examples including those from Withington, Glos. (Lysons ii, 1817, pl. XX) and Newton St. Loe, Somerset (Scarth 1864, pl.XLVII). The scale and opulence of the Woodchester villa is likely to have demanded the skills of imported workers, and it would seem likely that eminent mosaicists from the continent were employed.[1] Craftsmen of the Corinian *officina* continued practising into the middle of the fourth century, but their work became steadily poorer and less inspired.

The open Christian symbolism of the Hinton St. Mary and Frampton pavements in Dorset, attributed to the work of the Durnovarian school, is unlikely to date earlier than 313, after which Christianity could be openly professed. This *officina* therefore would appear to have been a little later established, perhaps, than the Corinian school. It has been suggested (Smith 1965, 100) that the Hinton St. Mary mosaic (No 61) was laid not earlier than *c.* 315/325 and not later than *c.* 340/350, which gives a broad possible date-range for their work. The Durobrivan school, based possibly at Water Newton, Hunts., is believed to have laid many pavements in Leicestershire, Lincolnshire and Northamptonshire. Pavements of this group have been compared with those at Great Casterton (Smith 1969, 107) dated by sealed coins to no earlier than *c.*350-65. A pavement from Denton, Lincs., sealed a coin of *c.* 370; together, this evidence suggests that this *officina* flourished during the third quarter of the fourth century. The Petuarian school is believed by Dr. Smith to have been responsible for the construction of mosaics at Brantingham, N. Humberside, and Horkstow and Winterton, S. Humberside, and to have operated, from the evidence of coins at Brantingham, not earlier than *c.* 330-50.

[1]Dr. Smith (Smith 1975, 113), however, prefers the reverse explanation. The similarity between panels at Woodchester and at the Palastplatz in Trier is a result, he suggests, of the Woodchester mosaicists moving onto the continent.

However, the writer must express doubt about the validity of this *officina*; although some of those pavements share common schemes and motifs and a *primitif* style, many differ technically, and this raises the prospect that they are unlikely to be products of the same contractor. The fact that pavements from as far afield as Lincoln and Malton, Yorks, could be products of the same mosaicist as that at Brantingham, not to mention the fact that Petuaria has so far yielded no evidence for mosaics, may argue not for a static workshop but for itinerant craftsmen.

CONSTRUCTION METHODS

The most common types of foundations are a bedding of mortared stone rubble or a bed of *opus signinum* (a compound of crushed tile and lime mortar). Apart from being very strong, the latter provided a damp-resistant membrane on which a thin levelling skin of mortar could be spread. However, variations occur in the quality of foundations; sometimes mosaics, particularly those of the fourth century and paving in non-hypocausted rooms, were bedded into mortar laid directly on rammed earth and unmortared rubble. Whether this was a means of cutting costs is uncertain, but it is possible that it was designed to allow the mosaic to settle without cracking.[2] Guide-lines for the design of the mosaic were either scored into the damp levelling-skin or painted. Painting would be the most convenient method, as the bedding could be allowed to set and be walked upon. Both types have been noted under Romano-British mosaics. Beneath a mosaic from Rudston (No 69) guide-lines were scored on the penultimate bedding of mortar, while beneath No 26 from Cirencester, red-painted guide-lines were found.

Laying a mosaic probably began in the centre of the room and worked outwards towards the borders. It would have taken many days to complete, for only a small area was worked at any one time. A fine lime-mortar bedding for the tesserae was spread over the guide-lines: once the tesserae had been placed in position, they were tapped and levelled by the use of a hand-weight, the action of which was to force the mortar up into the interstices of the tesserae. If the mortar became too dry a little water could be sprinkled upon the tesserae to aid their bedding. It is likely that, as work progressed across the floor, the motifs would be laid first and the background tesserae and guilloche forming the 'framework' of the scheme later. There are many instances, for example at Brantingham (No 12), where motifs have 'broken' into the surrounds of the panels, clearly indicating that they were laid first. Finally the floor would have been grouted with fine crushed tile mortar (*opus signinum*), providing a water-resistant surface, and then smoothed and polished with abrasive stones.

The direct method of setting tesserae into a bed of mortar has already been explained; but two other processes should be described — the indirect and reverse methods. In the indirect method the tesserae were first bedded in sand and then strong pieces of cloth glued to their upper surface. Once the glue was set the design could be lifted out of the sand and re-set in a permanent bed of mortar. The glued sheet could then be dissolved with hot water. The reverse method was similar; here the tesserae were glued face down onto a cartoon drawn on strong cloth. After re-setting and the removal of the cartoon, the picture would have been the reverse of that shown previously. An advantage with both the indirect and reverse methods is that sections of mosaic could be prefabricated in workshops. As with setting tesserae in the direct method, both the other processes would have required grouting and polishing.

Tesserae were usually made from stone local to the area, but occasionally stone was imported from further afield. For example tesserae of Kimmeridge shale and Purbeck marble from Dorset occur fairly widely in southern England, while examples in Pennant stone from the Forest of Dean can be found as far afield as Oxfordshire. White background tesserae were usually of oolitic limestone or rock chalk, and the black or dark grey/blue stones were of lias or shale. Frequently, however, tesserae were made from old or reject roofing-tiles, which provided a range of red tones and to a lesser extent pink, yellow, grey, black and (rarely) blue. Fine-quality red tesserae were also sometimes made from samian vessels. Stone was also roasted to obtain red tones. Glass tesserae were used, but only rarely in Britain; of the pavements in the collection

[2]Preservation of mosaics with these foundations is usually poor, as they are not resistant to worm or root action.

they are to be found in those from Aldborough (No 3), Cirencester (No 25) and Verulamium (No 74). In all cases glass tesserae are used most sparingly and they only highlight detail such as the blue inscription at Aldborough, the green speckles in the hare at Cirencester and green grapes garlanding Bacchus at Verulamium. On the continent, however, glass or frit tesserae were common, being derived not merely from broken vessels but from purpose-made strips of glass which could be cut on a small portable anvil. Such a device was probably used for cutting stone tesserae, although present-day mosaicists frequently use pincers. These also could have been used in the Roman period.

In Italy two types of construction can be found — *opus vermiculatum* and *opus tessellatum*. The former technique employed tesserae as small as 2-3 mm wide and imitated painting with tonal variations. The smaller pavements were sometimes mounted in stone trays set as *emblemata* into larger pavements, where they were often surrounded by geometric ornament of coarser *opus tessellatum*. The term *opus vermiculatum* was referred to in the second century B.C.: its meaning, 'worm-like' was explained by L'Orange and Nordhagen (1966, 8) with reference to the sinuous lines which formed in mosaic when very small tesserae were used. However, Oakeshott (1967, 10) more logically thinks that the term originally referred to the worm-like rods of glass used for cutting into tesserae. Whether fine mosaics are constructed in stone or glass, the same term is used today. Nowhere in Roman Britain has this technique been found, and although some pavements have tesserae as small as 4 mm they are always incorporated into figured work which includes *opus tessellatum* with tesserae as large as 10-12 mm square. This is about the average size of tesserae on Romano-British pavements; but frequently very large pavements have larger tesserae — this is true at both Brantingham (No 12) and Woodchester (No 87).

DESIGN AND THE USE OF 'NETS'

A study of the schemes illustrated here provides an insight into how patterns may have evolved and into the guide-lines which mosaicists could have used before starting construction. In analysing many of the schemes it is apparent that some construction guide-lines may have been based on a design visually different from the final product. Many of the simpler pavements would have required only a minimum of guide-lines with little recourse to a plan; but for mosaics with complex geometry it is likely that two drawings were necessary. One was perhaps in a copy-book which gave the finished impression of the general scheme (motifs were probably illustrated separately); this drawing could be shown to prospective clients. The other was a plan, used solely by the mosaicists, illustrating the guide-lines or 'nets' (see below) required to set out particular patterns.

There is no evidence that mosaics with similar schemes came in standard sizes, and therefore the layout must have varied with each mosaic. A mosaicist would have found it inconvenient for a client to specify an exact size for a mosaic, because it would have involved him in the problem of making a scale drawing. More likely the size of the mosaic was partly governed by the size of the initial plan, which could be scaled up on site, say by ten times. This practice would have avoided the complex mathematical task of working out the sizes of various elements in the pattern, and it possibly facilitated the use of prefabricated elements constructed in the *officinae*. It is clear that the designer of the patterns must have had mathematical ability, but it is not necessarily true that the mosaicist was always the designer.

The majority of schemes (but not necessarily the content) were clearly chosen by the client at random, and frequently are unsuited to the shape of the room. Make-up panels converting squares into rectangles, or unsightly wide plain tessellated borders, were often required. Occasionally, however, there are exceptions where the shape and content of the pavement has been intended for a specific room. The scheme of the Great Mosaic at Woodchester (No 87), with its column-bases set in spandrels, has obviously been designed to suit the architecture; while at Keynsham, Somerset, a hexagonal mosaic (FIG. 9a) fits a hexagonal room. Brantingham (No 12), its scheme so far unique in Britain, was also probably created for the room it embellished. The obvious examples of scenes (as opposed to schemes) being chosen for their position are aquatic pavements which so often decorate bath-houses.

How the mosaicist went about setting out patterns is open to conjecture; but it is probable
that for many schemes, to simplify construction, the area to be paved was divided by a series of
guide-lines known as 'nets' (Meyer 1888, 4) (FIG. 1). For a pattern based on rows of tangent or

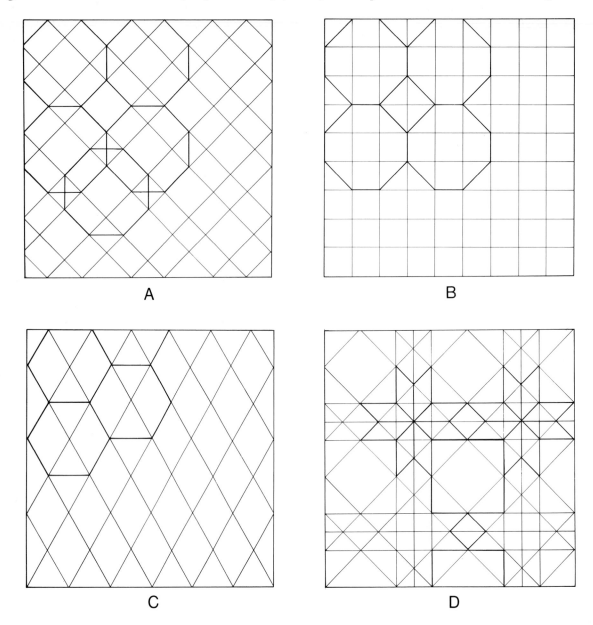

FIG. 1 The formation of patterns and the use of nets. A: 'Regular' octagons; B: 'Irregular' octagons;
C: hexagons; D: grid of spaced squares tangent to filled squares with eight-lozenge stars in the interspaces.

interlaced octagons (A), a 'net' at a 45° angle to the border is required, with the spaces between
lines alternating, the greater space being ⅓ larger than the smaller. If the octagons are required
to be diagonal to the border, so that the small tilted square interspaces are now at right-angles
to it (as in the Bonus Eventus pavement from Woodchester (Lysons 1797, pl. XIX)), an identical
net but at 90° to the border is required. Frequently, however, irregular 'octagons' (e.g. FIG. 1 B)
were favoured in preference to regular octagons, because the 'net' required to register the
pattern was simpler — merely a regular grid. This explains the irregular octagons from Combe
St. Nicholas, Somerset, and Aldborough for example (FIG. 7 D), and also why the panels
containing octagons between L-shapes around the Woodchester mosaic (No 87) and at Rapsley
(No 65) are not true octagons. For hexagonal schemes (FIG. 1 C) a 60° lattice is required. Nets

were probably also used to form eight-lozenge star-patterns (FIG. 1, D). They require a 90° grid of large squares, each separated by three right-angled lines, the space between each line representing one quarter of the width of a square. This net is then overlaid by another with diagonal lines at 45°. The spaces between lines alternate, the greater space being twice the width of the smaller. Alternatively, the pattern can be obtained from a closely-spaced net with a regular distribution of right-angled lines. The registration of these nets was probably obtained with the use of large set-squares and calipers: once a base-line had been drawn the mosaicist could simply measure others from it.

GEOMETRIC SCHEMES

A few of the more common geometric schemes are described below in order to show how, in some cases, the design could be adapted or changed radically by an enlargement or contraction of the basic pattern, or by rotating the design in relation to a static border.

Tangent Squares (FIG. 2)

In its basic form this pattern imitates a coffered vault, such as was represented in painted plaster on a ceiling from Gadebridge Park, Hemel Hempstead (Herts.), (Neal 1974, fig. 89 b). In mosaic, perhaps the simplest example is a pavement from Building IV, 8 at Verulamium dated 160-90 (Wheeler and Wheeler 1936, pl XLII), which has a grid of 16 panels (FIG. 2 A) each

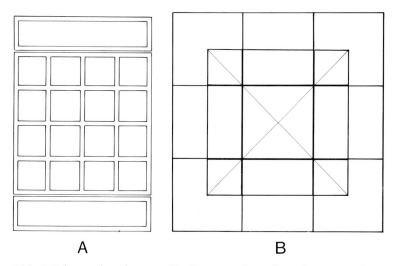

A   B

FIG. 2 Schemes based on a grid of squares. A: outline of pavement from Building IV, 8, at Verulamium; B: drawing showing how the basic scheme has been adapted to form a large central panel flanked by rectangles and with smaller squares in the angles

containing a circular medallion occupied by a flower or 'boss'. At Brislington, Glos (Barker 1900, pavement 1) there is an unusual variation of a coffered grid: it is outlined in simple guilloche and broken by small squares superimposed at each intersection. In the coffers are tilted squares occupied by buds. It has been assigned to the late second or early third century (Smith 1975, 286). Pavement B, Insula 2 at Colchester (Hull 1958, pl. XV) may also be quoted. A similar scheme, probably of the late third or fourth century, but in a more debased form, occurs at Carisbrooke, I.O.W. (No 18). Here abutting squares are linked to each other by short strips of guilloche. More frequently nine panels of the grid are truncated (FIG. 2 B) so that the scheme has a central square flanked on each side by rectangles and (within the angles) by smaller squares. The side and corner-panels are usually ½ and ¼ units of a square. It is a very common scheme in the second century and, as we shall see at Colchester for example (Nos 39 and 40), is sometimes further adapted by superimposing the grid upon a concentric arrangement of various repeating patterns.

In the fourth century the scheme was less common. At Frampton (Lysons 1817, pt. iii, pl iv),
however, we find an example of a nine-panel coffered grid without adaptation except for the
insertion of roundels into its central and corner squares, occupied by figures and representations of the gods of the winds. Classical scenes are represented in square panels at Brading
(Price and Price 1881, fig. iv 10) where a nine-panel grid is rotated 45° to the border to form a
large St. Andrew's Cross or saltire with a central square tangent to squares. Instead of
rectangular panels at the border, triangular panels are formed. Another mosaic in the same
room also has a nine-panel grid, with its marginal panels truncated into ½ and ¼ squares. The
latter are further elaborated by the insertion of quadrants.

Spaced Squares (FIG. 3)

Another variation is where the squares are not tangent to one another but spaced and
sometimes tangent to smaller tilted squares. In Britain the earliest representation of this type
appears on a pavement from Room N3 at Fishbourne, dated *c.* A.D. 75 (Cunliffe 1971, pl.
LXXVII *a*), but the scheme is a very common one and survives into the fourth century. For
example it appears at Gadebridge Park (No 51) in a context dated *c.* 325, and is particularly
popular in the Midlands, where it appears on many mosaics with elaborate arrangements of
lozenge stars (p. 81). In the fourth century, however, the scheme is frequently adapted by
enlarging the squares in relation to the scale of the mosaic and rotating them 45° to the border
(FIG. 3). The effect created, a saltire, is not dissimilar to the example quoted from Brading, but

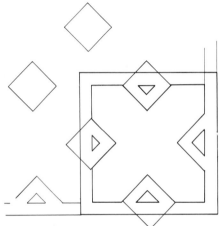

FIG. 3 Spaced squares rotated 45° to
margin of panel to form Saltire

without a square central panel and with the squares near the margins truncated into triangles.
Examples are to be found at Chedworth, Glos (Goodburn 1972, pl. 8), North Leigh, Oxon
(Hakewill 1826, pl. 2.1) and Tockington Park, Glos (McLean 1887-8, pl. vi). All these have
circular centrepieces.

We have looked at variations where the scheme, although modified in proportion and angle,
remains basically the same; but there are mosaics where the scheme has been extensively
modified — to such an extent that it ceases to be apparent. For example, an analysis of No 38
from Colchester, dated to the mid second century, reveals its pattern to be based originally on
squares separated by smaller tilted squares (FIG. 4 A). The latter remain in evidence, occupied by
squares of guilloche: along the border they have been cut diagonally to form triangles
containing a variety of peltae. The central interspace between a group of four squares, however,
which is commonly dominated by an eight-lozenge star, has been omitted and a square substituted. Consequently a quincunx of panels is formed — those in the angles having been inverted
at their internal corners to become L-shapes. At Bancroft, Bucks. (No 7) we can see a fourth-
century example. No 65 (see FIG. 4 B and further discussion on p. 91) although so alike has not
evolved similarly but from a grid of squares, octagons and cruciforms. No tilted squares can be
discerned.

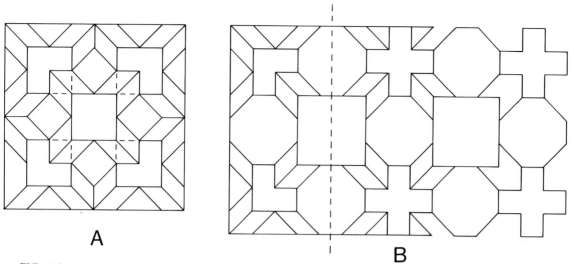

FIG. 4 Mosaic 38 from Colchester (A) and 65 from Rapsley (B) showing how patterns have evolved from other schemes. A began as a scheme of spaced squares tangent to smaller tilted squares and B as an arrangement of squares, octagons and crosses.

Interlaced Squares (FIG. 5)

Yet another variation are interlaced squares, a scheme exclusive to the late third to fourth century.[3] Frequently, as on No 36 from Cirencester for example, the motif occurs singly, with quadrants in the angles, or arranged in sets of four sometimes in a juggled composition (FIG. 5, B).

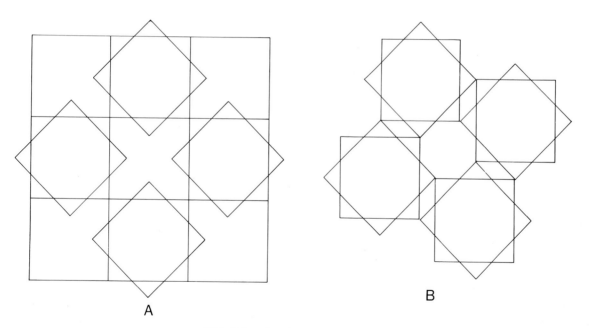

FIG. 5 Interlaced squares; variations.

The basis is two grids of squares, one with squares tangent to each other and the other a grid of spaced squares superimposed upon and at 45° to the first. When the pattern appears juggled, it is really two identical grids of spaced squares arranged in a staggered formation, but with one grid superimposed over and at 45° to the first. No 58 from Gloucester, and perhaps No 17 from Caerwent, had this arrangement.

[3]With the possible exception of a mosaic from Box, Wilts. (Brakspear 1904, pl. 1), for which Dr. Smith favours a late second or early third-century date (Smith 1975, 274). If so, it is the only example and therefore perhaps it would be wiser to assume a late third- or fourth-century date for this also.

Schemes based on Circles (FIG. 6)

Tangent Circles

This is a pattern (FIG. 6 A) with rows of circles each touching one another. As yet there are no mosaics in Britain with an overall pattern of circles, but (as in the examples of square schemes) we frequently find an arrangement of nine circles (three rows of three) truncated by a border to

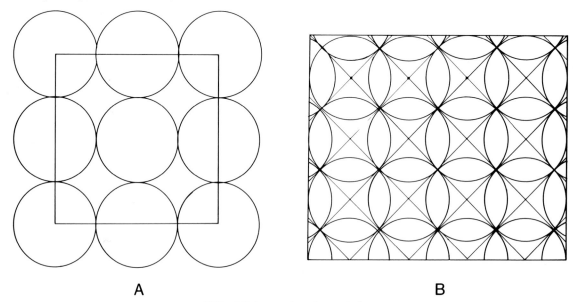

A   B

FIG. 6 Schemes based on circles.

form a central circle with lateral semicircles and with quadrants in the angles (FIG. 6,A). This arrangement first appears in Britain in a second-century context. For example the Cupid-astride-a-dolphin mosaic from Room 7 at Fishbourne (Cunliffe 1971, pl. XLVII) is dated to the mid second century and a similar date is probable, on stylistic evidence, for a mosaic from Dyer Street, Cirencester (Buckman and Newmarch 1850, pl. VI). It has hunting dogs in the central panel and fabulous marine creatures and Oceanus-masks in the semicircles and interspaces respectively.[4]

Four other examples are of or may be dated to the second century. They are: No 75 from Verulamium; Middleborough, Colchester (*Catalogue* 4, p. 6); North Leigh (Hakewill 1826, fig. 3); and Walton Heath, Surrey (Smith 1975, pl. CXXI, 1). An important difference between them and the basic schemes at Fishbourne and Cirencester, however, is that their semicircular panels are without outer margins (see No 75). Consequentially adaptation has produced a large curvilinear saltire, enhanced by the omission of the quadrants. They are also different in that their central panels are square, except that at North Leigh which is circular. The Walton Heath example, however, has corner-panels which are not quadrants but squares. It would seem that this is a hybrid of both square and circular schemes — the squares in the angles being ¼ units of the central panel. The square scheme at Frampton, already commented on (p. 24), with its spaced central and corner roundels would also appear to be a hybrid therefore, but of fourth-century date. Another hybrid from this site (Lysons 1813, pt. iii, pl. v) is very similar to the Walton Heath mosaic except that it has a circular central panel. Its semicircles are truncated, where the arcs meet the border, by large squares in the angles unusually equal in internal width to the semicircles. The central panel is occupied by a scene depicting Bellerophon killing the Chimaera. The presence of a Chi-Rho confirms a fourth-century date.

Apart from Frampton the variations described are exclusive to the second century and do not appear on any of the dozen or so fourth-century parallels, typified here by an example from

[4]Although there can be little doubt that the basic scheme at Dyer Street with its Oceanus-masks is original work, much is ancient repair, including the dogs, which could be as late as the fourth century.

Rudston (No 66). At Caerwent (No 16) and Hinton St Mary (No 61) we have a fourth-century variant where radial strips of guilloche link the central circles and the quadrants in the angles. They reflect the increased popularity of radial schemes, such as at Brantingham, for example, and those illustrated on FIGS. 10 and 11. A unique variant, also of fourth-century date, comes from Medbourne, Leicester (V.C.H., *Leic.* i, 1907, pl. VII). The conventional scheme has been adapted to fit a rectangle by removing a slice across its axis, resulting in the formation of a central ellipse flanked by half 'ellipses' on the narrow sides of the rectangle, and by semicircles and quadrants on the longer sides.

Interlaced circles

The most frequent form of circular pattern appears not in separate schemes such as those described but as repeating motifs forming interlaced circles (FIG. 6, B): it is a particularly common pattern especially in the fourth century and widely distributed. Of the pavements in the collection it occurs at Bancroft (No 6), Brantingham (No 12), Rudston (No 70) and Winterton (No 84). It is formed by placing the radii in a staggered arrangement at alternate junctions of a right-angled net. As far as the writer is aware there is only one mosaic in Britain where the overall scheme is based on interlaced circles — at Holcombe, Devon (Pollard 1974, pl. XXVIII). Here six circles drawn in guilloche are arranged around a hexagon. Its date is no earlier than 330 and probably of the second half of the fourth century.

Spaced circles

In this arrangement instead of the circles touching one another or being interlaced they are set apart. Only at Kings Weston, Glos., is there an unadapted example (Boon 1950, pl. VII) with five circles in a quincunx arrangement separated by ornate concave-sided octagons. It is dated between *c.* 270 and 300. The scheme can be seen in a modified form at Rudston (No 69) in a fourth-century pavement with a central circle enlarged to touch the smaller circles in the angles. More commonly, however, as we shall see below, spaced circles are associated within octagonal schemes, as roundels occupied by flowers. In this form the arrangement may date in Britain from the middle of the second century.

Schemes based on Octagons

Tangent octagons

This term is given to octagons touching one another and sharing common outlines. When two rows are joined together small interspaces are created. The simplest form is a series of tangent octagons (FIG. 7, A) imitating a coffered vault bearing flowered bosses similar to the square schemes. It is represented on two mosaics in the collection; No 57 from Gloucester and No 8 from Bancroft; further discussion and parallels are quoted under the latter. The scheme is most frequent in the second century; but the Bancroft example and another from Colliton Park, Dorchester (RCHM *Dorset* ii, pl. 220), attest its continuing popularity into the fourth century.

A pavement from Caerwent (Morgan 1855, pl. XXXIV) dated on stylistic evidence to the late second or early third century (Smith 1975, 287) is a variant where 13 octagons, tangent diagonally, are separated not by squares but a swastika of simple guilloche continuous with the guilloche bordering the octagons — an arrangement similar to a linear pattern from Combe St. Nicholas shown in part on FIG. 7, C. There is an identical pattern at Aldborough on a corridor pavement (Smith 1852, pl. XII) but with the octagons overlapping or interlaced with each other (FIG. 7, D). Similarly at York, where this arrangement borders a pavement at Micklegate Bar (R.C.H.M. *Roman York,* pl. 23), the mosaic has a quincunx-distribution of spaced octagons, the central octagon occupied by a pair of deer and the others, supposedly, by joints of venison (see p 39). Its date is doubtful: its scheme and the presence of chain guilloche would suggest a late second-century date; but the colourful rhomboids, so typical of fourth-century pavements, may suggest a later product, perhaps third-century. Another mosaic with linear interlaced octagons and open spaces without meander occurs at Widford, Oxon (No 77) in a

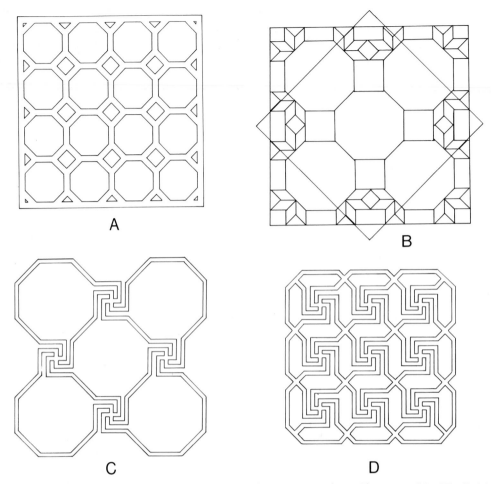

FIG. 7 Schemes based on octagons. A: pattern based on a mosaic from Gloucester (No 57); B: Mosaic
from Room 22, House 1, Insula XIV at Silchester with superimposed square outlining extent of mosaic
from Room 6, House VII at Caerwent. C: Combe St Nicholas, Somerset. D: Aldborough, Yorks.

fourth-century context. It is a fairly common type.

We have seen a variety of simple schemes with the octagons dominant visually. Mosaic
designers, however, contrived to vary and elaborate the pattern in as many ways as possible,
with the result that often the schemes became entangled within a confusion of geometric
elements so complex that the pattern's structure is hard to disentangle. It is also difficult in some
cases to establish whether a pattern has evolved from tangent octagons or from spaced squares
such as No 51 from Gadebridge Park. Here the scheme is spaced squares separated by tangent
tilted squares with the interspaces filled by eight-lozenge stars (see p. 81); but one can discern
within the design a series of coincidental linear interlaced octagons, each containing a square
panel and four tilted squares.

There can be little doubt that the dominant scheme of Panel B on No 39 from Colchester,
dated to the second century, is an arrangement of tangent octagons. Two rows are occupied by
flowered medallions, similar to the schemes imitating coffering. Its rectangular format is 2½
times larger than an identical scheme from Insula XIV at Silchester (FIG. 7, B), where the
emphasis is a quincunx distribution of roundels, those in the angles occupied by flowers of a
similar style to those at Colchester. It too is second-century. The earliest example, dated c. A.D.
75 comes from Room W8 at Fishbourne (Cunliffe 1971, pl. LXXVI). Instead of the octagons being
occupied by flowered roundels as at Colchester, they all contain small squares flanked by tilted
squares and lozenges.

On another pavement from Caerwent, House VII (Ashby et al. 1902, pl. X) there is an
arrangement identical to the Silchester mosaic but with the scheme rotated through 45°(FIG. 7, B:
scheme within superimposed diagonal square). Instead of the design being a quincunx of
octagons it is now a quincunx formed by a central octagon, with a lost figured subject, flanked

on alternate sides by four squares occupied by cupids holding torches. (At Silchester the equivalent to these panels merely contained swastika-peltae.) The remaining octagons each contain squares in the angles (not shown in FIG. 7, B) and on the axes, those in the angles being occupied by busts of the Four Seasons and the others by small animals. The background comprises a pattern of tilted squares and lozenges. The introduction of figured subjects and colour into the lozenges has made the scheme less formal. Its date must follow the Silchester example yet probably dates to the fourth century.

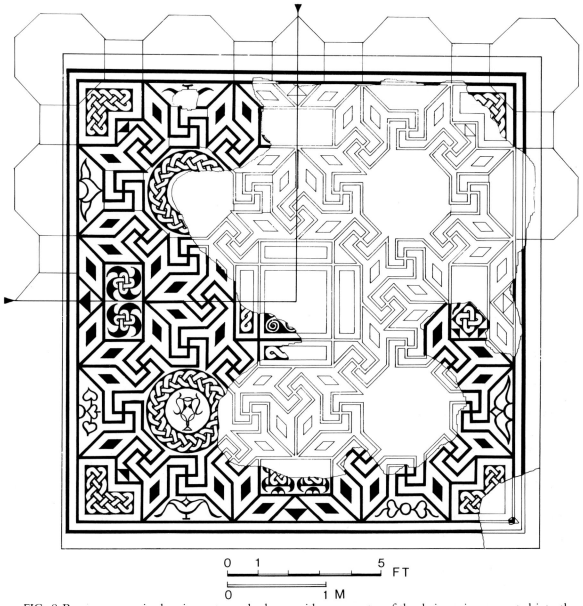

FIG. 8 Boxmoor mosaic showing octagonal scheme with one quarter of the design mirror-repeated into the remaining quarters

It does not necessarily follow that increased elaboration of the scheme is a pointer to date. A highly complex variation at Boxmoor, Herts. (FIG. 8), is dated to the mid second century. We can discern within the pattern a series of octagons, the most obvious containing roundels evidently occupied by canthari. Analysis of the design, however, reveals it not to be an all-over series of tangent octagons developing small squares, but four separate schemes each identical to the Silchester example but with the pattern filling one quarter mirror-repeated in the remaining quarters (see p. 33). The fact that the design is not continuous is demonstrated by the occurrence of rectangles (two square interspaces side by side), one of which contains two swastika-peltae, and by the formation of oblong hexagons along each axis. Further elaboration is achieved by surrounding the principal octagons with eight linked swastika-meander patterns — those 'above' and to the 'sides' fill what would otherwise have been square interspaces.

Schemes based on Hexagons (FIG. 9)

Adaptation of the hexagon is limited to only a few patterns. The simplest and most common form is an all-over arrangement of hexagons, outlined in simple guilloche, forming a cluster either around another hexagon or around an octagon, as represented at Fullerton (No 45) on a pavement dated to the fourth century, and at Keynsham (FIG. 9,A) within an hexagonal room.

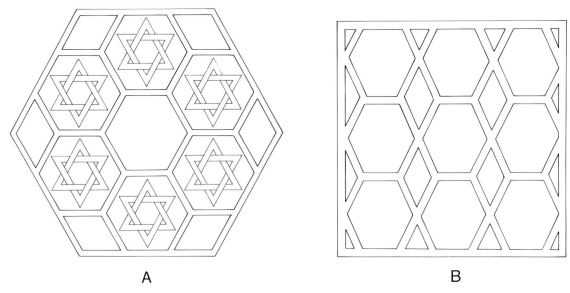

A   B

FIG. 9 Schemes based on hexagons

Although this is the most frequent variation, the scheme is uncommon and only appears on another five examples (see p. 79). A variant (FIG. 9, B), attributed to the second century, comes from Insula XIV at Silchester. Here there is an arrangement of nine irregular hexagons in three rows of three, each containing flowered motifs including two squared rosettes. The central panel is occupied by a cantharus with a swastika-meander on its neck, typical of canthari on second-century pavements including those from Colchester (No 39) and Verulamium (No 75.). The adaptation of the pattern has created lozenge-shaped interspaces occupied by swastika meanders. This variation also fits well into a square or rectangle which a standard scheme would not — hence the frequency of the hexagon as a cluster within a circle or hexagon. Neither does the shape lend itself to being interlaced like the octagon. A single row of linear hexagons on a corridor pavement from Brislington (Barker 1900, pl. VII) is the only example. It is not possible to interlace the shape both longitudinally and horizontally, although it is possible to have two rows of interlaced hexagons with one row abutting the other. One other pavement should be quoted — an *opus sectile* floor in hexagonal and octagonal tiles from Silchester (Fox and Hope 1901, pl. XXVII). In the centre of the floor the hexagons are arranged point to point to form lozenged interspaces set with tesserae, and on the border in fully interlocking segments.

Scheme with a combination of Squares, Octagons and Crosses (FIG 4, B)

This scheme consists a grid of spaced squares contiguous with octagons, the latter contiguous with crosses. It occurs in room N12 at Fishbourne (Cunliffe 1971, pl. LXXVIII) dated to c. A.D. 75, but with hexagons instead of octagons. Its pattern is similar to that shown on No 34 from Cirencester, dated to the late second or early third century. It is really a variety of a spaced-squares scheme, but it is described here separately since it lends itself to adaptation and has been the basis for many later pavements. FIG. 4 B shows how the standard pattern has been adapted with two arms of the crosses truncated to form chevrons or L-shapes separated by octagons.

(The scheme is similar to, but not to be confused with that shown on FIG. 4, A — which is based on large squares and tangent tilted squares (see p. 24), hence between L-shapes hexagons and not octagons are formed.) We find the basis of the scheme used on No 65 from Rapsley and No 87 from Woodchester.

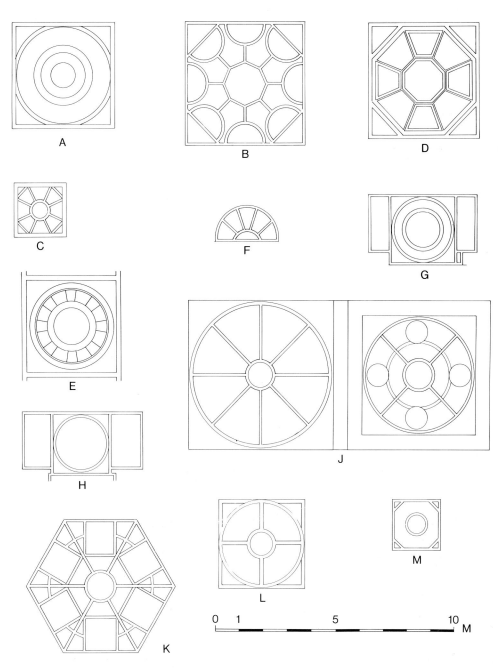

FIG. 10 Mosaics with schemes based on concentric circles and radial divisions (A-M)

A Barton Farm	E Colchester	J Horkstow
B Brantingham	F Dewlish	K Keynsham
C Bramdean	G Frampton	L Littlecote Park
D Chedworth	H Hinton St Mary	M Newton St Loe

Concentric and Radial Schemes

FIGS. 10 and 11 show a selection of radial and concentric schemes drawn to approximately the same scale; in many cases without their borders or attached panels. Two other radial schemes, but of a less obvious type, can be seen at Caerwent (No 16) and Hinton St Mary (No 61).

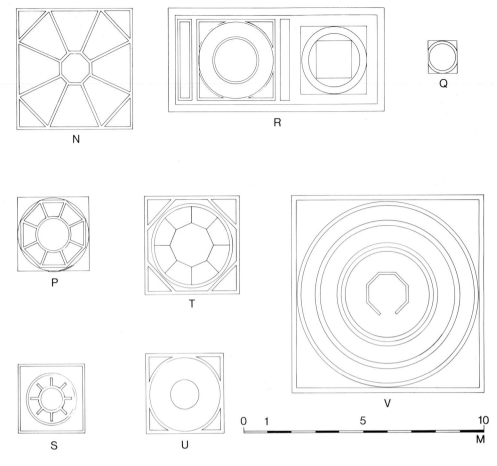

FIG. 11 Mosaics with schemes based on concentric circles and radial divisions (N-V).

N	Pitney	R	Stonesfield	U	Withington
P	Rudston	S	Thruxton	V	Woodchester
Q	Rudge	T	Winterton		

Concentric schemes were particularly popular in the late third to fourth century, but they are not exclusive to that period. We can see an example at Fishbourne (No 44) dated *c.* A.D. 75 for instance, and also see it superimposed by a grid of squares in a later second-century context at Colchester (Nos 39 and 40). The reason for the popularity in the fourth century is doubtful; but one of its advantages is that it could be fitted into a square of any size, and apart from compass-drawn guide lines required no complex 'net'. The larger the circle the more the bands of pattern that could be introduced. Another advantage is that, as on the Orpheus pavements from Barton Farm (A) and Woodchester (V), a continuous 'frieze' of animals could be illustrated. With radial schemes, commonly a circle within a square was divided into the form of a wheel with a central hub. For example at Horkstow (J) and Littlecote Park, Wilts. (L), a circle is divided into four panels, while at Thruxton, Hants. (S), it is divided into eight. Even more complex is No 41 from Colchester (E), with 16 panels. Octagons were divided similarly and formed an ideal shape for eight subdivisions as at Chedworth (D), Pitney, Somerset (N), and No 69 from Rudston (P). At Keynsham (K) a hexagon has been divided by six radial panels, further elaborated by a concentric band of guilloche superimposed by the insertion of squares into each of the panels. One of the advantages of these schemes is that the panels were large and ideal for figured content. Indeed, the examples of circles, octagons and hexagons with radial divisions which are illustrated here all contain representations of figures and animals.

Comparison between square schemes in mosaic and painted coffered ceilings has already been made (p. 23); but it is possible that some of the concentric and radial designs were also copying ceiling decoration. In Italy, the third century saw an increase in the construction of domes and the appearance of vault-mosaics. It should be expected therefore that the fashionable styles of architecture and decoration in Italy would soon be imitated in the provinces. It is unlikely that many villas in Britain had vaults in rooms other than bath-houses, but possibly the general effect was copied in painted plaster including the *'skylight'*, the latter represented in mosaic by circular or octagonal 'hubs' of the wheel designs. At Bignor a hexagonal scheme in mosaic has a hexagonal basin in its centre which, although only ornamental, is probably imitating an impluvium.

Swastika-meander Patterns

Also termed Greek-key, this is one of the most common patterns in mosaic and is also to be found decorating borders and corridors. In this context it may have been intended to represent a maze to ward off evil spirits. The design is based on two strands each with a double return. Where these cross, a swastika is formed. We have already seen two variations of swastika-meander at Combe St Nicholas and Aldborough (FIG. 7, C, D respectively), both uncommon varieties. We have seen it has been utilized at Boxmoor (FIG. 8), linking octagons and lozenges. More commonly meander is arranged in a staggered formation, developing square interspaces often occupied by small motifs as in the example from Chedworth (No 19 and FIG. 14). It is a very frequent type and is represented elsewhere in the collection at Bancroft (No 5, panel B), Cirencester (No 26) and Fullerton (No 50). On mosaics from Cirencester (Nos 21-37) we can see a wide variety of types ranging from continuous runs of swastika-meander with double returns (No 21) to more complex versions where the patterns are reversed to form mirror-repeats (p. 57). An unusual type with reverse return can be seen at Aldborough (No 2) and Winterton (No 82), while at Chichester (No 20) the meander alternates with squares but with the meander opposed and linked (FIG. 15) – similar to an example from Verulamium (No 74).

To construct the pattern the mosaicist probably laid out a right-angled net (FIG. 1, B), width of a square being the width of a line or spaces between lines. The mosaicist may have drawn each meander individually before setting, but for speed of construction more likely he used a cartoon or template. The advantage of a cartoon is that if the pattern was to be reversed, as in that on No 72, the cartoon could be used upside down. However, free-hand layout was frequent and resulted in errors of construction — as can be seen for example on No 26 from Cirencester. Not only is its pattern irregular but the line-thickness is variable.

Mirror Repeats

Under the last seven headings a few of the most common schemes have been discussed with particular reference to the various adaptations. In all cases the patterns have been obtained by a latitudinal, longitudinal or diagonal shift, or by superimposing one motif upon another. The variations are essentially dependent upon the orientation of the grid in relation to the border and where the border dissects the design. Another technique, already briefly commented upon in the discussion of octagonal schemes (p. 27), is where the design filling one quarter of the pavement is reflected in the remaining quarters, as in the Boxmoor mosaic (FIG. 8) dated to the mid second century. Its design is based on a grid of tangent octagons developing square interspaces. Where the pattern is mirrored along the axes, the interspaces have become rectangles. This mosaic is a particularly intricate example since the designer has also mirrored the meander surrounding the roundels. It was the designer's intention — a pattern-shift here would also link with the rest of the design. A mirror-repeat of the pattern has also been employed on a pavement of similar date from Insula 2 at Colchester (Hull 1958, pl. XVI). Here an overall diagonal grid of large squares tangent to small tilted squares has rectangles instead of tilted squares along the axes. In the centre of the design is a large eight-petalled flower occupying an octagon, itself flanked on each of its sides by short strips of guilloche in rectangles. It recalls the eight swastika-meanders around the octagons at Boxmoor, and it is tempting to suggest that they may be the work of the same designer if not the same mosaicist.

The adaptation of the more complex schemes using mirror repeats appears to be confined to the second century, but it was used frequently in conjunction with swastika-meander, where occasionally, as in the scheme already described, ¼ of the floor was repeated in the remaining quarters. At Woodchester for example (No 87), instead of the corner-panels comprising an all-over swastika-meander, it has been mirror-repeated — hence the rectangles instead of small squares at the axes.

Workmanship and Grading

One of the aims of the catalogue is to assess the standard of workmanship of each pavement so that technical as well as stylistic comparisons can be made. Stylistic similarities have been used in the past to relate pavements to a particular *officina* although their technical merit differs markedly, and they either cannot in fact be products of the same *officina*, or are earlier or later products of it. Following each mosaic description, therefore, is comment on its technical merit, and a grade of workmanship — Grades 1-3. These grades are based on the following factors: (a); the precision of geometric ornament and the portrayal of figures; (b); compactness or looseness of setting; (c); size of tesserae; and (d); range and use of colour.

None of these factors is considered individually. For example on some mosaics, such as Brantingham (No 12) and Woodchester (No 87), larger than average tesserae are used; but the point has been made (p. 122) that if smaller tesserae were used, the time and cost of construction would have been considerably greater. At Brantingham and Woodchester we find their portraits and animals constructed with smaller tesserae. Many other pavements include two standards, and this has to be considered in assessing grading — evidence perhaps for the workmanship of master and pupil. For example at Thenford, Northants. (No 72) the portrait is far better than the surrounding ornament; the common and obvious example is where the border decoration is appreciably inferior to the main panel, e.g. at Kingscote, Glos. (No 63).

A useful guide in assessing technical merit is the standard of guilloche. In all cases the finer the workmanship the more braids in a band — conversely the poorer the workmanship the looser and more extended the braids, so that there are fewer in a band of the same length. For example if we observe a Grade 1 mosaic (No 75) from Verulamium we find the chain guilloche extremely compact; but if we compare it with the same ornament at Thenford (No 72), on a pavement listed Grade 3, we will see that there the pattern is very loose.

Grade 1

Pavements in this category are infrequent. They would include the best of all the factors listed, particularly precision of setting ornament and fineness of tesserae. As a yardstick, the mosaic from Room 3 at Bignor, Sussex (Lysons iii, 1817), with its figure of Venus and its frieze of the Cupid Gladiators, is in this class. It is of exceptional quality and probably technically the best mosaic in Britain; its tesserae are particularly fine and compact, and not only are the figures superbly drawn but they are also executed with a wide range of colour including blue glass. The mosaic in Room 5 at Chedworth (R.C.H.M., *Glos.* i, pls. 4 and 5) is of somewhat poorer quality than Bignor but would still merit a Grade 1 rating. The figures include 'reticulated' setting of the tesserae. Only six mosaics in the collection are thus rated — they are Nos 7 and 8 from Bancroft, No 19 from Chedworth (perhaps broadly contemporary with that in Room 5 and by the same mosaicist), Nos 38 and 41 from Colchester and No 75 from Verulamium.

Grade 2

The majority of the mosaics in the catalogue are in this grade and are further subdivided by comment related to specific details. In all cases the pavements lack the precision of the Grade 1 mosaics, but may include well-drawn figures and a wide range of colour. Guilloche will be fairly tightly drawn but will include mistakes in the bands and at their terminals. No 61 from Hinton St Mary is listed as Grade 2. Its geometry and symmetry are inaccurate, as can be seen when comparing the juxtaposition of its two schemes. Its guilloche is reasonably well drawn, but errors have occured in linking the semicircles to the central medallion. The portrait of Christ is well-drawn in a bold yet simple style, in contrast to the personifications of the Winds in the quadrants which have awkwardly-drawn arms. The Bellerophon panel is well-drawn and includes a wide range of colour, but no attempt is made to employ small tesserae for detail or to use tesserae of similar shades to obtain blends, as has been done in the lion emblema on No 75 from Verulamium or can be seen in the gradation of colour at both Bignor and Chedworth.

No 87 from Woodchester is also listed as Grade 2. Its animals, collectively, may be worthy of a higher grade owing to the excellent way the artist has obtained a rhythmic harmony. However, when comparing the individual animals it will be found that they are very similar to one another, and if it was not for their markings the identity of some would be doubtful. Its geometry is precise but the tesserae are slightly larger than average. Although reticulated setting is also to be found in the legs of the reclining nymphs it is coarse when compared with that at Chedworth.

No 12 from Brantingham is also Grade 2, but it is inferior to Woodchester in many respects. Its tesserae are somewhat coarse, its guilloche is very loose, its range of colour narrow, and its reclining nymphs are poorly drawn. In contrast the bust of Tyche and the portraits occupying arched panels are fine and the work of a master. Its portraits, and so far unique scheme, are sufficient to exclude it from a Grade 3 category.

Grade 3

As a general rule Grade 3 pavements will include the majority of corridor mosaics, which are not only constructed in coarse tesserae but frequently include errors in setting and perhaps have only three colours. In these respects they are comparable to the borders around Grade 2 pavements. However, sub-standard work is to be found widely and frequently in houses occupied by pavements of higher quality. For example in Building XII 1 at Cirencester we can see Grade 2 workmanship represented by No 25; but adorning the bath-suite in the same building is a very coarse piece of workmanship represented by No 26. Two other floors in the same house had ever cruder floors — merely irregular red panels against a limestone background.

We can find a similar situation at Fullerton where the principal room of a small villa is paved with polychrome hexagonal scheme (No 45) of Grade 2. Elsewhere the rooms contain very crudely-worked monochrome pavements including what must be the worst example of a maze in Britain (No 48) — not only naively simple but crudely worked (Grade 3). It would appear that at Fullerton and Cirencester the owners could only afford one reasonable mosaic but were determined to have as many rooms paved as possible, no matter what the quality. The same may apply to Building XII 2 at Cirencester situated just south of XII 1. It is the opposite of most buildings, for the corridor pavement (No 27) is markedly superior in construction and originality to the rest of the pavements in the house — e.g. Nos 28-33, which are carelessly set out, crudely constructed and degenerate.[5]

---

[5]Degenerate workmanship is common, but not necessarily indicative of late date. When comparison of the workmanship is made for example between the first and second-century pavements from Fishbourne and the fourth-century mosaics at Bignor we find the Fishbourne examples decidedly inferior. This is particularly strange when compared to the grandeur and the fittings of the palace.

THE CATALOGUE

Note

Each entry is headed with the dimensions of the mosaic and, when known, the size of the room. The dimensions, if overall, are from the limit of the fine tesserae and do not include coarse tessellated borders, whether plain or decorated. If the overall scheme cannot be reconstructed, only the dimensions of the fragment are given. References to drawings already published follow each heading: if the drawing has not already been published it is followed by the initials NPP (not previously published). A select bibliography follows each entry. The first part of the description describes the pavement's scheme — its basic pattern as represented by the overall framework — usually, but not always, executed in guilloche. In some cases the visual appearance may differ from the description. This is because the scheme may have been debased, as demonstrated in the introduction dealing with a few of the various basic types (p. 23). In an attempt at standardization of terminology descriptions of schemes and ornament have been taken from Dr. Smith's translation of the *Répertoire graphique de décor géométrique dans la mosaïque antique* Bulletin IV of the Association Internationale pour l'Etude de la Mosaïque Antique (AIEMA, Paris, 1973). However, in some cases, to use that terminology would be at variance with the writer's ideas on how individual schemes underwent design-alterations, and therefore terminology of schemes does not adhere strictly to that glossary.

Following each description is an assessment of the workmanship (see p. 34) and the citation of parallels: In quoting parallels the writer has tried to follow a theme relating to the similarities and variations of schemes — the theme of the introduction — and not similarities of style between specific types of ornament. Nor is the list of parallels exhaustive. Quoting parallels for ornament, however desirable, would have considerably expanded each commentary; and since this subject relates to schools of mosaic (see p. 19), on which work is already published (Smith 1965, 1975), duplication has been avoided.

Old county names are not used: site-names conform to the new county boundaries of 1974.

Mosaics from Aldborough, Yorks. Nos 1-4.

Aldborough, Roman *Isurium Brigantum*, a small town 16 miles north-west of York, covers a rectangular area of some 55 acres. Intermittent excavation in the early eighteenth and mid nineteenth centuries revealed fragments of at least ten pavements many of which are illustrated in H.E. Smith's *Reliquiae Isurianae* of 1852.

Mosaic 1. Aldborough. Lion beneath a tree

From a town-house. Second century. Dimensions excluding coarse border 11 ft 4 in by 9 ft 7 in (3.46 by 2.92 m), room 12 ft 7 in by 10 ft 10 in (3.85 by 3.30 m). *In situ,* on display. Drawn and painted 1969. Charlesworth 1970, pl 2.

This mosaic was discovered in 1832 when a hole was being dug to bury a dead calf, and was subsequently fully exposed and recorded by H.E. Smith. It comes from the same building as No 2 and possibly No 3. Its almost square central panel contains a reclining feline, probably a lion, facing a tree with widespread overhanging branches. Much of the creature is damaged but part of its tail, chest and front paws remain. These are depicted with the left paw resting upon the right. Colours include yellow ochre, yellow and dark red — the latter possibly samian. Beneath the lion and forming part of the tree-trunk is a band of yellow ochre possibly depicting the ground. The tree-trunk is tall and slender with three branches, each with a cluster of leaves finely worked in yellow ochre, pale grey and dark grey. An unusual technique is that the leaves on the right side of the panel are white and barely distinguishable from the background. The subject is contained in a linear square surrounded by bands of right-angled Z-pattern, stepped triangles and a wide band of chain guilloche outlined in grey with red, yellow and white links, and white, grey and brown scallop-shaped centres. At the 'top' and 'bottom' of the scheme are strips of four-strand guilloche, — in grey, red, yellow and white with the alternate braids in brown, pale grey and white — designed to convert the hitherto square scheme into a rectangle, more suitable for the shape of the room. The chain border and strips of four-strand guilloche are surrounded by a wide band of white tesserae, two opposing grey castellated bands and a white external border. Around the finer work is a coarse brown border.

There is no distinction between the workmanship (Grade 2) of the central panel and the surrounding patterns. The pavement has been heavily grouted in modern times but the wide interstices of the tesserae indicate considerable wear and long use. There are small areas of modern patching above the lion's head, and the white borders are also likely to have been relaid. The workmanship is much finer than in Mosaic 2 and clearly that of a different mosaicist.

The arrangement of concentric squares, although so simple, is uncommon. The writer knows of another 11 examples, two of which are at Aldborough — No 2 with a central flower and the Wolf and Twins pavement (Toynbee 1962, pl 220) with a single border of lozenge patterns. Two other examples are in the collection; these are No 60 from Gorhambury and No 68 from Rudston with a central panel occupied by four swastika-peltae. The other examples include a

37

pavement from the Royal United Hospital, Bath (Cunliffe 1969, pl. LXXXII), with a central eight-petalled flower and six borders of ornament; a mosaic from Brantingham (Slack 1948-51, fig IV) with two bands of ornament including triangles and scales; a pavement found at Castle Hill Farm, Ipswich, in 1854 (Reid Moir and Maynard 1931-3, plan c) with seven bands including superposed triangles and axe-heads; a small panel from Threadneedle Street, London (R.C.H.M. *Roman London*, pl 50) with only two borders, and a coarse mosaic from Woolstone, Berks (Hamilton 1959, facing p. 84), with at least four bands including a scroll. No 56 from Gloucester may be another example but it is too fragmentary to be positive.

Apart from No 2 from Aldborough all the other examples are probably of the fourth century. The infrequency of the scheme compared to arrangements of circles or octagons is perhaps because the scheme limited more than a single panel for a principal motif. A client or a mosaicist may have found this too restricting. The Aldborough Wolf Twins pavement is so similar to No 1 that it is tempting to suggest its format was inspired by it.

References. Smith, 1852, pl. XVI; Toynbee 1964, 284; Charlesworth 1970, 6.

Mosaic 2. Aldborough. Eight-petalled flower.

From a town-house. Probably second century. Dimensions; panel 8 ft 10 in by 8 ft 7 in (2.70 by 2.62 m), room 12 ft by 11 ft 9 in (3.67 by 3.60 m). On display, *in situ*. Drawn and painted 1969. Charlesworth 1970, pl 3.

This mosaic was excavated in 1848 and probably belongs to the same building as No 1. Its scheme contains a square central panel with an eight-petalled flower outlined in grey and shaded white, yellow and with red tips. Around the flower is a band of out-turned stepped triangles in a dark grey linear square, and a border of four-strand guilloche, outlined in grey, and shaded white, yellow and red. Around this is an arrangement of alternating swastika-meanders and swastika-meanders with reverse returns and a surround of simple guilloche. Around the guilloche is a white band of unequal width; the reason is uncertain but possibly it was an attempt to make the mosaic appear central to the room following an error in the setting. The standard of workmanship (Grade 2) is coarser and inferior to Mosaic 1 and includes a number of mistakes. The mosaicist has omitted some yellow tesserae in part of the four-strand guilloche and used red tesserae instead. He has also incorrectly linked the outer bands of the swastika-meander border at the 'bottom' of the pavement. However, the use of swastika-meanders with reverse returns is unusual on Romano-British mosaic and only occurs on No 82 from Winterton,[1] a pavement dated to c. 180. Our example is probably likewise, but possibly early third-century. Nearby York is likely to have been the centre, perhaps for only a short duration, of a flourishing *officina* when we consider the existence of an imperial palace of Severus there and the demands a palace would have created.

The similarity of its scheme to No 1 has already been noted (p. 37) together with parallels.

References. *Illustrated London News,* 20 Jan, 1849; Smith 1852, pl. XVII; Charlesworth 1970, 9.

[1] But see No 52 from Gloucester with a staggered formation set in a lozenge.

Mosaic 3. Aldborough. The Muses Mosaic

From a town-house. Late third to early fourth century. Approximate dimensions of complete mosaic including borders 36 ft 6 in by 24 ft (11.12 by 7.29 m). Lifted, drawn 1975, painted 1978. NPP.

Discovered in 1846 this mosaic lies to the south-west of Nos 1 and 2 and may come from the *triclinium* of the same building. Like pavements 1 and 2 it was published by Eckroyd Smith in his *Reliquiae Isurianae* of 1852, although published earlier in 1849 as a separate engraving. It has suffered from considerable disturbance and since 1846 more has been lost. The illustration shows the extent of the pavement in 1975 and areas lost from 1846.

The fragmentary remains consist of a rectangular panel bordered by a double fillet containing

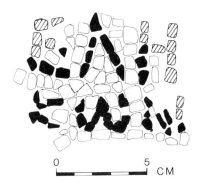

0   5
⊢—————————⊣ C M

FIG. 12 Aldborough. No. 3. Greek inscription in blue glass
tesserae reading EΛH/KωN (missing hatched tesserae
restored from photographs).

the lower part of a standing female in a girdled tunic seen from and facing towards a wide apse.
The left arm is flexed across the breast and holds one end of an open scroll. To the right of the
figure are irregular areas of red and grey, possibly stylized rocks. Above the rocks and
immediately beneath the left elbow is an inscription (FIG. 12) in two rows of Greek lettering set
in blue glass tesserae, reading EΛHKωN (HELIKON).[1] Parts of the second figure survive in
another panel to her right. In a quadrant below the main figured panel and bordered on one side
by a linear band of superposed triangles, is an amorphous design[2] coloured red and yellow
ochre. The interpretation of this feature is speculative but the writer favours it being a jelly-fish
although he can quote no parallels.

Dr. David Smith believes that there were in all nine figured panels, which, together with the
inscription referring to Mount Helicon, is evidence for the subject being the Nine Muses. The
figure in the inscribed panel is interpreted as Clio, the Muse of History, and the more
fragmentary figure as Melpomene the Muse of Tragedy.

Another fragment survives about 25 ft (7.62 m) away from the first and is almost certainly
the corner of the same pavement. It is decorated by a female bust shown by Eckroyd Smith to
have been gazing forwards. Her shoulders and chest are naked and outlined in red and infilled in
two tones of pink. The right breast is exposed and coloured red with a black nipple. Tightly
drawn across the neck is a red and brown necklace bearing a small black pendant. Over the left
shoulder are wavy red and brown lines, probably a lock of hair. The bust is set on a white
background and is surrounded by a band of wave pattern, simple guilloche and a meander.
Between the meander and the walls of the room is a coarse border in bands of red and grey
tesserae. Workmanship Grade 2.

The fragments were lifted in 1979 for eventual display beneath a cover-building. Dr. S.
Johnson, who carried out subsequent excavations, has kindly reported that the pottery evidence
would favour a later third-century date both for the construction of the room and its pavement.
A late third- to fourth-century date is compatible with its figured content — the use of fairly
small tesserae (c. 10 mm) would hint at the earlier fourth century rather than later.

References. Smith 1852, pl. xviii; Smith 1977, fig 6.1, pl. 6.1 a and b.

[1]At the time of the 1975 survey the inscription was separated from the pavement and set in plaster of Paris.
Considerable loss has occurred over recent years.
[2]This feature recalls the so-called 'Haunches of venison' on the pavement from Micklegate Bar, York engraved by
W. Fowler, 1814 (R.C.H.M. *Roman York,* 1962, pl. 23). Perhaps it represents the work of the same mosaicist — its
complex border pattern of interlaced octagons with alternate sides broken and returned to form a swastika (see FIG. 7D)
also occurs at Aldborough (Smith 1852, pl. xii).

Mosaic 4. Aldborough. Guilloche Mat.

From the same town-house as No 3. Probably fourth century. Dimensions, panel 3 ft 5 in wide
by at least 5 ft 8 in long (1.03 by 1.73 m), room 9 ft (2.74 m) wide. *In situ.* Drawn 1975, painted
1978. NPP.

This fragment lies south of and immediately adjacent to the Muses mosaic (No 3) and probably paved a corridor. It comprises two adjoining panels both oulined in red. In the larger rectangular panel is a mat of guilloche in grey, red, buff and white. In the smaller oblong panel, at 90° to the former, is an open grey square, set lozengewise, containing a grey curvilinear square on a red background. Contiguous with the ends of this panel and the open square are solid grey peltae.

The workmanship is coarse and the tesserae about ¾ in (20 mm) square. The panel has a broad, coarse, warm grey border. Lozenges, or squares set lozengewise, appear to have been a popular pattern at Aldborough occurring frequently on corridor pavements. On a long corridor illustrated by Eckroyd Smith (Smith 1852, pl. XIV) the motif repeats at least five times alternating between squares, while on another pavement (*ibid.* pl. XIX) it is also flanked by peltae. The pattern borders the Wolf and Twins pavement from Aldborough (Toynbee 1962, pl. 220), but also occurs on a number of other pavements in the north of England, including Brantingham (Nos 12 and 13) and Winterton (No 83). Although the pattern predominates in the north of England in the fourth century it is not exclusive to that area. For example it also borders the Orpheus mosaic from Newton St Loe, Somerset (Scarth 1864, pl. XLVII) and is represented on a corridor pavement from Withington, Glos. (Lysons ii 1817, pl. XXI) both attributed to the fourth century. In Dorset the pattern occurs on two pavements from Dorchester, one from Olga Road, (Colley March 1900, pl. facing p. 162), and the other from South Street (Hutchins 1863, facing p. 692). It also borders the fourth-century Bacchus mosaic from Thruxton, Berks. (Ingram 1849, pl. facing p. 241).

It is likely that our example is contemporary with No 3 and therefore dates to the early fourth century.

Reference. Smith 1852, pl. XVIII a.

Mosaics from Bancroft, Milton Keynes, Bucks. Nos 5-8.

Bancroft[1] Roman villa, Milton Keynes, lies on the west bank of the Loughton Brook valley just north of Bradwell village. The villa, of winged corridor plan, has a hall in its main range approached *via* an eastern corridor with a central porch. It was discovered by D. Mynard in 1971 and excavated since 1973 by H.S. Green and J. Barnbrook. Nos 5 and 6 were first exposed in 1973-4 and Nos 7 and 8 in 1978. A fragment of a fifth mosaic (Green 1975, fig 3 pl. ic), with a white meander on a red background, is not illustrated.

[1]The Site was known originally as Bradwell villa but the name has been changed to Bancroft because the site lies in the Bancroft square of the new Milton Keynes City development.

Mosaic 5, Bancroft. Corridor pavement.

From the eastern corridor. Fourth century. Overall length of fragment 79 ft 11 in (24.40 m), panel A; 34 ft 6 in by 3 ft 11 in (10.50 by 1.20 m), panel B; 6 ft 11 in (2.10 m) square, panel C; at least 20 ft 10 in (8.35 m) long by 4 ft 1 in (1.25 m) wide. *In situ,* buried. Drawn 1978. Painted 1979. NPP.

The corridor mosaic is in three sections, two long rectangular panels (A and C) on either side of a threshold (B). With the exception of five small squares in Panel B, which are grey, the pavement is worked entirely in coarse red brick tesserae on a pale cream background. Panel A is sub-divided into three unequal rectangles, two containing an overall pattern of running peltae on either side of a smaller panel containing interlaced circles situated in front of a door into Room 8. Panel B, a threshold approached from a porch, comprises an overall pattern of swastika-meander developing squares in a quincunx arrangement. The squares in the angles each contain four inturned stepped triangles, separated by pure white tesserae set corner-to-corner. The central square has four grey ellipsoids with red centres forming a flower. The design is bordered with a row of out-turned stepped triangles and a plain band. Panel C consists of an overall and continuous pattern of swastika-meander. Unlike its opposite panel it lacks a border. Together with the evidence of a cill separating it from Panel B, and a wider interval between designs here than between panels A and B this may suggest different periods. Panels A and B are likely to be contemporary with No 6.

Although the threshold is of finer quality than the adjacent panels, the standard of workmanship is coarse and typical of corridor pavements of the later third and fourth centuries. There is no exact parallel for the general layout, but running peltae, a common pattern, occur on a number of villa corridor pavements including for example Whittington Court, Glos. (O'Neil, 1952, pl. III), Box, Wilts. (Brakspear 1904, pl. I) and Fullerton (No 46). Interlaced circles, also a common pattern, occur for example on corridors at Woodchester, Glos. (Lysons 1797, pl. XI), West Park, Hants. (Hewitt 1971, pl. XXXV), Great Casterton, Lincs. (Corder 1954, fig. 25) and, further north, at Scampton, Lincs. (Fowler Coll. No 8, 1 May, 1800: Illingworth 1808, pl. 6). Panel B occurs six times along corridor 2 at Woodchester (Lysons 1797, pl. XI) but without central ellipsoids.

The decoration of Panel C is unusual in that the pattern is continuous and not broken by staggered squares. Usually, if meander is depicted as a continuous pattern, its width is confined to a single meander such as at Withington (RCHM *Glos.* i pl. 16); on Panel C the width of the pattern comprises two swastika-meanders. Of the examples quoted, the only pavement dated archaeologically is that from Great Casterton which from coin evidence cannot be earlier than *c.* 350/65 and is perhaps as much as 20 years later (Corder 1954, 35-39). A similar date-range for the Bancroft pavement is possible.

Reference. Green 1975, pl. 3A, 3B, fig 3.

Mosaic 6. Bancroft. Hall pavement.

From Room 1. Fourth century. Dimensions of fragment 27 ft 3 in by 17 ft (8.30 by 5.20 m), room 32 ft 10 in by 26 ft 11 in (10 by 8.20 m). *In situ,* buried. Drawn 1978, painted 1979. NPP.

A most unusual feature of this pavement is that its pattern of red-brick interlaced circles with small squares at the centre is worked around a flagged hearth set slightly to one side of a hall occupying the main range. On the north and west sides of the hearth the width of the pattern is confined to the diameter of a circle (3 ft 2 in (0.95 m)), but on the south side a larger area of pattern occurs.

Its shape is irregular. Along the west side is a dog-leg, reflecting the presence of a doorway (the main entrance into the room was on the east side). At the dog-leg the margin of the pattern, a narrow band, is absent and the circles meet a wider outer band surrounding the scheme. Here the mosaicist has drawn one circle incorrectly, and omitted a small central square. The workmanship is very coarse and probably by the same hand as laid the corridor pavement (No 5). Affinities at Great Casterton (Corder 1954, fig 25) would suggest a date no earlier than *c.* 350/65 (see comments on No 5). Apart, possibly, from another fragmentary mosaic (not illustrated, Green 1975, pl. 1c, 1d, and fig. 3) in Room 2 immediately north and contemporary with that under discussion, the writer knows of no parallel for a mosaic surrounding a central hearth.

Pavements comprising all-over interlaced circles, although not uncommon, are mainly confined to a belt extending from Dorset to Yorkshire. Usually the pattern is executed in smaller circles than the Bancroft example (eg Rudston, No 70) often with the ellipsoids and concave-sided squares formed by the interlaced circles infilled with colour. The pattern occurs frequently in the Midlands, with four examples from Leicester — Blackfriars Street (V.C.H. *Leic.* i, pl. IV), Cherry Orchard, Norfolk Street (V.C.H. *Leic.* i, fig. p. 197), Dominican Friary (drawing by W. Stukeley in S.A.L. Red Portfolio, Leicester p. 11) and Sarah Street *Trans.Leic. A. &H.S.* 9, 1904-5, facing p. 174). It also occurs for example at Haceby (Fowler Coll iii, 22), Scampton (Illingworth 1808, pl. 6) and Great Casterton (Corder 1954, fig. 25). With the frequency of the pattern in and around Leicester it is tempting to suggest that the pavements are the work of a single *officina* perhaps in Leicester, rather than in Durobrivae—Water Newton, the centre of the postulated Durobrivan school (Smith 1969, 107).

Reference. Green 1975, pl. 1A, 1B, fig 3.

Mosaic 7, Bancroft. Geometric square.

From Room 9. Fourth century. Dimensions, 7 ft 1 in by 6 ft 6 in (2.16 by 1.87 m), room 9 ft 8 in by 7 ft 9 in (2.95 by 2.36 m). *In situ*, buried. Drawn 1978, painted 1979. NPP.

Although fragmentary, sufficient survives to enable a reliable reconstruction. Its square scheme is derived from a grid of large squares and small tilted squares with eight lozenge stars in the interspaces (see FIG. 4 A). On this example, however, instead of an eight-lozenge star in the centre, the mosaicist has substituted a square and converted the 'squares' in the angles into L-shapes, here enclosing chevrons of simple guilloche worked in blue, red, yellow and white. Each lozenge is filled with either a solid red or blue rhomboid (if red, outlined blue, if blue outlined red) and with red and blue triangles in the triangular compartments around the margin. The only surviving tilted square contains four inturned stepped triangles in red and blue. Along two opposite sides of the square, converting a square scheme into a rectangle, are bands of right-angled Z-pattern in blue, red, yellow and white. At either end of each Z-form are three blue tesserae in a stepped arrangement. The small rectangle between each Z-shape is chequered with blue, yellow, white and red tesserae. Bordering the mosaic is a band of three-strand guilloche, in the same colours as elsewhere, a double fillet of white, a broad blue band and a coarse border of creamy-grey limestone. The workmanship is very fine and precise (Grade 1) and indicates a most accomplished mosaicist. The general scheme is not unusual; it occurs at Colchester (No 38) in a context dated *c.* 150, but with the lozenges containing rhomboidal swastikas. On a small panel from Silchester (Hope and Fox 1896, pl. XV; Fox Coll. Box 5, 9) and a pavement from Victoria Road, Cirencester, (Smith 1975, pl. CXI, 2) both mosaics being of probable second-century date, the central square has been enlarged at the expense of the small tilted-squares and rotated through 45° to be lozengewise to the pattern. In a third-century context at Rapsley (No 65) we find a similar scheme but with octagons between the L-shapes. Likewise octagons have also been placed between the L-shapes on eight panels around the Great Mosaic at Woodchester (No 87), perhaps of the early fourth century. Scampton, Lincs. (Illingworth 1808, pl. 6) may also be quoted.[1]

Although there are these variations, the prototype remained in favour into the fourth century. It is to be found on a 'restored' pavement from Spoonley Wood (R.C.H.M. *Glos.* i, pl. 15),[2] but the closest parallels both stylistically and geographically are a panel on pavement B from Stonesfield, Oxon. (Smith, 1969 pl. 3.15) and a mosaic from Cotterstock, Northants. (Artis 1828, pl. LX). At Stonesfield the central panel is occupied by a mat of guilloche and the small tilted squares have guilloche knots; the lozenges also contain multi-coloured rhomboids. At Cotterstock the central square has been enlarged and rotated through 45° to be contiguous with the L-shapes — at the loss of the small tilted squares.

With such close stylistic affinities to the Stonesfield pavement there can be little doubt that the pavement under discussion is probably fourth-century and may be a product of the Corinian *officina* which Stonesfield is considered to be (Smith 1969, 97). However, although stylistically and certainly technically there are strong grounds for suggesting the same *officina* for these pavements, the more northerly Cotterstock example raises the question whether the same contractor was possibly working from the Durobrivan or Leicestershire area? At least this might explain both the technical and stylistic similarities and the presence of the blue tesserae — Switherland slate from the Charnwood Forest, Leicestershire. Of the elements in the pattern, only one is worthy of comment. The form of the right-angled-pattern with its stepped terminals and chequered centres is most unusual, and as far as the writer is aware to be found on only one other mosaic — the Kingscote pavement (No 63).

[1]Although the Bancroft mosaic with its irregular hexagons between L-shapes appears similar to the Rapsley and Woodchester examples, the structure of the designs is different. Pavements with hexagons are derived from a grid of spaced squares with lateral cubes set lozengewise (FIG. 4 A), while pavements with L-shapes separated by octagons are probably derived from a grid of octagons, squares and crosses (FIG. 4 B), the basis for the scheme used on No 34. For further discussion see p. 30.

[2]The reference quoted beneath pl. 15 in R.C.H.M., *Glos.* i is incorrect. It does not appear in Dent 1877. The correct reference is *Winchcombe and Sudeley Record* 4, 1893, fig 7.

Mosaic 8, Bancroft. Grid of octagons.

From Room 3 of the villa. Fourth century. Dimensions, fragment 19 ft 8 in by 6 ft 7 in (6 by 2 m), room 27 ft 11 in by 19 ft 8 in (8.50 by 6 m). *In situ*, buried. Drawn 1978, painted 1979. NPP.

Its scheme consists of a grid of octagons, tangent, outlined in simple guilloche in blue, white, yellow and red throughout, containing circular panels. Regrettably parts of only two panels survive. One is drawn in three-strand guilloche and contains the remains of a flower — originally with eight red-tipped petals, and the other bordered with a row of L-shapes in the same colour as the guilloche, surrounding a circular laurel wreath worked in deep maroon with white and very pale grey leaves. Inside and outside the wreath are rows of small blue stepped triangles and in the centre is a yellow circle containing a blue quatrefoil. The angular interspaces between the medallions and octagons bear small angled 'crescent'-shapes alternating blue and red. A single remaining triangular interspace has a chequered arrangement of three blue triangles set in a thin yellow frame. Around the scheme is a band of waves, a band of three-strand guilloche and a coarse border of local limestone decorated with a red swastika-meander and a chequered rectangle on the axis.

Grids of octagons tangent to one another on Romano-British mosaics occur on eighteen examples(see Appendix 2, p. 125). The most usual form is a grid of three rows of three octagons (seven examples) followed by four rows of four (two examples), three rows of four (two examples), two rows of three (one example), one row of two (one example) and perhaps four rows of five (one example). The dimensions of the pavement under discussion are uncertain, but if the mosaic filled the whole room and the width of the border remained constant, there would be room for three rows of five octagons — making more octagons than in any other scheme so far known in Britain. However, there is no reason to assume that the grid covered the whole floor; the border adjacent to the door on the east side (at the bottom of the drawing) could have been wider or alternatively filled with a separate panel.

Until further excavation takes place the date of the pavement must remain problematical. Grids of octagons have been ascribed on stylistic evidence to the later second or possibly early third centuries (Smith 1975, 281-5). On a mosaic from Room H at Keynsham, Somerset (Bulleid & Horne 1926, pl. XII; and fig 2) a grid of two rows of three is associated with figured pavements assigned to the fourth century. The remaining pavement to be considered is that from a four-by-four grid scheme from Room 10, Building I, Colliton Park, Dorchester (R.C.H.M., *Dorset*, pl. 220). It is surrounded by a band of swastika-meander alternating with chequered rectangles not observed on any of the previously quoted examples, but present in a simple form at Bancroft. Other mosaics from the Colliton Park building are attributed to the fourth century, so it would seem likely that this example is of the same date. A fourth-century date is also probable for the Bonus Eventus pavement at Woodchester (Lysons 1797, pl. XIX). Here, what was once a three-by-three octagon grid has been rotated through 45° to form a quincunx pattern. It is perhaps to Woodchester (No 87) that we should look for further affinities with the Bancroft pavement, for it is one of the few sites with a laurel pattern: it surrounds the parade of birds there and one also surrounds Orpheus at Barton Farm (Buckman & Newmarch 1850, pl. VII). Other examples of laurel wreaths are known in Britain at Colchester (No 41) and Winterton (Stead 1976, fig. 136). They are not known on any pavements attributed to the second century. On the present evidence an early fourth-century date is favoured for the Bancroft mosaic.

Excepting the border, the standard of workmanship is fine (Grade 1), though slightly inferior to the mosaic in Room 9 (No 7) in that the tesserae are a little larger, resulting in the motifs, e.g. the width of the guilloche, being larger. The background tesserae of white limestone are harder than in Mosaic 7 which suggests that it may not be contemporary. Reliably to attribute the pavement to a workshop is not possible, but the occurrence of wreaths at Woodchester and Barton Farm may indicate that the mosaicist came from the Corinian school. However, as in No 7, the blue framework tesserae have been identified as Switherland slate from the Charnwood Forest, Leicestershire, which may suggest a more northerly base for the mosaicist.

Mosaic 9, Beadlam. Geometric

From a villa at Beadlam near Helmsley, Yorks. Fourth century. Dimensions; excluding borders, 13 ft 10 in by 8 ft 4 in (4.23 by 2.54 m), room 21 ft 3 in by 13 ft 6 in (6.47 by 4.11 m). Lifted,[1] drawn 1969, painted 1978. NPP.

This mosaic came from a domestic building on the north side of a courtyard flanked by outbuildings, and was discovered in 1969 during an excavation directed by Dr. I.M. Stead. The site is to be consolidated by the Ancient Monuments Inspectorate for display to the public. Unfortunately the long axis of the mosaic is damaged, but sufficient remains to enable a reconstruction of the pattern. Its scheme is divided into three fields — a central square between two oblongs. The central square consists of a grey, all-over, swastika-meander pattern developing squares in a staggered arrangement containing squares of simple guilloche with alternating grey, buff-white, and grey, red and white braids. In the only surviving square are four L-shapes set in the angles with a cross in the centre. Two of the squares have been patched in antiquity.

'Above' and 'below' the design is a strip of simple guilloche in alternating grey, red and white, and grey-buff, and white braids. The oblongs on either side of the mosaic are identical and are bordered with four-strand guilloche, in grey, buff, red and white, [2] enclosing an oblong compartment with a red strip surrounded by a band of grey inturned stepped triangles, similar to the central oblong on No 13 from Brantingham. Surrounding the whole scheme is a row of red out-turned stepped triangles, two red bands and a cream-coloured border, all in coarse tesserae. The workmanship is fairly coarse (Grade 3) and the small tesserae are irregular in size. A number of mistakes have occured in the meander resulting in more lines along the 'left' side than the 'right'.

The arrangement of staggered squares and meanders is a design more common in the second century. It occurs on a pavement from Verulamium (Wheeler and Wheeler 1936, pl. XLV) dated c. 160-190, and at Chichester (No 20) on a pavement possibly of comparable date. The squares on both pavements contain rosettes. A pavement from North Street, Colchester (Benham 1923, pl. facing p. 251), probably also of the second century may be quoted. The writer knows of no certain fourth-century examples of this general scheme except possibly for a pavement from South Street, Dorchester (Hutchins 1863, fig. facing p. 692) with a staggered arrangement of at least six squares and meanders. It has a border of lozenges which, as we have already seen (p   ), are common in the fourth century particularly in the north of England. A distinction between the pavement under discussion and the second-century examples quoted, however, is that the arrangement of squares and meanders is reversed. The squares no longer occupy the corners and centrepiece.

A pavement from Hovingham[3] only six miles from Beadlam and originally comprising a square mat of guilloche flanked 'above' and 'below' by squares of swastika-meander, is a truncated version of the same scheme. The style of meander and the use of stepped triangle borders is so similar that it raises the possibility that it was the work of the same contractor; especially so since the sites are so close. A variation of the pattern and a design fairly common throughout the Roman period is the all-over swastika-meander, for example at Chedworth (No 19), Cirencester (No 26) and four panels at Woodchester (No 87).

References. *The Ryedale Historian* 3 (April 1967) Cover plate, pp. 10-11. *JRS* lvii (1967), 179. *Britannia* i (1970), 278.

[1] At the time of writing the pavement is in temporary store in Helmsley Castle.
[2] A minor variation in the guilloche is that the mosaicist has shaded the braids in the 'right-hand' panel erroneously — grey, white, red and buff. Red in guilloche, if used, is usually placed along the margin of the braid.
[3] An engraving of this mosaic is preserved in the Yorkshire Museum.

Mosaics 10 and 11. Bishopstone Down. Fragments

From a villa at Starveall Farm, Bishopstone Down, Wilts. Probably datable to c. 300-350.[1] Dimensions of pavements uncertain, Room 1 containing Mosaic 10, 14 ft 7 in by 12 ft 9 in (4.44 by 3.90 m), Room 2 containing Mosaic 11, 10 ft 6 in by 8 ft (3.20 by 2.44 m). *In situ*, buried. Drawn 1972, painted 1978. NPP.

These two fragments, from separate rooms, are recorded on a single drawing, in correct relationship to one another. No 10 was first recorded in a photograph by A.D. Passmore in 1938, but a reference would suggest that the pavements were known as early as 1880.[2] They were rediscovered in 1972 following a survey and small-scale excavation by B. Phillips, but were found to be seriously damaged by plough-action and, in the case of No 10, collapsed into a hypocaust.

All that survives of No 10 are fragments of a band of spaced swastika-meander with a rectangular strip of guilloche in each space. The meander is in two tones — red and pale grey (an unusual treatment also found at Combley for example (No 42)) and bordered by alternating bands of red and very pale grey worked in coarse tesserae. Although so fragmentary the pavement is of interest since fragments of mosaic from the hypocaust channels indicate it to have been figured. One fragment shows what appears to be the open jaws of a hound with its tongue hanging out and another possibly the spine of a boar with coarse bristles. It is not known whether they formed part of a small Orpheus scene, as the excavator has suggested to me, or merely a hunt. The remaining fragment, No 11 from Room 2, appears to have had a square panel bordered by three-strand guilloche surrounded by broad white, yellow ochre, grey and yellow ochre bands.

[1]The date, kindly provided by B. Walters, is based on pottery dated *c.* 320-350 from a pit sealed by destruction-material.
[2]*W.A.M.* xli (1920-22), 390.

Mosaics from Brantingham. Nos 12-15.

The Roman villa at Brantingham, N Humberside lies about a mile north-west of Brough (Roman Petuaria). Two fragmentary mosaics were discovered in 1941 during the removal of topsoil for quarrying. In 1948 arrangements were made to lift them. One was successfully raised and transported to Hull museums (Slack, 1948-51, fig. IV) but the other (PL. 88) (Slack, *op. cit.* fig. II) was unfortunately stolen from the site. In 1961, following the observation of tesserae in a ploughed field adjacent to the quarry, local archaeologists dug a trial pit and revealed part of a figured mosaic. Consequently, to forestall further damage, a rescue excavation was mounted in 1962 by Dr. I.M. Stead. Owing to the spectacular nature of the principal pavement (No 12) it was decided to transport it to Hull Museums; fragments of three other pavements (Nos 13-15) were also found then.

Mosaic 12. Brantingham, Tyche and Nymphs

From Room 1. A.D. 330-350. Overall dimensions of pavement and room 36 ft 6 in by 25 ft (11.13 by 7.60 m). Lifted, fragments on display Hull Museums. Drawn 1962, painted 1970. Stead *et al.* 1973, pl. VI B; Smith 1977, pl. 6 VIII a.

Its scheme of decoration can be divided into three fields — a very large central square flanked by two rectangles. The central field comprises a square, in simple guilloche (blue, red and white throughout), with its four corners made into triangles — the result is the formation of an octagon. From the inside faces of the octagon spring eight semicircles, each surmounted by radial 'spokes' linked to the angles of a central octagon or 'hub'. The flanking rectangles are each divided into four arcaded compartments.

The central field

The octagonal central panel contains the bust of a female wearing a white dalmatic, with red facing, across her right shoulder. Her face and neck are coloured cream and, apart from a crescent-shaped area of white beneath the chin (which is outlined in black), have no shading. Her head is turned slightly to her right but her gaze is forwards and consequently appears to be looking at the spectator. The hair is blue with dark red outlines and set into twelve curls. On her head is a mural crown. Behind the figure is a white nimbus and this, together with the figure, is set against a circular red background surrounded by a linear band of inturned stepped triangles in grey.

The semicircular panels each contain reclining female figures, outlined in deep maroon and shaded yellow ochre with white highlights, with the left arm resting upon white circular cushion-like objects, misrendered overturned vases, and with the right arm extended, holding a sprig of leaves. From the waist downward they are swathed in white garments and are shown with their right feet protruding below them. The garments have red bands at the waist and feet. In at least four examples the waist-band runs beneath the figures to form part of a cloak draped over the left arm. The hair of the figures is blue.

In each of the eight interspaces between the semicircular and central panels is a large bulbous cantharus with a round belly and trumpet-shaped neck. The perspective is unusual — not only is the cantharus depicted from above, so that its interior is partly visible, but its small pedestal is portrayed as if seen from the underside. Its handles are straight, but where they join the body they hook outwards and at the rim turn inwards at right angles. All the vessels have red bodies but are shaded brown and grey on the left side. Two vessels are highlighted in white. The triangular corner compartments each contain a large pelta with a knop and triangular pedestal resembling the stem of a goblet. The pelta is split axially by a straight white fillet. The colouring in the two halves differs — if a particular area in one half is red the opposite side is brown and *vice versa*. Flowing outwards from the side of the peltae are tendrils terminating in red or brown circles.

The reclining figures, canthari and peltae all differ in size, so it is likely that they have been freely drawn rather than copied from a cartoon. They also impinge upon red fillets within the panels, which indicates that they were laid before them.

The side fields

Each of the side fields is divided into four arcaded compartments, with horseshoe-shaped arches, each containing a female bust wearing a white dalmatic with grey bands across the shoulders, in a style similar to that of the figure in the central panel. Their hair is wavy and less severely set than on the central figure and their colours are more variable — ochre, blue and deep maroon. Two have locks of hair falling behind the neck and all wear a topknot tied with a narrow red ribbon. Their faces are in pale ochre and are highlighted in white on the nose, forehead and cheeks. As on the central bust and the reclining figures, the neck is white below the chin (which is outlined in deep red) but shown in relief by a grey shadow. Similarly, the busts also have a white numbus but are set on an arcuate red background which extends around and beneath them. Beneath the busts are bands of superposed and inturned triangles. In at least one panel in the 'top' field there were alternating red and white squares instead of superposed triangles.

In the spandrels above the arcading are various types of canthari. Those in the bottom field contain foliage, while those in the top have lids with conical handles.

The borders

Bordering two sides of the pavement is a series of oblong compartments containing lozenges, outlined in red, filled with circular motifs. The strip on the dexter side has seven compartments and the strip on the sinister side nine. The panels at the 'top' and 'bottom' of the mosaic contain patterns of interlaced circles forming quatrefoils and tilted curvilinear squares. At the 'bottom' the curvilinear squares are shaded red and the quatrefoils white, but at the top the shading is reversed. A point of detail in this panel is the way in which the pattern has been broken, suggesting prefabrication, although such an error could occur if two mosaicists worked inwards. The panels in the corners of the room contain a guilloche mat, a running-pelta pattern, a scale pattern and possibly a chequerboard.

Interpretation

From the evidence of the mural crown and the nimbus, the central bust is interpreted as Tyche, 'the personification and quasi-divine protectress of a province, tribe, city or any body of people bound together by ties of kinship' (Stead *et al.* 1973, 97). The eight reclining figures are water nymphs such as those depicted on the Woodchester pavement (No 87). The identity of the nimbed busts in the arcuate panels is not known, but the presence of the *nimbi* would suggest that they are dead and rank as deified. Dr. Smith believes them to relate to Roman funerary portraiture and iconography.

The standard of workmanship is variable (Grade 2). The craftsmanship and form of the busts is very fine, particularly the surviving one in the top field. Considerable skill has also been shown in the simple yet powerful gaze of the faces and the use of white highlights and shading.

The faces of the nymphs are inferior and suggest the work of a less experienced hand — as do the crudely executed borders. The size of the tesserae used in the detailed work is larger than on most other pavements and measures between 10-12 mm square; the background tesserae are also relatively coarse — c. 15 mm square.

There is no precise parallel for the scheme of decoration in Romano-British mosaic, but it falls into a class of mosaic confined to the fourth century[1] where a square scheme, containing either a circle, octagon or hexagon, is divided radially into 4, 8 (e.g. Horkstow (FIG. 10 J)), or 16 (e.g. Colchester, (FIG. 10E)) compartments. The Brantingham example is further elaborated by the introduction of the eight semicircles springing from the angles of the central octagon and partially 'truncating' the radial divisions. A form of this pattern occurs at Hinton St. Mary (No 61) where the scheme is based on a grid of nine tangent circles (three rows of three with radial lines through the interspaces).

Dr. Smith has proposed (Smith 1976, 270) that the pavement may be a product of the so-called Petuarian school, responsible for the Winterton Orpheus mosaic (No 83); but the workmanship of Brantingham, exemplified by the portrait busts, is far superior to Winterton and the writer therefore can see no justifiable reason, except for the radial schemes, for attributing the work to the same *officina*. There can be little doubt, however, that the Brantingham mosaic, as Dr. Smith has suggested (Smith *op. cit.*), has affinities with the Horkstow pavement. Comparison between the workmanship of both pavements suggests they might be the work of the same contractor, if not mosaicist. Also, both pavements include coloured backgrounds, a feature found elsewhere only at Woodchester. Dr. Smith believes the Brantingham and Horkstow pavements to have been influenced by the Corinian school. This may be so, though the influence need not be direct but rather, perhaps, related to the transfer of plans and schemes from one contractor to another. Moreover the Brantingham pavement has close affinities in a mosaic found within the precincts of Lincoln Castle in 1846 (Whitwell 1970, pl. III). This had four canthari almost identical with that sprouting leaves at Brantingham. Not only is their form similar but they also have necks ornamented with similar striping. Again, the occurrence and method of arranging superposed triangles in bands delineated by thin lines at Lincoln is matched precisely at Brantingham. There can be little doubt that these two floors were by the same mosaicist.

Pottery sealed by the Brantingham mosaic belongs no later than the first half of the fourth century. This, together with a coin of 330+ found in mortar contemporary with the construction of the room, suggests a date in the second quarter of the fourth century.

References. Stead *et al.* 1973. For discussion of the mosaic see *ibid.*, Pt. II, 'The Mosaics' by D.J. Smith p. 90; Toynbee, 1964, 286; Smith, 1976, pp. 19-21.

[1]A monochrome example from Chester with eight trapezoids arranged around an octagon (Watkin 1886, fig. p. 137) could be earlier. It has a solid black central roundel; its scheme is also drawn in black lines and not guilloche, which suggests association with monochrome pavements of the first and second centuries.

Mosaic 13, Brantingham. Corridor

From a corridor (Room 2) A.D. 330-350. Original dimensions 31 ft 6 in by 6 ft 9 in (9.60 by 2.05 m). *In situ*, buried. Stead *et al.* 1973, pl. VII B.

The illustration represents only the end of a corridor-pavement extant for 28 ft (8.60 m). Its original scheme consisted simply of a long oblong, with two rectangular panels at either end set at 90° to the first.

From the outside inwards, the long oblong contains concentric bands of blue, blue inturned stepped triangles, simple guilloche in blue, red and white, another band of blue inturned stepped triangles, and finally a long red strip outlined blue. In the rectangular panel at one end is a blue lozenge containing a blue circle, quartered red and white with two 'spears'; these project from either side and point into the sharper angles of the lozenge. In the interspaces between the outer frame and the lozenge are solid red right-angled triangles. The two long sides of the pavement are decorated with a bold chequer-pattern in white, blue and red, with each similarly coloured square set corner to corner in a stepped arrangement.

The quartered circle motif with 'spears' is similar to the border motifs around the Tyche mosaic (No 12). The long central oblong with its surround of stepped triangles has affinities at Beadlam (No 9) 45 miles north, and the general scheme also occurs at Aldborough (No 4), where a corridor terminates in a rectangle set 90° to the main panel. Chequered borders are not found at Aldborough but the pattern occurs for example at Malton (Mitchelson, 1963–66, pl. IX) and Rudston, Yorks. (No 70); on these two examples the chequers are confined to two colours, not three.

The workmanship is neat but bold (Grade 2) and almost certainly the work of the same mosaicist as No 12 and therefore of the same date.

Reference. Stead *et al.* 1973. For comment on the mosaic see *ibid.*, Pt. II. 'The Mosaics', by D.J. Smith, p. 90.

Mosaic 14. Brantingham, fragment

From Room 3. Probably fourth century. Fragment 6 ft 11 in (2.10 m) long, room 16 ft by 15 ft 10 in (4.90 by 4.85 m). Stead *et al.* 1973, pl. VII A.

This mosaic, found in pieces collapsed into a hypocaust and robber trench, is too small to make possible a reliable reconstruction. The remains, in blue tesserae on white, appear to suggest a row of spaced open squares (or rectangles) containing smaller open squares, each alternating with squares (or rectangles) containing chequers. However, it is possible to

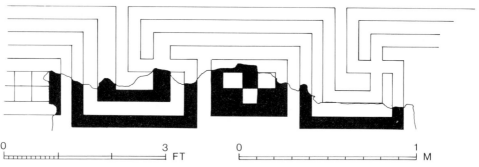

FIG. 13 Brantingham. No 14. Reconstruction

reconstruct the pattern as a swastika-meander developing rectangles (FIG. 13). If this interpretation is correct it is only the second example known in Yorkshire. The other comes from Harpham[1] situated 23 miles to the north. The workmanship is coarse; the discovery of the fragments around the sides of the room suggests a border.

Reference. Stead *et al.* 1973. For comment on the mosaic see *ibid.*, Pt. 11, 'The Mosaics', by D.J. Smith, p. 90.

[1]Collier 1906. An illustration of the mosaic in question appears in a typescript report on the excavations in August–September 1950 preserved by the Augustinian Society of Bridlington.

Mosaic 15. Brantingham, fragment

From Room 5. Probably fourth century. 16 in (41 cm) long. NP.

Fragment worked in red tesserae with the remains of a rectangular panel containing a lozenge and a central motif similar to some within lozenges on the Tyche mosaic (No 12).

The fragment was found in the rubble filling of Room 5, but its proximity to the damaged corridor pavement (No 13) prompted the excavator to suggest it might have been displaced from this, and that it matched the lozenge at the opposite end of the floor. This hypothesis is unlikely, however, because the outline of the lozenge is only two and not three tesserae wide, is in red and not blue/grey, and because the rectangular panel, if complete, would be smaller — 27 in (0.68 m) wide internally as opposed to 43 in (1.09 m) wide. It is likely therefore that the fragment belonged to a pavement in Room 5.

Reference. Stead *et al.* 1973, pl. VIII A.

Mosaic 16, Caerwent. Cantharus and Dolphin

From a courtyard-type town-house in Caerwent (Venta Silurum), Gwent. Possibly fourth century. Original dimensions excluding coarse border 9 ft (approx.) by 8 ft 4 in (2.75 by 2.53 m). *In situ*, buried. Drawn and painted 1969. NPP.

In 1947-8, excavations along the east side of Pound Lane by G.C. Dunning revealed fragments of two mosaics: No 16, from House XXVII N. and No 17 from House XXVI N. At the time of the excavation only the border of No 16 could be recorded as the remainder underlay adjacent property and it was not until 1969, when parts of the site were being consolidated, that the opportunity arose to expose more. The area of the pavement has still not been fully explored as it runs beneath Pound Lane.

Its scheme, in simple guilloche, consists of a square containing a circular central panel tangent to four lateral semicircles and four triangles in the corners and with, on one side at least, a narrow oblong. This basic scheme is further elaborated by a band of simple guilloche running concentric with the semicircles and parallel to the triangles and interlaced with that of the central circle, thereby forming a St. Andrew's Cross. In the four interspaces in the arms of the 'cross' are short radial strips of guilloche projecting from the central panel towards the corners of the mosaic but not linked to the ends of the cross. All the guilloche is outlined in grey with the colours of each plait alternating — green, pale-grey and white, and red, pinkish-yellow and white.

The central panel contains a fragmentary cantharus depicted as if its interior were visible. Its rim is decorated with red and white 'millefiori' and its body fluted in grey, pale-grey, white and pinkish-yellow. The bowl is gadrooned in grey, red and white, and has a band of 'millefiori' across its body. It is supported on a knop and a triangular pedestal and has S-shaped handles. Falling from the surviving handle is a stalk bearing a heart-shaped leaf in white, pale grey and with a green tip. In the two surviving semicircles are dolphins (it is likely that all four were similarly decorated) with their beaks, 'eye-brows' and outlines in grey, their bodies pale-grey and their teeth, fins and tails, in red. The triangular panels each contain a chequer-pattern of grey and white triangles and in the oblong is a grey line. Around the pavement is a coarse border with bands of white, grey, white and red tesserae.

The work is very carefully executed (Grade 2) and the dolphins are well drawn. The guilloche is particularly fine with its alternating colours. One of the features which sets this pavement apart is the use of green tesserae, but their use may be merely the result of stone of this shade being found locally. Its scheme, based on an overall grid of circles, is also unusual, for the parallel band of guilloche around the semicircles and triangles has introduced a saltire pattern emphasised by radial strips. There is no exact parallel for the scheme, the closest being the fourth-century Christian pavement from Hinton St. Mary (No 61). On this however, the radial strips of guilloche follow through to link up with quadrants in the angles. It can also be compared with radial mosaics such as Brantingham (FIG. 10 B). The association of canthari with dolphins is comon. On two mosaics from Verulamium (Wheeler & Wheeler 1936, pl. XLVII and No 73 below) and one from Downton (Rahtz 1963, pl. 1), the dolphins are entwined with the handles, but more commonly, eg Cirencester (No 34), dolphins and canthari are situated in separate panels — as on the Caerwent example. The sharply angled waist and narrow neck of the cantharus is a fourth-century characteristic. But the design, only partially radial, is not so evolved as at Hinton St. Mary (No 61) and therefore an early fourth-century date is likely.

Toynbee, commenting on a lost cantharus from Carisbrooke (No 18), has suggested (Toynbee 1964, 258) that 'such dominant, centrally placed chalices may allude, here and else-where, in the apse at Frampton for example, and on many other pavements . . . to the soul's refreshment in the heavenly banquet.'

Mosaic 17. Caerwent. Fragment

From a town-house at Caerwent, Gwent. Probably fourth century. Dimensions uncertain, length of fragment 6 ft 6 in (1.98 m). Destroyed. Painting made in 1969 from a rubbing. NPP.

The small fragment, from Room 7, Building XXVI N, was exposed during the 1947-48 excavations along the east side of Pound Lane (see No. 16). It consists of a right-angled border of four-strand guilloche in coarse grey, red, yellow and white tesserae around the finer work of the main scheme which is represented here merely by another right-angled band of three-strand guilloche (in the same colours) and part of a quadrant. In the quadrant are traces of a lotus bud. Tangent, and at 30° to the inner guilloche, is a grey right-angled line forming an isoceles-shaped compartment containing an open triangle.

Although fragmentary it is possible to visualize the overall scheme as comprising a square containing four pairs of interlaced squares with quadrants in the four angles and semicircles midway along the sides: a similar scheme perhaps, although larger, to Mosaic 36 from Cirencester, which has only one pair of interlaced squares. There is no direct evidence for more than one pair of interlaced squares at Caerwent but the size of the pavement, at least 13 ft 6 in (4.12 m), leaves room for more than one. A fragmentary pavement with four pairs of interlaced squares is No 58 from Gloucester. A reconstruction of it (FIG. 22), based on parallels from The Avenue, Cirencester, (Lysons ii 1817. pl. v), and Bramdean, Hants. (V.C.H., *Hants.* fig 19, facing p. 308), for example, provides a clearer impression of the overall scheme.

With the possibly single exception of a mosaic from Room VI, Box, Wilts. (Smith 1975, 274, pl. CXII), considered by Dr. Smith to date to the second of even third century, interlaced squares are confined to the fourth century, occurring on at least 60 pavements — nine examples in this collection alone. Their distribution is confined mainly to the south and west of England with outlying examples at Wroxeter, Shropshire (Fox 1897, pl. 2), Lincoln (Whitwell 1970, pl. III), Malton, Yorks. (Mitchelson 1963-6, pl. IX), and in a debased form at Winterton (No 84).

Mosaic 18. Carisbrooke. Fragment

From Room D of the Carisbrooke villa, Isle of Wight, Fourth Century. Dimensions, 9 ft 10 in (3.0 m) long by about 7 ft 9 in (2.36 m) wide. Room approximately 15 ft (4.57 m) square. *In situ*, buried. Drawn 1973, painted 1978.

Carisbrooke Roman villa lies in the grounds of the vicarage and was excavated by W. Spickernell in 1859. The villa, an aisled building with living apartments to the north and a small bath-suite to the south-west, was on display to the public for many years, and the principal mosaic was protected by a shed, but regrettably the site has since become dilapidated. The mosaic has suffered serious damage and now only about a quarter of it remains. The mosaic has also been extensively relaid in modern times with a cross-shaped pattern (not shown on the drawing) without regard to its original scheme. In describing the mosaic it will be assumed that it is complete — its reconstruction is based on a plan by G. Hillier from which a drawing by Roach Smith (Roach Smith 1868, vi, pl XIX) was prepared.

Its scheme is a grid of adjoining squares, but the pattern has been so considerably adapted that its scheme is scarcely apparent. The rectangular field is divided into nine panels, in three rows of three. Along the central axis is a row of three almost square panels, contiguous to one another, each bordered in simple guilloche and linked to one another by short strips of guilloche at 90°. Along each side of the mosaic are three rectangles also linked to the central row of panels by short strips of guilloche but not linked to one another.

The central panel has a blue inner margin (a colour not found elsewhere on the fragment) surrounding a cantharus viewed from the bottom of the drawing. It had S-shaped handles and a gadrooned bowl and was depicted with foliage sprouting from within.[1] The other larger panels 'above' and 'below' the cantharus had bands of four superposed thorns in a guilloche frame. The oblong panels along the sides of the mosaic contained a lotus bud with curled petals in red touching flanking leaves also with red tips; and a large heart-shaped leaf enveloped on either side with smaller leaves. Instead of the inner margins of these panels being bordered by guilloche, they are framed in black and white 'millefiori' and red stripes which further obscure the grid-like structure.

The quality of the geometry and workmanship is good and technically more accomplished than the pavements from Brading (Price and Price 1881) and Combley, I.O.W. (No 42). This mosaic is almost certainly the work of a different craftsman.

The only Romano-British mosaics known to the writer with squares linked by short strips of guilloche are pavement No 1 from Brislington, Glos. (Barker 1900, pl. XIV) and Pavement B from Insula 2, Colchester (Hull 1958, pl. XV). Both mosaics consist of a grid of guilloche bands with superimposed squares exceeding the intersections but with tilted squares occupying the interspaces, absent on our example. The Colchester pavement is dated on stylistic evidence to the mid second century (Smith 1975, 285) and the Brislington pavement may be likewise (*ibid.* 286). However, on the Carisbrooke example the rigid grid-line structure is absent — the heavy use of guilloche, the wide use of 'millefiori' and the stylized buds would all suggest a fourth-century date.

References. Roach Smith 1868, vi, 121-129, with plan and plate (XIX) of the mosaic. V.C.H., *Hampshire* I, 316, fig. 26.

[1]Roach Smith shows the cantharus placed asymmetrically to the panel and with the pedestal 'breaking' the blue margin. It is more likely that the cantharus was symmetrical but it is possible that the drawing of the pedestal is correct. There are examples, including No 25 from Cirencester, where they break into the surround.

Mosaic 19. Chedworth. Meander pattern

In the Chedworth villa, Glos. Fourth century. Overall area of fragments 16 ft 9 in by 6 ft 3 in (5.10 by 1.90 m), room 22 ft by 7 ft 6 in (8.70 by 2.29 m). *In situ*, on display. Drawn 1978, painted 1979. NPP.

Chedworth Roman villa, a National Trust monument, was discovered in 1864, and lies at the head of a small valley about seven miles north of Cirencester. It was largely excavated between 1864 and 1866, with intermittent excavation since 1935. Including corridors, at least 13 rooms had mosaics of which five are displayed, including the famous pavement from Room 5, with Bacchic scenes and personifications of the four seasons (R.C.H.M., *Glos.* i, pls. 4 and 5). The pavement to be described comes from Room 22 in the bath-suite of the north range; really two adjoining rooms of a double *laconicum* with a pair of apsidal plunge-baths both obsolete when the mosaic was laid. The rooms were entered from a door in the south-east side opening onto a panel of mosaic (Panel 1) almost totally lost except for two fragments of simple guilloche, in grey, red, yellow and white, bordering a square damaged in antiquity and resurfaced with *opus siginum*. Around the mosaic, not shown on the drawing, is a flagged border.[1] Entry into the adjacent room was via a threshold of coarse tesserae decorated with what was perhaps a rectangular panel with a pale blue/grey frame. It was infilled with white and divided along its long axis by a red band and surrounded by a coarse red border. In the northern room, only three fragments of a second panel (Panel 2) survive. They all have a pattern of grey swastika-meander developing small squares in a staggered arrangement. The squares, outlined in red or black, contain four inturned stepped triangles, one pair black and the other red. Around the pattern is a very pale blue/grey line followed by a surround of simple guilloche in coarse grey, red and white tesserae, and white, red and another white band. The remainder of the border is paved with red brick tesserae clearly contemporary with the threshold panel between the rooms. It is doubtful whether panels 1 and 2 are contemporary. Apart from the methods of paving their surrounds, the guilloche in Panel 1 is finer.

Although the fragments of Panel 2 are disturbed, it is possible to visualize the overall scheme (FIG. 14) as a continuous pattern of swastika-meander developing staggered squares unbroken by rectangles such as on the four similarly ornamented corner-panels at Woodchester (No 87), or the larger version of that scheme from Room 5 at Chedworth. Less skilfully worked versions are represented in the collection by Nos 26 from Cirencester and 50 from Fullerton, both dated to the fourth century. Frost-action obscures the quality of Panel 2, but apart from its surround the workmanship is very fine and it is comparable in class (Grade 1) to the mosaics in Room 5. The technique of introducing a very pale blue/grey band around the borders occurs on the 'Seasons' mosaic (but in pale buff) and therefore could be the work of the same contractor. An early fourth-century date is probable for Panel 2. Perhaps the earliest version of the overall

FIG. 14 Chedworth, No 19. Reconstruction

scheme[2] in Britain is a monochrome pavement from Silchester, Hants. (Hope & Fox 1896, pl. XIII). On this example the squares are infilled with such a variety of geometric forms that they dominate the pattern at the expense of the meander. A second-century date is likely. Possibly another broadly contemporary pavement, but a simpler monochrome version with plain open squares comes from Room 3 at Wingham, Kent (Dowker 1882, fig. between pp. 136-7). This has a striped black and white border typical of first- and second-century floors, and very notable e.g. at Fishbourne (Cunliffe 1971). The other examples of mosaic with continuous swastika-meander are mainly confined to the Dorset, Gloucester and Oxfordshire areas with outlying examples at Bignor, Sussex (Lysons iii, 1817, pl x) and Bancroft, Bucks. (No 5); stylistically all would appear to date to the late third or fourth century.

References. Goodburn 1972, p. 21 and 25. R.C.H.M. *Glos.* i 1976, pls. 7 and 25.

[1]This is the only example known to the writer of a mosaic bordered with flags and not with coarse tesserae.
[2]It occurs as a repeated insert in a mosaic from Room W3 at Fishbourne (Cunliffe 1971, Vol. i, pl. LXXV).

Mosaic 20. Chichester. Squared rosette

In the south aisle of Chichester Cathedral, Sussex. Mid to late second century. Fragment 5 ft (1.52 m) long, original dimensions 7 ft 8 in (2.34 m) by at least 8 ft 2 in (2.50 m). *In situ*, on display. Drawn and painted 1969. Down and Rule 1971, pl. 13.

This fragment, probably from a town-house, was discovered in 1969. Although only partially complete, its scheme can be reconstructed with reliability (FIG. 15); it is based on an all-over meander pattern, the swastikas alternately reversed, but developing squares in a staggered arrangement. The squares enclose square panels, bordered in simple guilloche in grey, red, brown and white, in a quincunx arrangement, containing (at least in the corner-panels) squared rosettes.[1] These have heart-shaped petals with four short and four long pointed excrescences with a chequered centre surrounded by concentric circles of yellow, grey, white and yellow. The tips of the petals are red and the excrescences white and two tones of pale

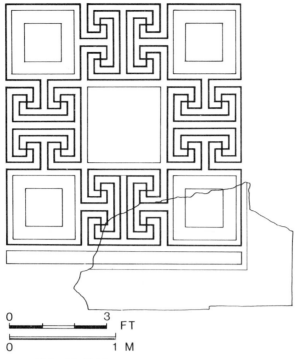

FIG. 15 Chichester, No 20. Reconstruction

grey. Along one side is a strip of simple guilloche in grey, red, yellow and white, and around the mosaic a coarse grey border. The workmanship is fairly fine (Grade 2).

One of the earliest forms of the scheme is a mosaic dated *c.* A.D. 75 from Room W3 at Fishbourne (Cunliffe 1971, Vol. i, pl. LXXV). On this example 20 panels are set in a profusion of running swastikas with the spaces containing repeating patterns but also, curiously, miniature all-over spaced swastika-meander patterns - a reflection of the overall scheme. In a second-century context we can find an example in Building IV, 8, at Verulamium, dated 160-90, with a central panel occupied by the head of Oceanus (Wheeler and Wheeler 1936, pl. XLV). Unlike No 20 however, on this example the squared rosettes are in panels outlined with thin lines and not guilloche. The alternate reversed swastikas have also been 'opened-out' to insert small panels with canthari. The design also occurs on a pavement discovered in 1880 at North Street, Colchester (Benham 1884, between pp. 188-9). For fourth-century examples see No 5 from Beadlam, Yorks, and No 50 from Fullerton, Hants.

The latest samian sealed by the mosaic is Trajanic. This, together with the stylistic evidence of the Verulamium example would suggest a mid second-century date.

References. Down and Rule 1971, 132, pl. 13; Smith 1975, 275, pl. CXIII 2.

[1]A motif consisting of a rosette of four heart-shaped petals, or eight petals when the hearts are divided longitudinally, with four or eight pointed excrescences between the rounded ends of the petals, so that the essentially circular form of the rosette is nicely adapted to occupy a square panel (Smith 1975, 274). For discussion on the form see the paper cited. Another mosaic with this flower in the collection is No 39 from Colchester.

The Cirencester Mosaics. Nos 21-37.

By far the largest single group of paintings in the collection is of pavements discovered in Cirencester since 1968 and (apart from No 37) all found on excavations carried out, in advance of development, by the Cirencester Excavation Committee directed by A.D. McWhirr.

Drawings 21-24 are of pavements discovered in 1968 in the garden of 17 The Avenue and came from Building 2, a courtyard town-house in Insula XIV (Brown *et al.* 1969). Evidence for pavements here was first observed during the laying of a water main in 1964. A second, larger group Nos 25-33, came from two associated buildings, Buildings 1 and 2, both of winged corridor plan, excavated in 1972 and 1973 respectively on a threatened allotment site at Beeches Road, Insula XII, close to the eastern defences of the city (McWhirr 1973 and 1978). Building XII, 1 contained four mosaics, two of which are illustrated[1] (Nos 25-6) and Building XII, 2, eight, seven of which are illustrated (Nos 27-33).

Excavations in 1974, on a town-house at Admiral's Walk, St. Michael's Field, on the west side of Insula VI (McWhirr 1978), revealed another four pavements, three illustrated, Nos 34-36; the other pavement (No 37) was found in 1972 during the construction of a supermarket on the site of the Congregational Church, Dyer Street.

In numbering the drawings throughout this catalogue sequentially it has not been possible to give the pavements from The Avenue and Beeches Road their excavation numbers. These are set out below.

Cat. No.	Exc. No.	Cat. No.	Exc. No.
21	1	27	6
22	2	28	7
23	3	29	8
24	4	30	9
25 (Panel A)	1	31	10
25 (Panel B & C)	2	32	11
26	3	33	12

[1] The unillustrated pavements in Building XII, 1 consisted of a solid red oblong set in a panel bordered in red, with a wide plain surround, and the other a solid red oblong (similar to the first) also with a wide plain surround. The unillustrated pavement from Building XII, 2 had traces of guilloche with a meander pattern.

Mosaic 21. Cirencester. Meander and Labyrinth

From Room 4, Building XIV. 2. Second century. Fragment 13 ft 6 in (4.12 m) long. Overall dimension uncertain but possibly about 15 ft 6 in (4.74 m) square (excluding border). *In situ*, buried. Drawn and painted 1968. (Brown *et al.* 1969, pl. XXXVII *b*.)

This fragment consists of an all-over meander in dark grey against a cream-coloured background. A continuous uninterrupted band of meander borders the mosaic, but further inwards the meander is spaced to allow the insertion of a square and a rectangular panel. The square contains a flower, outlined in grey with four red-tipped petals and shaded in white and yellow, and the rectangle a strip of four-strand guilloche outlined in dark grey with red, yellow and white, and grey, pale grey and white alternating braids. Around the mosaic is a white border with a series of concentric grey lines (a paler grey than the meander). The lines do not run around the whole pavement however but do a [- turn opposite the rectangular strip of guilloche suggesting, possibly, that this point is the axis of the design. One of the bands is joined to the meander indicating that the border decoration may represent a labyrinth.

The writer knows of no parallel in Romano-British mosaic. The scheme is not an all-over swastika-meander developing squares, such as Chedworth (No 19), for it is broken by a single square *and* a rectangle and in places the meander is reversed in the form of a mirror repeat. An

FIG. 16 Cirencester, No 21. Reconstruction

interpretation of the overall design can only be speculative but a reconstruction (FIG. 16) would suggest that the fragment represents a quarter of the total floor area and that the remaining quarters were filled with mirror repeats of the first. The guilloche strip, therefore, is only half its original length. Again it is only speculative, but the floor possibly had a square central panel. The workmanship is good (Grade 2); the complicated meander indicates an experienced designer and craftsman.

No firm dating evidence was forthcoming during the excavation of this pavement, but on stylistic grounds it would be reasonable to assign a second-century date to it. The conclusion is strengthened by the fact that in the fourth century it was sealed by a new mosaic (No 22).

References. Brown *et. al.* 1969

Mosaic 22. Cirencester. Saltire pattern

From Building XIV, 2. Fourth century. Fragments 12 ft by 9 ft (2.66 by 2.75 m), dimensions of pavement and room uncertain. Lifted, on display in foyer of Carter Contracting, 159 Clapham Road, London S.W.9. Drawn and painted 1968. Brown *et. al.* 1969, pl. XXXVIII *a*.

Although largely fragmentary, enough survives to enable a reconstruction which shows the scheme as a grid of spaced squares at 45° to the border. From the evidence of the surviving square they contained squares of guilloche; at the margins the squares are converted into open triangles outlined in simple guilloche linked to the border, and occupied by small grey triangles. In alternate staggered spaces, between and tangent to each group of four squares, are circles and eight-lozenge stars.

The circles appear to contain a common type of conventionalized flower with four inward-pointing heart-shaped petals linked at their 'stalks' by the flared leaves of outward-facing buds. Around the circles are four petal-shaped motifs with triangular pedestals and with their midpoints drawn up into volute-like tendrils. The eight lozenges forming the star contain (in the two surviving examples) a chequered arrangement of red and dark grey triangles. Around the mosaic is a wide border of coarse yellow limestone tesserae.

The saltire-scheme with peltae in association with circular panels is common in and around the Cirencester area and occurs for example at Chedworth and Tockington Park, Glos. and North Leigh and Stonesfield, Oxon. It is typical of many pavements assigned to the Corinian School, a type discussed and illustrated in a paper by D.J. Smith (Brown *et. al.* 1969, 235).

The workmanship is very coarse (Grade 3), and although it paves a room its quality is more akin to the workmanship of corridor-pavements. Technically it does not compare with either the Chedworth or Northleigh examples and therefore is likely to be a later product, probably mid fourth-century. It appears to have remained in use until well towards the end of the fourth century as it was patched in antiquity with roofing tiles; no attempt was made to restore the design. The pavement was laid over No 21.

Reference. Brown *et. al.* 1969.

Mosaics 23. Cirencester. Corridor pavement

From Building XIV, 2. Fourth century. Length about 17 ft (5.19 m), width of decorated area 5ft (1.52 m). *In situ*, buried. Drawn and painted 1968. (Brown *et. al.* 1969, pl. XXXVIII *b*).

This fragment was found in a corridor (Room 5) on the north side of a courtyard and was approached via a porch situated directly opposite the meander pattern, here possibly intended to represent a maze (see comments on No 27). Its design consists in part of a row of three sets of swastika-meanders with double returns between two large mats of guilloche 4 ft 3 in (1.30 m) square in grey, red, yellow and white. The pavement was bordered in coarse yellow limestone tesserae and heavily patched in red sandstone tesserae without regard for the original design.

The workmanship is coarse (Grade 3) and comparable to Nos 22 and 24 which are probably contemporary. Corridor-mosaics with this general scheme appear to be confined to Gloucestershire and the fourth century, and are likely to be products of the Corinian school. An example at Chedworth (R.C.H.M., *Glos.* i, pl. 6) has panels of open guilloche instead of mats and in corridor 8 at Woodchester (Lysons 1797, pl. XII) guilloche mats alternated with right-angled 'spirals' in squares. The workmanship of this Woodchester example would seem equally coarse. A corridor from Beeches Road, Cirencester (No 28) is another example.

Reference. Brown *et al.* 1969.

Mosaic 24. Cirencester. Corridor mosaic

From Building XIV, 2. The Avenue. Fourth century. Length of fragment 8 ft 4 in (2.53 m), width of panel 4 ft 6 in (1.37 m). *In situ*, buried. Drawn and painted 1968. Brown *et. al.* 1969, pl. XXXIX *a*.

This fragment comes from Room 10, a corridor on the side of the courtyard opposite No 23, and would appear to have been similarly decorated. All that remains is a series of grey and white concentric right-angled lines which almost certainly come from two sets of swastika-meanders with double returns (FIG. 17), a reconstruction different from that in the original publication. It has a coarse yellow limestone border; its workmanship is equally coarse (Grade 3) and it is probably contemporary with Nos 22 and 23. (See comments on No 23).

References. Brown *et al.* 1969.

Mosaic 25. Cirencester. Hare mosaic

From Building XII, 1, Beeches Road, third to fourth century. On display in Corinium Museum. Drawn and painted 1972. NPP.

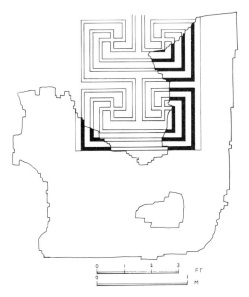

FIG. 17 Cirencester, No 24. Reconstruction

The three main panels on this pavement are of two periods. The earliest, Panel A, probably dated to the later third century, measures 10 ft 10 in by 9 ft 5 in (3.30 by 2.87 m) (measurements taken from outer edges of a band of stepped triangles) in a room 15 ft 2 in by 12 ft 2 in (4.62 by 3.70 m). It has a concentric circular scheme. Panel B, a rectangle with a cantharus flanked by birds, and Panel C, with a central medallion containing a hare, were added in the second half of the fourth century contemporarily with a southward extension to the room. Panel B measures 6 ft 10 in by 3 ft 2 in (2.08 by 0.96 m) and Panel C 10 ft 10 in by 8 ft 7 in (3.30 by 2.62 m) (measurements taken from the outer edges of the coarse decorated border) in a room 14 ft 6 in by 11 ft (4.42 by 3.35 m).

Panel A (PL. 25b)

Its scheme comprises a linear square with a central medallion surrounded by concentric bands of simple and three-strand guilloche. Along two opposite outer sides of the square are strips of guilloche converting its square into a rectangle all framed by a broad band of four-strand guilloche.

The central medallion is almost lost but the fragmentary evidence suggests that it had a guilloche knot at its centre. The braids in the guilloche circles are shaded grey, red/brown and white. In the three-strand guilloche every third strand is grey, red, blue and white. The four angles between the circles and the linear square frame contain slender canthari with fluted necks and semicircular scalloped bodies outlined in dark-grey and shaded blue, red and white. They have S-shaped handles and tiny triangular pedestals. Flowing from the top of each vessel to the left and right, are two dark grey lines which form voluted scrolls each with a red bud between the volutes. The scrolls springing from each cantharus link with those springing from the adjacent canthari. On either side of the canthari are small 'three-forked twigs'. Around three sides of the outer four-strand guilloche is a band of inturned stepped triangles. When the south wall of the room was breached for the extension, the mosaic alongside the wall was damaged and was patched with an irregular dark-grey line.

Panel B (PL. 25c)

Panel B is a threshold between pavements A and C and was designed to be viewed from the north. Its design is dominated by a large highly ornate cantharus outlined in grey, with a semicircular scalloped body, a rounded stem, and a red 'fish-tail' pedestal which projects into the simple guilloche frame. On the body, red, yellow and white flutes alternate with purple, grey and white flutes. The narrow but very flared neck, separated from the bowl by red and white 'millefiori', looks more like a stylized plant than a cantharus and is divided into two white and red petals, outlined grey. Their tips turn sharply downwards to form voluted S-shaped handles attached to the outer edges of the bowl. The upper outline trails away to form tendrils terminating in red and yellow leaves, (?) pomegranates, and grapes. In the scroll on either side of the cantharus and facing it are two almost identical birds with long black, red and yellow tail-feathers flowing towards the corners of the panel. Both birds are pecking at a bunch of grapes sprouting from the handles of the cantharus; their species is doubtful, but they are most probably peacocks.

Panel C

The scheme of Panel C comprises a circle inside two interlaced squares of simple guilloche, surrounded by a bold geometric pattern of squares and lozenges. In the central medallion is a naturalistic figure of a hare, crouching and facing left. In front of its head is a leafy stalk and from behind its back rises a bush or shrub, both in grey. The hare is expertly shaded in white, yellow, pale and ¹ mauvish-grey, the darker colours working up towards the spine. Here the mauvish-grey tesserae are mixed with translucent green glass giving the creature a speckled appearance. The front paws are unfortunately damaged; its right ear is shaded mauvish-grey and yellow and its left ear mauvish-grey, red and white. The shaded frame of the medallion, unusual in Britain, is bordered with a single grey fillet and (from inside outwards) coloured with white, yellow and red concentric circles and surrounded by two interlaced squares. The guilloche in one square is in red, yellow and white and the strands in the other mauvish-grey, grey and white. Curiously, instead of the braids flowing from the top left to bottom right, which is customary, they flow from top right to bottom left.

The geometric pattern has four squares each 15 in (38 cm) internally, set lozengewise, two at the 'top' and two at the 'bottom', in an arrangement of lozenges and triangles. The squares at the 'top' contain a stylized eight-petalled flower and a four-petalled flower on a grey square, and at the 'bottom' a guilloche mat and another four-petalled flower. The triangular compartments on the sides enclose a guilloche twist, chequered triangles, and a solid triangle. The lozenges are designed to show the squares as cubes, i.e. three-dimensionally, and each *pair* of lozenges is similarly decorated. In both lozenges in the top left corner is a rhomboid divided into nine smaller lozenges each containing red and yellow arcs, and in those in the top right, a black lozenge with a guilloche knot. The side lozenges also contain smaller lozenges; one on the 'right' side is divided into four smaller lozenges, with arcs of yellow and red, one on the 'left' side has a circle and another has a guilloche knot. The lozenges in the 'bottom right' corner are each subdivided into lozenges and triangles in red, white and grey. Damage on the left side of the pavement has destroyed all save a small part of the lozenges here, but the remains would suggest that they contained rhomboidal swastikas similar to those in lozenges on the mosaic from Room IX at Tockington Park, Glos. (Smith 1969, pl. XLI). Around three sides of the scheme is a band of simple guilloche in grey, red, yellow and white and, at the south end, a row of grey inturned stepped triangles and a dark-grey band, all in coarse tesserae.

Discussion

The concentric scheme of Panel A is not uncommon; a number of examples are shown in outline on FIGS. 10 and 11. The earliest example in Britain is a first-century pavement (No 44 and FIG. 21) from Room N20 at Fishbourne (Cunliffe 1971, pl. LXXXI). It has amphorae in the four corners superimposed over volutes; these however, do not link up with one another since the circular centrepiece fills the square frame. The writer knows of no examples of second-century date, but a crude pavement from Room 33 at Bignor (Lysons iii 1817, pl. XXIV), could — on stylistic and archaeological evidence (it is partly sealed by the corridor steps) — be a third-century 'do-it-yourself' example. Among the pavements in the collection we can see fourth-century examples from Sparsholt (No 71) and Woodchester (No 87), but although their basic schemes are similar their ornamentation differs markedly. A closer example both of the scheme and content can be found in Room LXIV, Lydney, Glos. (Wheeler and Wheeler 1932, pl.

XIX B), but the scroll here terminates in heart-shaped petals and not volutes. It does however have a guilloche knot as a centre piece — which is possibly also the content of the central panel on our example. The Lydney pavement has been dated from the coin evidence to no earlier than 367, a later date than our example, which could be as early as the late third century and contemporary with the constructions of the house. It is perhaps significant that it was followed by two other mosaics — panels B and C and by another mosaic paving a hypocaust laid over panels B and C.

The different shading of every third strand in the treble strand guilloche is of interest since this technique is uncommon. Of the mosaics in the collection it occurs only on No 36, also from Cirencester, but it is a technique employed frequently at Bignor, especially in the borders of the Ganymede and Cupid Gladiators panels (Lysons iii 1817 pl. VII and XIX). The use of red/brown instead of yellow in the guilloche gives the pavement a darker tone; the introduction of alternate braids, partly in blue, is not unusual, but generally if blue or pale-grey is employed a mosaicist will complement it with a paler grey, seldom with red. These differences set the work apart from other mosaics at Corinium and it is tempting to suggest that its creator was not a master or pupil of the Corinian school. Its workmanship is superior to that of Panels B and C.

Panel B, with its highly ornate cantharus, has no close parallels. Canthari are frequent; in the second century they are more commonly found as an element in the pattern, although on two examples from Verulamium (No 73, and Wheeler and Wheeler 1936, pl. XLVII), canthari in the form of a fountain have handles entwined with dolphins, while at Cirencester (No 34) dolphins are set in isolated panels beneath canthari. In the fourth century the motif remains common, and increasingly becomes a focal point, sometimes found in association with dolphins (e.g. at Brislington, Somerset (Barker 1899, pl.v), Caerwent (No 16), and Fifehead Neville, Dorset (Smith 1969, pl. 3.30)). On some examples the cantharus is set between two confronting felines (e.g. at Rudston (No 69), Littlecote Park, Wilts. (Smith 1969, pl. 3.16) and possibly Wellow (V.C.H. *Somerset,* fig. 71)), while on others, such as the panel under discussion, it is flanked by birds, e.g. at Rudston (No 67), London (Hinks 1933, fig. 138) and Wellow.

The significance of the scene remains speculative. At Fifehead Neville finger-rings with the Christian Chi-Rho monogram have been unearthed, which raise the possibility that here at least the occupants of the villa were Christians and that the cantharus, originally symbolic of the mystic communion between Bacchus and those initiated into his cult, was seen as a chalice and the symbol of the Eucharist. There is no parallel in Cirencester for the form of the cantharus; but No 52 from Gloucester, while not depicting a cantharus as such, has two stylized bowls, without pedestals or handles, from which sprout flared petals terminating in heart-shaped buds. A closer parallel stylistically, although remote from Cirencester, are three bowls on the Broad Street mosaic, London (R.C.H.M., *Roman London,* pl. 48); here petals imitate the 'body' of the 'cantharus'. The similarity between No 52 and that from Broad Street might suggest the same workshop (see p. 83).

As far as the writer is aware, the portrayal of a hare as in Panel C is unique as a centrepiece. An animal at Pit Meads, Wilts., was so interpreted (Hoare 1821, pl. facing p. 113, fig. 3), but this example occupies a narrow panel and is not a dominant part of the design. A long-eared animal on a mosaic from Room 6. House VII at Caerwent (Ashby *et. al.,* pl. X) may also be a hare, but again this occupies a perimeter panel. A running hare occurs on the Orpheus mosaic from Horkstow, in the elephant panel (Hinks 1933, fig. 112).

For further comments on interlaced squares see Nos 17 and 58.

References. McWhirr 1973, pls. XXXI *a* & *b* and XXXII a. (For discussion, see *ibid.* Appendix II by D.J. Smith, pp. 214–18).

Mosaic 26. Cirencester. Meander pattern

From Building XII, 1, Beeches Road. Fourth Century. Length 6 ft 1 in (1.85 m) width 4 ft 9 in (1.45 m); room 11ft by 9 ft (3.35 by 2.75 m). Displayed in Corinium Museum. Drawn and painted 1972. NPP.

This small mosaic was found in the changing-room of a bath-suite on the west side of the house. Its decoration comprises an all-over swastika-meander pattern in grey, developing six small staggered squares. Four squares are quartered diagonally, and the triangles shaded red and grey; the remaining squares are filled with concave-sided squares turned lozengewise, with a red centre and a grey outline. The pattern is surrounded by a band of red and a coarse grey border.

The workmanship is very crude and the geometry irregular. It seems that the mosaicist may have laid the border tesserae before the panel, because he has reduced the width of the bands (from the bottom to the top) from three tesserae to one in width — possibly to fit the design into the chosen area. Had the panel been laid first there would have been no need to truncate the bands. The inexperience of the mosaicist is further suggested by his failure to link up the pattern; instead of two ends of the meander joining he has allowed them to 'float'. However, a reason for this may have been an attempt to create the illusion of a maze. Although meanders are common in the repertory of the Corinian school, the quality of this example does not compare with that of others.

The incorrect layout is unusual, especially since the mosaicist prepared guide-lines. When the pavement was lifted for transfer to Corinium Museum, red painted guide-lines were found on the penultimate bedding of mortar. This is the only example known to the writer of painted guide-lines in Britain, but scored lines have been found at a number of sites including Rudston (see No 69). Red-painted guide-lines have been observed, however, beneath pavements in Tunisia including those from the House of the Cascade at Utica (Alexander and Ennaïfer 1965, pl. A1).

The meander scheme is common in the repertory of Corinium school[1] but the quality of this example (Grade 3) does not compare with that of others, and it must either be regarded as degenerate and a late example of their work or else the work of an amateur. The pavement is probably contemporary with the construction of the bath-suite and dates to the middle of the fourth century.

Reference. McWhirr 1973, pl. xxxii, *b*. (for discussion see *ibid*. Appendix II by D.J. Smith, pp. 214–18).

[1]For further discussion on meanders of the Corinian school see No 19.

Mosaic 27. Cirencester. Labyrinth mosaic

From Building XII, 2, Beeches Road, Fourth century. Fragment 25 ft (7.62 m) long, corridor 46 ft by 9 ft 6 in (14.03 by 2.90 m). *In situ*, buried. Drawn and painted 1972. NPP.

This mosaic paved a corridor (Room 2) on the north side of the building, and was approached via an entrance porch opening onto a threshold panel which was decorated with a highly complicated labyrinth, much damaged, and probably flanked on both sides by repeating patterns of swastika-meander. Both the meander and the labyrinth have a common border of three-strand guilloche, shaded grey, white and red. With the exception of the guilloche the mosaic is monochrome — grey on white.

The basic scheme of the labyrinth is a square quartered, with a central open cross-shaped compartment containing a small grey square. In each quarter is a series of zig-zag lines reflecting the shape of the cross. A reconstruction (FIG. 18) shows the maze to follow an anti-clockwise route; in practice, the spectator's eye is likely to have been drawn from an 'entrance', situated opposite the porch, towards the central cross. Entry here was blocked and the spectator would have to follow the corridors of the pattern back towards the perimeter, where he would have found himself, not back at the entrance, but in the adjacent quarter. This progression would have had to be repeated in the remaining quarters before entry into the central cross was gained — via a 'passage' immediately left of the entrance-way.

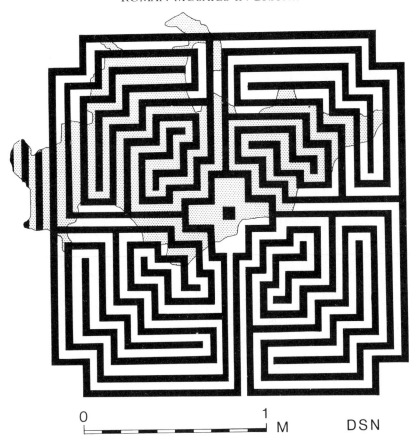

FIG. 18 Cirencester, No 27. Reconstruction of labyrinth threshold panel

Including the pavement under discussion, the total number of labyrinth mosaics known in Britain is six. Two others are represented in the collection — a second-century example from Cirencester (No 21) and a crude fourth-century pavement from Fullerton, Hants. (No 47), both of which are simple by comparison. Closer affinities are to be found at Caerleon, Gwent (FIG. 19) (Smith 1958-60. pl. II) and Harpham, Yorks (FIG. 20) (Collier, 1906, fig. 4). These are almost identical to one another except that entry into the Caerleon maze, a pavement from the *principia* of the legionary fortress, is via a clockwise movement as opposed to anti-clockwise movement at Harpham. Neither is so complex as the pavement under discussion, because their mazes run concentrically around a square and not a cross. There is no evidence for decoration in the square at Caerleon, but at Harpham it was a conventionalized four-petalled flower. A buried labyrinth pavement from Oldcotes, Notts (*Arch. Journ.*, 28 (1871) pp. 66-7) would seem to have contained a representation of the victory of Theseus over the Minotaur, a scene with many continental parallels in painting and mosaic.

A fourth-century date is also likely for the Harpham pavement as another mosaic from the site sealed a coin of 304 'in mint condition'. Dr. Smith (Smith 1958-60, p. 306) has suggested a third-century date for the Caerleon example, but the simple form of its surrounding scroll may indicate an earlier construction conceivably contemporary with the rebuilding of the fortress in *c*. A.D. 100. The discovery of a mosaic from the legionary bath-house at Exeter (Bidwell 1979, pl. XVI A) in a context *c*. 55-60 obviates surprise that pavements should adorn military buildings as at Caerleon.

Both the construction (Grade 2) and the geometry of the Cirencester pavement indicate a most accomplished mosaicist and designer, and for a corridor-pavement the standard of work is good. The evidence so far recovered suggests a later third-century date for the construction of the house, but the corridor appears to have been a fourth-century addition. The quality of the mosaic, superior to the other pavements (Nos 28-33) in the same house, would suggest it was earlier fourth-century rather than later.

Reference. McWhirr 1973 (for comments on the mosaic see *ibid.*, Appendix II by D.J. Smith, p. 214).

0 _____ 1 M

FIG. 19 The labyrinth mosaic from Caerleon, Gwent. Revised reconstruction of drawing by
G.C. Boon (Smith 1958–60, fig. 1)

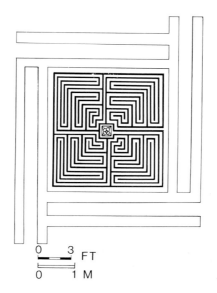

0   3 FT

0   1 M

FIG. 20 The labyrinth mosaic from Harpham, East Yorks.

Mosaic 28. Cirencester. Meander

From Building XII, 2, Beeches Road, Fourth century. Dimensions; fragment 15 ft (4.57 m) long, room 20 ft by 6 ft (6.10 by 1.82 m). *In situ*, buried. The guilloche square is preserved in Corinium Museum. Drawn and painted 1972. McWhirr 1973, pl. xxxv, *a*.

This narrow mosaic paved a passage (Room 13) linking the north corridor (see No 27), to a small room on the south side of the range, paved with No 29. Its design consists of a band of opposed and linked swastika-meander with a square in each space. Of the two surviving squares, one has a border of three-strand guilloche in grey, red and white, and contains a small solid square, and the other a border of simple guilloche enclosing a guilloche mat. The construction of the meander is inconsistent — at the 'bottom' a line is narrower than elsewhere. Compared with the corridor-pavement the work is crude (Grade 3) and unlikely to be by the same mosaicist: it is more likely to be by the mosaicist who laid Nos 30 and 32.

There is a very similar corridor-mosaic leading to Room 14 at Chedworth (R.C.H.M., *Glos.* i pl. 6): the published illustration would suggest it to be superior in quality, however. In reporting on No 28 Dr. Smith has suggested (McWhirr 1973, 218) that such patterns can be regarded as having been devised for corridors by a designer of the Corinian school.'

References. McWhirr 1973 (for comments on the mosaic see *ibid.*, Appendix II by D.J. Smith, p. 214).

Mosaic 29. Cirencester. Guilloche mat

From Building XII, 2, Beeches Road. Fourth Century. Dimensions, length of fragment 8 ft 8 in (2.64m), panel 5 ft 7 in by 2 ft 8 in (1.70 by 0.81m). Room 11 ft 6 in by 5 ft 6 in (3.50 by 1.67 m). *In situ*, buried. Drawn and painted 1972. McWhirr 1973, pl. xxxiii *a*.

This simple yet strikingly effective panel comes from a passage or vestibule (Room 16), and consists merely of a rectangular mat of guilloche with blue/grey, red and white braids. Apart from its distorted shape, many elementary mistakes have occured in the pattern — red tesserae have been substituted for white, and *vice versa*, and mistakes made in the interlacing of the braids.

Around the panel are two wide bands in coarse tesserae, the first in dull yellow limestone and the second in Pennant (mauve) stone. The width of the first band is not constant; furthermore tesserae of various other colours are interspersed in it. The work, particularly the borders, is very poor and was done either by an amateur or by a third-rate apprentice. Workmanship, Grade 3.

Reference. McWhirr 1973 (for comment on the mosaic see *ibid.*, Appendix II by D.J. Smith p. 214).

Mosaic 30. Cirencester. Roundel with flower

From Building XII, 2, Beeches Road. Fourth century. Dimensions of panel including decorated border 12 ft 3 in by 12 ft (3.73 by 3.66 m). Room 20 ft (6.08 m) square. *In situ*, buried. Drawn and painted 1972. McWhirr 1973, pl. xxxiv *a*.

This occupied the main room (Room 12) of Building XII, 2, and was approached from the labyrinth corridor (No 27). Its scheme of decoration consists of a large circle of simple guilloche, in grey, red and white, within a square of treble-strand guilloche forming spandrels in the four corners. Unfortunately most of the central medallion is missing, but it seems to have contained a large multi-petalled flower (possibly with 16 petals) with the tip of each petal alternating in colour — red and white. Around the motif is a thin circular grey band, and between this and the circular guilloche frame is a band of inturned stepped triangles.

The spandrels (two are missing) contain red and white heart-shaped leaves. Surrounding the guilloche border is a band of spaced swastika-meander with an oblong panel in each space. On opposite sides the oblongs contain short strips of guilloche and on the other sides grey chequers. The pavement has a coarse yellow surround. As on many mosaics from Corinium the workmanship of the meander border is inferior to that of the main panel. Grade 3.

The general scheme, with a circle in a square surrounded by swastika-meander developing rectangles or squares, can be matched at the Weymouth House Schools, Bath (Cunliffe 1969, pl. LXXXIII *a*.), at the Bank of England, London (Merrifield 1965, pl. 69) and at Building XXVII, 2 from Verulamium (Frere 1958, pl. III). Neither the Bath nor the London example is dated, but at Verulamium it is found in a late fourth-century context and it is likely that the other quoted examples are also fourth-century. At Verulamium the medallion encloses a flower with eight interlaced petals, but the use of large multi-petalled flowers as a central motif is common to mosaics of all periods. However, in the fourth century there is a tendency for the flowers to become much larger and to develop more petals. At Kenchester, Hereford (Jack 1916, pl. 23), at London (R.C.H.M., *Roman London*, pl. 48) and at Tockington Park, Glos. (MacLean 1887-8, pl. VII), for example, 16-petalled flowers occupy interlaced squares and in all cases have guilloche knots in their centre. It is tempting to suggest that the Cirencester example may have been such a flower. The Kenchester, London and Tockington Park mosaics have other stylistic similarities which provide evidence that they may be the work of the Corinian *officina* (p. 19); so too may be No 30, but its degenerate quality would make it a late product and not attributable to the same contractor.

Reference. McWhirr 1973 (for comments on the mosaic see *ibid.*, Appendix II by D.J. Smith, p. 214).

Mosaic 31. Cirencester. Chequered pattern

From Building XII, 2, Beeches Road. Fourth century. Dimensions; panel probably 13 ft 8 in by 8ft 4 in (4.17 by 2.54 m), room 19 ft 6 in by 13 ft (5.95 by 3.98 m). *In situ*, buried. Drawn and painted 1972, McWhirr 1973, pl. XXXV *b*.

No 31 occupied Room 8, situated in the south-east corner of the main range. Its design is an all-over chessboard pattern, of large red-brick and creamy limestone squares 13 in (33 cm) wide. Around the pattern is a grey outline, and along one side a rectangular compartment outlined in red. When the boldness of the design is considered, the workmanship is precise (Grade 2) and superior in execution to some other pavements from the same house — No 29 for instance. The tesserae of the chequers are smaller than those of the border.

Examples of the design, or variants of it, are fairly common. The earliest representation in Britain, dated *c*. A.D. 75, is a mosaic from Room N 4 at Fishbourne (Cunliffe 1971, pl. LXXV), with a grid of bands with a chequered arrangement of large and small black squares with white rectangles. A more closely-related example, possibly dated to the second century on account of its black and white striped border, is a mosaic found in 1850 at Colchester (Hull 1958, pl. XXIV) with large regular black and white squares. Fourth-century examples of the pattern, all from villas, can be found at Haceby, Lincs. (Fowler Col. iii, 22), at Norfolk Street, Leicester (V.C.H., *Leics.* i, fig. p. 197), and at Newport, I.O.W. (Stone 1929, pl. XIII). On these examples coarse red tesserae have been employed throughout.

Reference. McWhirr 1973 (for comments on the mosaic see *ibid.*, Appendix II by D.J. Smith, p. 214).

Mosaic 32. Cirencester. Conventionalized flower

From Building XII, 2, Beeches Road. Fourth century. Dimensions; panel 5 ft 6 in (1.68 m) square, room 9 ft (2.75 m) square. *In situ*, buried. Drawn and painted 1972. McWhirr 1973, pl. XXXIV *b*.

This pavement occupied Room 7, an addition to the east side of the house. Its scheme, in simple guilloche, in grey, red and white, consists of a square with quadrants in each corner. In the interspace formed between the quadrants is an open concave-sided square bearing a conventionalized flower with four red-tipped heart-shaped petals with serrated stalks. Two opposite quadrants, although damaged, appear to have contained calices and the other two red-tipped, heart-shaped leaves, similar in form to the petals on the central flower. On two opposite sides of the panel are bands of white tesserae, and surrounding the whole is a coarse border with bands of yellow limestone and Pennant stone tesserae, similar to those in the borders of No 29 with which the pavement is probably contemporary. Its workmanship is very coarse, Grade 3.

For the design the writer knows of no parallel in Britain. More commonly it has semicircles separating the quadrants with circles or interlaced boxes in the centre (e.g. No 66). Here however the mosaic is so small that space restricts anything more than the quadrants — the mosaicist has merely adapted a common scheme to fit the room.

Reference. McWhirr 1973 (for comments on the mosaic see *ibid.*, Appendix II by D.J. Smith, p. 214).

Mosaic 33. Cirencester. Fragment

From Building XII, 2, Beeches Road. Fourth century. Length of fragments 4 ft (1.22 m), room 20 ft by 5 ft (6.10 by 1.52 m). *In situ*, buried. Drawn and painted 1972. McWhirr 1973, pl. XXXIV *c*.

This fragment comes from a passage (Room 9) on the east side of the house and seems to have consisted of a row of alternating open grey rectangles and tangent squares, set lozenge-wise, which contained small solid grey circles and squares respectively. In angles between the panels are red triangles, and bordering the pavement is a red band. All the tesserae are large. Workmanship, Grade 3.

The design is a variation of alternating square and rectangular compartments, containing squares and lozenges respectively, found on a corridor pavement (H) from Withington, Glos. (Lysons ii, 1817, pl. XXI). Here the interspaces between the lozenges and outer frame also contain triangles.

Reference. McWhirr 1973 (for comments on the mosaic see *ibid.*, Appendix II by D.J. Smith, p. 214).

Mosaic 34. Cirencester. Dolphins and Canthari

From Building VI, 4. Admiral's Walk, St. Michael's Field. Possibly third century. Dimensions; panel 14 ft by 13 ft 9 in (4.27 by 4.20 m), room 20 ft by 17 ft 9 in (6.10 by 5.40 m). Lifted, in store, Corinium Museum. Drawn 1974, painted 1978. NPP.

Building VI, 4 was either the rear of a shop fronting Ermine Street or one wing of a large courtyard house occupying the south corner of the insula. Although damaged, the scheme of the mosaic is apparent. It is derived from a grid of spaced octagons set at 45° to the border, but further elaborated by the introduction of a central square and rectangular panels around the margin and four staggered crosses: infilling the spaces between the crosses are lozenges. For the basic scheme see FIG. 4, B.

The largely missing central square would appear to have contained a linear circle and, in spaces between the circle and the square, dark-grey spandrels. On either side of the central square are four octagons, two lost. In one is an elaborate cantharus with a semicircular gadrooned body, in white, red and mauvish-grey, above which are two fillets with opposed and staggered dentils. It has a stem and a splayed red and white pedestal. The neck is narrow near the body, but towards the rim it flares out widely and is surmounted by a conical red lid divided into two sections by a vertical line. Its handles are voluted and have 'crests' at the top and bottom of the scrolls. Curling up from either side of the pedestal is a stem terminating in a diminutive grey bud. In a fragmentary octagonal panel opposite are the remains of a pedestal, indicating that this panel also contained a cantharus.

In the cross-shaped panels are correspondingly-shaped strips of guilloche shaded on one strip red, brown and white, and on the other brownish mauve, grey and white. In two opposed rectangular panels on the sides of the scheme are grey and white dolphins with red beaks, crests and dorsal fins; and in the other (one is missing) is a conventionalized fish. In trapezoidal panels also at the side is a mural crown with a sperm motif (or ? a ribbon), a pelta, a half-flower, and a leaf-arrangement. One of the two surviving square corner compartments contains a heart-shaped bud and the other a heart-shaped leaf. Each lozenge contains a solid brownish-mauve rhomboid.[1]. The scheme has a yellow, pale-brown and red guilloche border and a wide surround of pale yellow limestone tesserae broken by two grey bands. On one border, white tesserae have been used instead of pale yellow;[2] and there is also a crude repair perhaps marking the position of a door. The workmanship is very good (Grade 2) and the tesserae are closely set. Unusually, the surround is laid in small tesserae. The red tesserae in the detailed part of the pavement are cut from samian but the red tesserae in the guilloche border are of brick.

The mosaic has no exact parallel; it appears similar to a first-century pavement from room N 12 at Fishbourne (Cunliffe 1971, pl. LXXVIII). This example, however, has a more frequent distribution of crosses separated not by octagons but by irregular hexagons. It is to the later mosaics that we must look for parallels.

At Lullingstone, Kent, we find the scheme employed in a context dated after c. 330 (Meates 1955, 45-6) but with such a profusion of motifs in its panel that its geometric structure is not immediately apparent. Although there are no other examples where the scheme remains 'intact', cross-shapes can be detected on a third-century pavement from Rapsley (No 65) and on panels around the early fourth-century Great Pavement at Woodchester (No 87). On these the two arms of the cross nearest the corners of the scheme have been omitted, resulting instead in the formation of L-shapes. Also on these two examples less of the overall pattern is contained within the surround, with the result that rectangles (essentially repeats of the central square) around the margins are absent. Typologically the scheme would appear to be earlier than the Colchester example (No 38) but a second or early third-century date is probable. Of the motifs two are of particular interest. The peltae with swollen terminals are a rare motif occurring on only two other mosaics — at Victoria Road, Cirencester (Clifford 1946-8 pl. III), and on the Colchester mosaic referred to above. Both the sperm motif and mural crown are so far unique in Romano-British mosaics.

Reference. McWhirr 1978, pls. XXXIV a, b and pls. XXXV a, b

[1]Except three lozenges which are grey.
[2]The variation in colours of the borders may indicate the work of two mosaicists starting on different sides of the pavement and using different shades. Possibly, however, the mosaicist simply ran out of white tesserae and used cream tesserae (or *vice versa*) instead.

Mosaic 35. Cirencester. Corridor fragment

From Building VI, 4. Admiral's Walk, St. Michael's Field. Probably fourth century. Original width of panel 3 ft 6 in (1.07 m), corridor 8 ft (2.44 m) wide by at least 40 ft (12.20 m) long. *In situ*, buried. Drawn 1974, painted 1977. NPP.

From the same building as No 34. this mosaic paved a corridor along the south-east side of the house. Owing to its fragmentary nature its scheme is not fully understood, but it was probably a long rectangle bordered by a grey fillet and an outer band of simple guilloche in grey, red, yellow and white. At one end of the rectangle is part of a rosette with red petals and pale grey pointed excrescences within a grey linear circle. Outside the circle are two grey lines radiating into the corners of the rectangle, with the space between lines infilled with radiating bands of various colours.

Interpretation of the pattern remains speculative, but it is possible that there was a row of rosettes in spaced circles joined to one another by ♦ -shapes — a variant of the egg-and-dart motif common on second-century pavements (e.g. Gloucester, No 54). The evidence for this may be found in an examination of the motif linking the circle to the end of the panel. It appears to comprise a 'dart' cut in half by the panel's frame. An alternative interpretation, but less likely, is that the 'flower' and 'circle' are really part of a scroll.

The date of the floor is problematical; but the rosette, originally with eight petals and with the hearts divided longitudinally and with pointed excrescences, is a distinctive motif termed 'squared rosette' (see p. 54). It appears on a number of second-century pavements, e.g. Chichester (No 20), Colchester (No 39), Silchester (Hope and Fox 1896, pl. XIV) and Verulamium (Wheeler and Wheeler 1936, pl. XLV). This evidence, and the presence of the egg-and-dart motif would suggest the second or possibly the early third century, in other words perhaps a date broadly contemporary with that of No 34.

Reference. McWhirr 1978, p. 75, pl. xxxiii *b*.

Mosaic 36. Cirencester. Interlaced squares

From Building VI, 3, Admiral's Walk, St. Michael's Field. Probably fourth century. Original dimensions of panel 8 ft 3 in (2.51 m) square. Room 11 ft (3.36 m) ? square. *In situ*, buried. Drawn 1974, painted 1977. NPP.

The scheme of this pavement, possibly paving an entrance-porch, comprises a square with small quadrants in the angles containing two interlaced squares forming an eight-pointed star. On at least two sides are strips of three-strand guilloche, perhaps originally bordering the whole pavement but more likely forming two long rectangles containing rows of superposed thorns. Within the interlaced squares is a circular compartment bordered by a band of waves and in the two surviving quadrants are flower-motifs — one with a single petal with volutes and the other a calyx. The treatment of the guilloche is very imaginative and varied in colour, and the standard of workmanship and geometry is precise (Grade 2). One interlaced square is red, yellow and white and the other pale grey and white — both with dark-grey outlines. The braids in the framework guilloche also have these colours but alternating. The three-strand guilloche is grey, red, yellow and white with every third strand grey, pale-grey and white.

Interlaced squares are exclusive to the late third- and fourth-century pavements (see comments on No 17). No 36 cannot be matched precisely but its general scheme occurs for example at Lydney no earlier than *c.* 367 (Wheeler and Wheeler, 1932, p. 65, pl. xxi). The Lydney mosaic is inferior to the Cirencester pavement and probably later.

Reference. McWhirr 1978, p. 75.

Mosaic 37. Cirencester. Octagons with flowers

From the site of the Congregational Church, Dyer Street. Second century. Fragment 7 ft (2.13 m) long, but dimensions of mosaic not known. Lifted, in Corinium Museum[1] Drawn and painted 1972. McWhirr 1973, pl. xxxiii *b*.

The scheme of decoration consists of an overall grid of abutting octagons in simple guilloche. They contain circular panels bordered in simple guilloche or waves enclosing flowers. In the only surviving panel is a four-petalled flower with four pointed excrescences between the petals. On one side of the fragment are the remains of a broad grey band and a scroll with a red-tipped leaf. The pavement is possibly from the same building (XVII, 1, McWhirr 1973, 201) as the 'Hunting Dogs' and 'Seasons' pavements discovered in 1849 (Buckman and Newmarch 1850, pls. vi and ii).

Its scheme falls into a class of design common in the second century and discussed earlier (p. 44). Parallels are listed in an appendix (p. 125).

Reference. McWhirr 1973, 201 (for comments on the mosaic, see *ibid.*, Appendix II by D.J. Smith p. 214).

[1]This fragment is now on display in the foyer of the new Congregational church constructed over the site.

The Colchester Mosaics. Nos 38–41

Nos 38–40 were found in 1965 during excavations directed by Miss R. Dunnett in advance of the construction of a multi-storey car-park at North Hill. The pavements decorated a town-house of rectangular plan bordering a street on the south side of Insula 10 (Dunnett 1967, fig. 1 (plan)) and situated on the upper level of a terrace; they are dated archaeologically between the middle and end of the second century and are believed to be contemporary with one another, although variations in workmanship may preclude the work being by the same mosaicist.

Excavations by P. Crummy at Lion Walk in 1972 revealed a fourth-century courtyard house situated in Insula 36. The house contained a figured pavement (No 41) unfortunately mutilated by a large pit, but originally of exceptional quality and with an inscription.

Mosaic 38. Colchester. Four-petalled flower

From a town-house at North Hill. Mid second century. Dimensions of panel 11 ft 6 in by 9 ft 11 in (3.51 by 3.03 m), room 13 ft 8 in by 11 ft 3 in (4.18 by 3.44 m). Lifted, in store Colchester Castle Museum.[1] Drawn and painted 1966. Dunnett 1967, pl. VI; Smith 1975, pl. CXI, 1.

Its square composition consists of a central square tangent to four lateral cubes, set lozenge-wise, contiguous with four chevrons in a field of lozenges and lateral triangles. Its central square contains a very finely-worked flower outlined in black with four inward-pointing heart-shaped petals shaded white and yellow and with red centres. Between each petal is a pointed excrescence, in blue-grey; attached to the cleft of each petal and at the tip of each excrescence, filling the angles of the panel, are four sinuous black tendrils with blue-grey leaves. Each lateral cube has a guilloche knot and each chevron an L-shaped compartment bordered in simple guilloche in red, yellow and white, occupied by an L-shaped line. Two of the lateral triangles contain solid black peltae, and another two black open peltae with lobed terminals; one contains an open triangle flanked by peltae. Rhomboidal swastikas occupy the lozenges. Around the main composition in slightly coarser tesserae is a row of spaced L-blocks and on two opposed sides of the pavement are strips of simple guilloche and grey bands. The pavement has a border of coarse grey tesserae. The workmanship is exceptional (Grade 1) and the tesserae, especially those used in the central *emblema*, remarkably fine; it represents the work of a master mosaicist. The other mosaics from the house (Nos 39 and 40) are not of such quality.

In the description of the Bancroft mosaic (No 7) affinities and variations of the scheme have been discussed. It is worth noting, however, that this is the only example where rhomboidal swastikas have been used to fill the lozenges. Other rare motifs include the lobed peltae, a type noted on No 34 and occurring with a more bulbous stem on a second-century monochrome pavement from Silchester (Hope and Fox, 1896, pl. XIII). The arrangement of peltae around a triangle has no parallel, although solid peltae are frequently-used motifs in the first and second centuries. The flower, of exceptional quality, is of interest stylistically. Although its conventionalized form occurs elsewhere, e.g. at Woodchester (No 87), it is the only example which sprouts trailing stems with leaves. Two flowers on No 39 from the same house may have been influenced by the work, for their inward-pointing petals are also attached to undulating though leafless stems.

References. Dunnett 1967 (for a provisional report on the mosaic by D.J. Smith see *ibid.*, pp. 40–42). Smith 1975, 273.

[1]A section of this mosaic is also in the possession of the writer.

Mosaic 39. Colchester. Cantharus

From a town-house at North Hill. Mid second century. Original dimensions; Panel A, 15 ft 9 in by 15 ft 5 in (4.80 by 4.70 m), Panel B, 15 ft 7 in by 6 ft 6 in (4.75 by 1.98 m). Room, 30 ft by 25 ft (9.16 by 7.63 m). Lifted, in Colchester Castle Museum. Drawn 1965, painted 1966. Dunnett 1967, pl. VIII; Smith 1975, pl. CXVI.

No 39 is in two parts. Panel A has a square field divided into nine compartments — a central square flanked by four lateral rectangles and tangent to four squares at the angles, all overlying a concentric circular arrangement of bands of various patterns. The decoration of Panel B is based on a scheme of abutting octagons (FIG. 7A) infilled with canthari or flowers and by small squares flanked by four tangent tilted squares between pairs of lozenges.

Panel A

Occupying the central square is an elaborate yellow cantharus outlined in yellow ochre perhaps simulating gilding. It is shown in perspective with the interior of its bowl in red, possibly to represent wine; its neck is grey and without fluting. Its yellow handles are also outlined in yellow ochre, voluted at the rim and unusually thick. The cantharus is set in a grey linear medallion bordered in simple guilloche in grey, red and white, within a square linear frame. In spandrels between the angles of the square and the medallion are blue-leafed calices with triangular pedestals and red buds.

Around the square is a band of egg-and-dart pattern with dark grey ovoids containing red-tipped leaves. The darts are blue. Occupying the two surviving corner-panels are squared rosettes with eight red, yellow and white petals with four blue-pointed excrescences similar to the squared rosette on No 20 from Chichester. The rosettes are bordered with a band of dark grey thorns. The concentric bands of pattern underlying the grid and appearing in the side-panels consist, from inside outwards, of simple guilloche in grey, red and white, a grey floral scroll with white, yellow and red leaves and a band of dark grey waves.

Panel B

The panel comprises predominantly three rows of tangent octagons. Occupying the central octagons in the outer rows are two canthari, one considerably damaged but probably similar to its neighbour. The neck of the surviving vessel is decorated with a swastika-meander pattern in black with the spaces between the meander infilled either in red or blue. The body is decorated with three gadroons, the central one in white and blue and those on either side in red with white centres. It has a red knop and triangular pedestal from which spring two sinuous stems terminating in red-tipped leaves. The handles are black near the open neck but red lower down.

In octagons on either side of the surviving cantharus are stylized flowers with four slender red petals alternating and interlocking with four heart-shaped inward-pointing leaves in white and grey with blue tips and connected to one another by a black trailing stem not dissimilar to the tendrils in the central compartment of No 38 but without leaves. The other octagons in this row originally contained an eight-petalled flower in white, yellow and red, and with white and pale grey excrescences; but one panel is crudely patched in yellow ochre and red tile bearing little similarity to the original. The octagons flanking the damaged cantharus contain eight-petalled flowers similar to the surviving original flower at one end of the row already described. The remaining end-panel here is occupied by a red multi-petalled flower, but this too is a repair which may bear little resemblance to its predecessor. Panel A has a repair in its guilloche border which, to judge from its colours, is contemporary with that just described. Four octagons between and tangent to the ornamented panels contain guilloche squares and an arrangement of lozenges.

The workmanship of both schemes is technically inferior to that of No 38 and the tesserae are coarser. Panel B is very slightly wider than A, which raises the possibility that it may have been laid later, but if so after a very short period. Its workmanship and colours are the same as No 40 and it is probably the work of the same mosaicist.

Schemes with nine panels in the arrangement illustrated here, but without concentric bands, are fairly common, particularly in the Antonine period. Apart from No 40 from the same building, there are three other examples from Colchester alone; one found in 1763 at the Three Cups Inn (Hull 1958, pl. XXIII, A), another in 1922 at North Hill (Benham 1923, pl. facing p. 251) and one in 1923 at Bury Field (Hull 1958, pl. XXXIV).[1] The first two pavements have squared rosettes in their corner compartments and large lozenges bordered in guilloche in two or more of their side-panels. The latter motif can also be found at Verulamium (No 73) in another nine-panel arrangement. Apart from No 40, however, which also combines underlying concentric bands, none of the other examples quoted includes this addition to the scheme. It is to a mosaic from Building IV, 1 at Verulamium (Wheeler and Wheeler 1936, pl. XLIV B) dated to the late second century that we must look for a parallel. On this the concentric bands include waves and guilloche but no floral scroll; a band of 'dog's tooth' pattern has been substituted instead. This is the only other example of concentric bands 'underlying' a nine panel grid in Britain, and it raises the question whether these designs were products of the same *officina* working in the Colchester-Verulamium area. It must be said, however, that the workmanship of the Verulamium pavement is coarser and the guilloche wider than in the Colchester examples, and it is therefore unlikely to be that of the same mosaicist. Finally, the cantharus is worthy of comment — it is the only example known to the writer where the contents are visible.

The scheme of panel B occurs in Room W 8 at Fishbourne dated *c.* 75-80, but with every octagon infilled with smaller squares and a profusion of lozenges. A closer parallel, perhaps, is from Room 22, House 1, Insula XIV at Silchester (Hope and Fox, 1896, pl. XII), assigned to *c.* 140-60, where a quincunx arrangement of octagons has been infilled with stylized flowers and swastika-peltae occupying small square interspaces (FIG. 7 B). Lozenges in half-octagons around the borders contain small black rhomboids. One of the eight-petalled flowers on this pavement compares exactly with three on the Colchester mosaic. The swastika-meander motif on at least one of the canthari recalls the decoration on four canthari on No 75 from Verulamium dated to the late second century. It is not found on fourth-century canthari.

References. Dunnett 1967 (for a provisional report on the mosaic by D.J. Smith see *ibid.*, pp. 40-41): Smith, 1975, 277.

[1]For a fuller discussion on nine-panel schemes see No 73.

Mosaic 40. Colchester. Dahlia flower

From a town-house at North Hill. Mid second century. Panel A, 12 ft 4 in (3.76 m) square, Panel B, 12 ft 4 in by 3 ft 7 in (3.76 by 1.09 m). Overall; excluding border, 12 ft 4 in (3.76 m) by at least 16 ft 10 in (5.13 m), room 30 ft by 20 ft (9.16 by 6.12 m). Parts lifted, in Colchester Castle Museum. Drawn 1965, painted 1966. Dunnett 1967, pl. VIII: Smith 1975, pl. CXVII.

This pavement also has two schemes, one of which bears a striking similarity to Panel A of No 39. Its principal design is a square divided by simple guilloche into nine compartments — a central square flanked by four lateral rectangles tangent to four squares at the angles, all overlying an arrangement of concentric circular patterns. Panel B is rectangular.

Panel A

In the central panel is a 'dahlia' type of flower with 16-petals alternating in colour — white, yellow and red, and white and grey, surrounded by a bold chain-pattern with pairs of links alternating in colour — grey, red and white; grey-brown, pale blue-grey and white; and grey-brown, yellow and white. Around this is a row of white thorns set on a dark grey band. The corner panels are lost, but the fragments of one suggest that, like No 32, they contained rosettes. The underlying concentric circular patterns consist, from inside outwards, of an unusual dark grey bead-and-reel, simple guilloche in grey, red and white (similar to the guilloche of No 32), a floral scroll with white, yellow and red-tipped leaves, and a band of dark grey waves — apart from the bead-and-reel an arrangement almost identical to that of No 39.

Panel B

Panel B is bordered by a band of grey superposed triangles surrounding a wide strip of four-strand guilloche, in grey, white, pale blue-grey and brown; and grey, white, yellow and red. Like No 39 this panel may also be secondary since it appears to have been slightly wider than Panel A. However, against this theory is the similarity of workmanship and colours of the chain border around the 'dahlia' and the four-strand guilloche. Why the panel is slightly wider is not understood. The workmanship is good (Grade 2) and the pavement is almost certainly by the mosaicist who laid Panel A of No 39. Although bold, the setting of the chain-pattern is irregular and the alternating colours of the braids somewhat confused. The edge of the mosaic at the 'top left' has been patched with large red-brick tesserae.

Comment on the similarity to No 39 has already been offered and no further discussion is necessary. However, the central flower is remarkably similar to that occupying the central panel on the Verulamium example (Wheeler and Wheeler 1936, pl. XLIV). Both 'dahlias' are distinctive in that their petals are very slim compared to other flowers of the period, e.g. those on No 39 and pavement 10 dated *c.* 160-90 from Building IV, 8 at Verulamium (Wheeler and Wheeler 1936, pl. XLII). Another unusual motif is the bead-and-reel — the innermost concentric band. The only other example in Britain occurs at Caerwent (Ashby 1905, pl. LXVIII), where it appears in a 'negative' form — white on black. It is probably also second-century (Smith 1975, 271).

References. Dunnett 1967 (for a provisional report on the mosaic by D.J. Smith see *ibid.*, pp. 40-42); Smith 1976, 277.

Mosaic 41. Colchester. Radial mosaic

From a town-house at Lion Walk. Fourth century. Approximate dimensions 12 ft 9 in (3.88 m) square. Lifted, on display in Colchester Castle Museum. Drawn and painted 1972. *Britannia* iv (1973), pl. XXXIX.

Little of the mosaic survives, but the fragments include two large and seven smaller pieces, found *in situ* but somewhat displaced and clinging to the sides of a later pit. Sufficient remains to attempt a reconstruction.

Its scheme consists of a central circle surrounded by 16 compartments — eight large panels, apparently occupied by figured subjects, alternating with eight smaller panels containing floral arrangements, separated by radial lines within a larger circle in a square. On one side is a rectangular compartment.

Of the central circle only part of an internal band of out-turned stepped triangles remains, but its border was a laurel wreath which seems to have been subdivided into eight sections by reversed S-shaped bands possibly intended to represent ribbons. Only two survive, one red and the other yellow and white. The laurel between each ribbon is coloured differently — red leaves with white serrated tips in one section and (? only) white leaves in the next — all outlined in dark grey.

Only one of the smaller compartments survives intact. It is occupied by a highly formalized acanthus outlined in dark grey, with its thick lower leaves white and pale grey and the smaller upper leaves red and white. The acanthus is depicted as having been 'trained'; its lower heavier outward-flowing leaves are enclasped by a white collar which also holds the ends of the upper branches. These curve outwards and then spiral inwards again to touch one another: here they are fixed by another collar which also holds a 'crest'. Fragments of acanthus in two other panels appear to have been identical in form and colour. Parts of three larger radial panels survive, but only one hints at its figured content. It is occupied by a headless figure, probably female, with her arm and shoulder naked and with her arm extending forwards as if in a gesture. She faces right and wears about her legs a flowing dress and behind her shoulders a billowing red robe in a style reminiscent of the dress of a Maenad. The arm and dress of a second figure immediately in front of the first are just visible. Above the figures is a grey inscription reading Λ D [★] ṆP̣VIΛ [★ ★ ★ All that remains of a second panel is another fragmentary inscription set in two lines and reading ★ ★ ★] DRIΛ [★ ★ ★ | ★ ★ ★ I] LLIC [★ ★ ★ ★ (Wright & Hassall 1973, 331, fig. 20). A brown base-line occupies traces of a third panel.

Encircling the radial compartments is a row of out-turned stepped triangles which are surrounded by a band of chain guilloche, with white and pale-grey braids and red and white thorn-like centres, and another band of inturned stepped triangles. In a spandrel occupying one of the angles is a highly formalized acanthus-scroll. Like the acanthus in the radial compartment its 'lower' leaves are white and pale grey and its 'upper' leaves red and white. Although less than half is complete it would appear to have been similar, probably with a 'collar' about a central stem. Decoration in a tiny part of a second spandrel would indicate all panels to have been similarly ornamented. The mosaic is framed with an unusual double band of simple guilloche, inturned stepped triangles and a coarse red border.

The workmanship is exceptional (Grade 1), particularly the figures, which are worked in tesserae as small as 3-5 mm and include a wide range of subtle shades. Of the pavements in the collection this is one of the finest and hints at a most accomplished mosaicist. The overall scheme is unusual and brings to mind not only the earlier nine-panel grids with underlying circles (Nos 39 and 40) from the same city, but also the fourth-century schemes based on concentric or radial compartments (FIGS. 10 and 11) including for example Woodchester (No 87), Rudston (No 69) and Winterton (No 83). The style (but not the shading) of the acanthus is very similar to the pavements from Woodchester, Chedworth (R.C.H.M., *Glos.* i, pls. 4 and 5) and Barton Farm (Buckman and Newmarch 1850, pl. VII); so it is possible that the mosaicist had connections with the Corinian school. The workmanship, however, is superior to that of Woodchester and Barton Farm and marginally finer than that of Room 5 at Chedworth.

It is also to the Corinian school that we must look for affinities for the laurel wreath. It occurs at Woodchester and Barton Farm and also in an Orpheus mosaic found in Dyer Street, Cirencester (Beecham 1886, pl. facing p. 266). The only other parallels known to the writer are the Bancroft mosaic (No 8) and a fragment at Winterton (FIG. 25) bordering a medallion. None of these examples, however, has ribbons, nor does the colour of their leaves vary in different sections, although laurel wreaths with ribbons do occur on the continent — at Piazza Armerina, Sicily, for example (Dorigo 1971, pl. 127). Although not a close parallel, a pavement discovered in 1857 in the Red Lion Yard, Colchester (Hull 1958, pl. XXIV), is worthy of note. It had a circular compartment containing a flower, bordered by what appears to have been a shaded band wound with ribbons and, it is recorded, was of exceptional quality (Hull 1958, 196). Another pavement having a shaded band with a ribbon was discovered at Caerleon in 1877 (Boon 1960-62, pl. III).

The quality of the workmanship and its affinity to both the Barton Farm and Woodchester mosaics would suggest an early fourth-century date, perhaps no later than *c*. 325.

Reference. *Britannia* iv (1973), 304.

Mosaic 42, Combley. Octagon and peltae mosaic

From a villa at Combley, Arreton, Isle of Wight. Possibly third century. Dimensions, 9 ft by at least 15 ft 7 in (2.75 by 4.75 m); room, 32 ft by 11 ft 2 in (9.75 by 3.40 m). *In situ,* buried. Drawn 1971, painted 1972. Neal 1976, pl. 374.

This villa is first mentioned in the *Gentleman's Magazine* of 1867 (p. 791) and later in Lockhart's *Guide to the Isle of Wight* of 1870; but serious archaeological excavations do not appear to have taken place until 1911, when part of the villa and two mosaic pavements were exposed and duly recorded by A. Arnold.[1] One pavement (not illustrated) decorated a small bath-suite and comprised a row of spaced swastika-meanders with two fishes in a rectangular compartment. The other pavement, to be described, occupied Room 3 in the main house. Excavations by L.R. Fennelly since 1968 have re-exposed the mosaics and have established that the mosaic drawn in 1911 in Room 3 was merely part of a larger fragment with a rectangular field divided into at least three square panels. Waterlogging and unstable subsoil have caused the wall-foundations to subside, leaving the mosaic on a steep camber, cracked and distorted. For convenience, the best surviving panel will be described first.

This occupied one end of the scheme and had a large octagon containing four very large colourful peltae outlined in yellow with crossed points towards the frame; the undersides of the 'top' and 'bottom' peltae were coloured black, possibly in an attempt to show perspective. The peltae are infilled in concentric bands of colour — red, pale grey and black. In a curvilinear square compartment in the centre of the panel is a circle, outlined in pale grey, containing a guilloche knot with red, dark red and white braids and, curiously, yellow outlines. Within eight semicircular areas formed by the cusps of the peltae and the edge of the octagon are semicircular panels bordered in red and brown 'millefiori', sometimes with an open centre but sometimes partly infilled black. The background to the two opposed peltae at the 'top' and 'bottom' is very pale grey; the other is white. Outside the octagon, in two opposed 'wing-shaped' panels at the angles of the outer frame, are peltae with voluted handles outlined in black, one with a red and the other with a black pedestal. They are infilled with concentric lines of colour — red, brown and white, and red and yellow. The other 'wing-shaped' compartments contain red-sepalled calices, also voluted and with triangular pedestals. One has a band of red and white 'millefiori' — typical of canthari which this motif is imitating.

The panel to the right is damaged, but is occupied by a flower outlined in yellow with four white, pale grey, and red heart-shaped petals. The tips of the petals impinge upon an encircling band of red and white 'millefiori'. The latter is itself encircled by a pale grey band and the whole is contained within two interlaced squares; one square is black and the other pale grey. The interlaced squares are in a square black frame, with the spaces between it and the interlaced squares infilled with guilloche knots in red, pale grey and white, against pale grey or black backgrounds.

Between this panel and the other is a rectangular area filled with a swastika-meander in pale grey and red and, at one end, black. To the 'right' of the flowered panel are two separate fragments of guilloche, one with a chequered edge. The panels have a surround of four-strand guilloche in red, pale grey and white, and a coarse red-brick border.

The workmanship (Grade 2), although in places technically poor e.g. in the swastika-meander, is highly imaginative both in its scheme and in its wide use of colour. Apart from No 66 from Rudston and No 87 from Woodchester, no other pavement in the collection has such a colour-range, nor are the other pavements from the Isle of Wight, notably Brading (Price and Price 1881), similarly varied. Another feature which sets Combley apart from most other pavements is the wide use of fired clay: all the black tesserae have been made from the core of over-fired tile, and a close examination of them reveals traces of the red outer surfaces left untrimmed. Apart from the red, which is also brick, the remainder of the colours are from local stone. Widespread use of fired clay was also noted at Gadebridge (No 51).

The writer knows of no parallel for the design of this mosaic. There is a number of affinities which might suggest that its design was influenced by work in the Dorset area. A mosaic from Olga Road, Dorchester (Colley March 1900, pl. facing p. 162), now re-laid in Dorset Country Museum, has a linear square occupied by a large octagon in guilloche. Instead of large peltae it is occupied by a guilloche knot. 'Wing-shaped' panels occupy the four corners and each contains a voluted pelta. This same mosaic also has rectangles of guilloche with chequered edges. Another pavement from Dorset, from the Dewlish villa (Putnam & Rainey 1975, fig. 7), has two-coloured swastika-meander. This is uncommon and only appears on one other mosaic in the collection, No 10 from Bishopstone Down, Wilts.

It is not possible to date the pavement with any precision. The excavator prefers a late third-century date for the villa (Fennelly 1969, 282), but the wide use of colour infilling is perhaps more likely to favour a fourth-century date.

References. Fennelly 1969. Neal 1976 p. 242.

[1]The drawings are in the possession of the landowner, Mr. J. Willis Fleming.

Mosaic 43, Eccles. Gladiator mosaic

From a villa at Eccles in Kent. Late first to early second century. Dimensions uncertain. Fragments in DOE store. Drawn and painted 1964. Detsicas 1965, frontispiece and fig. 4: Smith 1969, pl. 3.1: Smith 1975, pl. CVIII.1.

The reconstruction of the Eccles mosaic is based on a large number of loose fragments from Room 46, but assumed to have been stripped from a *frigidarium* (Room 30) of a large and elaborate bath-suite of exceptionally early date (Detsicas 1965, p. 71). Most of the fragments have lozenge patterns while others have flower-motifs, simple and three-strand guilloche and parts of what may be human figures.

The overall scheme is totally conjectural, but it would appear to have comprised a principal panel, probably square, upon an overall scheme of spaced squares tangent to tilted squares and forming a composition of eight-lozenge stars. Some of the larger squares contain quatrefoils with red, yellow and white petals and the tilted squares a single leaf upon a curled stalk. Painstaking reconstruction of the figured fragments suggests a square panel bordered in simple guilloche containing two gladiators; these are represented by fragments of their legs, an arm and wrist bound with leather thongs, and possibly a red sword-pommel.

Although the composition of the gladiators must remain controversial, the basic scheme as reconstructed is probably fairly reliable. It occurs on a mosaic in Room N3 at Fishbourne (Cunliffe 1971, pl. LXXVII *a*) dated *c.* 75-80. The pavement under discussion was originally believed to date *c.* A.D.65, but doubts about such an early date have recently been expressed and Dr. Smith suggests that the mosaic is probably nearer to 120 (Smith 1975, p. 271).

Apart from a gladiatorial contest on a frieze at Bignor dated to the fourth century (Toynbee 1962, pl. 225-6) and another associated with the Abraxus mosaic from Brading (Price and Price 1881, fig. 22) this is the only other example in Britain. Neither of these can be closely compared, but the figures would appear to be very similar to gladiators on a pavement from Reims (Stern 1957, pls. XII.9 and XII.15). The general scheme is a common one. In a fourth-century context it occurs at Winterton (No 86) but here the lozenges have been infilled with colour. The Gadebridge Park mosaic (No 51) may also be quoted.

References. Detsicas 1965 (for a report on the mosaics by D.S. Neal see *ibid.*, Appendix, 'The *Frigidarium* Mosaics'
         p. 90). Smith 1969, p. 75: Smith 1975, p. 271.

Mosaic 44. Fishbourne. Amphorae and fishes

From the Roman palace at Fishbourne, Chichester, Sussex. Dated *c.* 75-80. Mosaic and room 17 ft (5.18 m) square. *In situ*, on display. Drawn and painted 1962. NPP.

The chance discovery of the Roman palace at Fishbourne during the cutting of a water-pipe trench in 1960 and the excavations by Prof. B. Cunliffe between 1961 and 1969 brought to light fragments of at least 20 mosaics many of an exceptionally early date. The building, its luxury unparalleled in Britain, was built *c.* 75-80, and is almost certainly associated with the British Royal House of Tiberius Claudius Cogidubnus. The mosaics are of four main periods *c.* 75-80, *c.* 100, *c.* 150-200 and *c.* 200; the earliest and the majority are executed in monochrome, black on white, and comprise geometric designs — lozenge or eight-pointed-star and meander patterns. However a noteworthy exception is this finely worked polychrome mosaic, one of the earliest polychrome mosaics in Britain.[1] The illustration is of only part of the mosaic, but FIG. 21 shows the overall scheme, based on a series of concentric circles within a square.

The central circle is unfortunately lost, but it was bordered with concentric black, grey, red, and black lines surrounded by a wide zone containing eight-petalled flowers and leaves alternating. The petals are traditionally rendered in white, yellow, brown and with red tips. The same colours are employed in the leaves, which are unusually large and heavy with thick black outlines and curled stalks similar to the stalks of the Eccles pavement (No 43). The next concentric zone contains an original variety of a very wide and bold simple guilloche with the braids alternating in colour — red and sienna, and steel-grey, grey and white, outlined in black

FIG. 21 Fishbourne, No 44. Copy of reconstruction by E. Baker

and very finely worked with a gradation of colour unparalleled in Britain. In the four quadrants are tall amphorae, one with a conical lid. Two are flanked by very heavy black scrolls terminating in roundels and sprouting the occasional leaf. The other two amphorae are flanked by fine and realistically-portrayed fish and one of them also by part of a black scroll. The arrangement of these motifs is unusual. For two quadrants on one side to have amphorae and fishes, while the quadrants on the other side have amphorae and black scrolls gives the design an unbalanced appearance — unusual on Romano-British mosaic, where usually the designs have symmetry.

The workmanship, Grade 2, is fine — the tesserae range from 5-10 mm in size with the smallest tesserae used in the guilloche — but it was not the best at Fishbourne. Fragments of a finer technique were found in the audience chamber, Room W. 14. It is, however, technically superior to all the other pavements from Fishbourne which are, curiously, of a relatively poor standard when compared to the exceptional grandeur of the building and its architecture.

References. Cunliffe 1971, p. 99 and pls. XXVI, XXVII, LXXXI and XCI. Smith 1969, p. 74-5.

[1]A fragment of mosaic discovered in the legionary *thermae* at Exeter and dated A.D. 55-60 must be the earliest mosaic recorded in Britain. It shows two diminutive horses confronting a sphere. (Bidwell 1979, pl. XVI A).

The Fullerton Mosaics. Nos 45–50

Fullerton Roman Villa, Wherwell, Hants, lies on the west bank of the River Anton adjacent to the route of a disused railway. In 1905 it was recorded (Haverfield 1905, 250) that 'A Roman villa near Fullerton railway station in Hampshire, previously known, has been further examined, and a fine figured mosaic discovered, taken up, and relaid in a modern house' — the nearby Fullerton Manor. A description of 21 June, 1930 (*Hants. Chron.*), implies that the figured mosaic was lifted in 1895 'by expert workmen from Bristol'. Other fragments were probably lifted at the same time because the manor also houses part of three other mosaics — Nos 46 and 47 a and b. In 1963–4 excavations by Dr. D. Whitehouse revealed a small corridor villa with remains of three pavements, Nos 48–50, No 48 clearly the same floor of which No 47a formed part. At about the same time, Fullerton Manor was converted into private flats and regrettably No 45 was partially built upon by a partition wall. It still lies in the house, together with other fragments, but sealed beneath fitted carpets! It is probable that all mosaics from Fullerton illustrated here are of the same date and by the same contractor.

Mosaic 45, Fullerton. Mars

From a villa at Fullerton, Hants. Fourth century. Original dimensions 14 ft (4.25 m) square. Lifted and set in Fullerton Manor. Drawn and painted 1969. Rainey pl. 2 B.

The scheme of this pavement comprises a large circle containing eight irregular hexagons arranged around a central octagon all within a square and inscribed in simple guilloche in grey, red, yellow and white.

Occupying the central octagon is a figure of Mars facing forwards but looking slightly to his left. He wears a helmet, with a projecting comb, and a red and yellow cloak drawn across his chest and hanging behind his back. In his raised right hand is a spear and in his left a red and yellow shield with a white boss and a red and white chequered rim. Of the surviving hexagons, three are complete and two damaged; they each contain a satyr, semi-nude, wearing a grey cloak. In a clockwise direction, one figure holds a *pedum* over his right shoulder, another a staff across his back, another holds a tambourine or sieve, and one a *pedum* with the crook down. All that remains of a fifth figure is an arm and leg in a prancing position. The figures are in red, yellow and white and outlined in grey. In two surrounding spandrels in the angles are female busts[1] without attributes but possibly representing the Seasons. One has dark grey hair and wears a yellow looped necklace and the other has red and yellow hair. On at least two sides of the pavement is a very bold border of opened guilloche forming circles,[2] each circle containing a smaller circle bordered in alternating red and dark grey inturned stepped triangles.

The workmanship is fairly coarse (Grade 2), and the guilloche is very irregular in the number of twists in a given space — sometimes five twists fill a band separating the hexagons, sometimes four. Mars and the Satyrs although very small and detailed are crudely drawn and their stance unnatural. The female busts are more accomplished both artistically and technically.

The scheme is unusual in Britain. Apart from a fragmentary mosaic from Room 26 at Bignor, Sussex (Lysons iii, 1817, pl. xix), which could possibly be reconstructed similarly, the only other example known to the writer is a pavement from Caerwent, found in 1881 (Morgan 1882, facing p. 22). Its overall layout is almost identical to our example but it has a circular and not an octagonal central panel. Much of the design is missing but three adjoining hexagons contain fishes. A fish also occupies the remaining spandrel. Although these are the only two examples of eight hexagons around a central panel, the general scheme can be found on a number of other mosaics, but with a circle of hexagon sub-divided into seven hexagons, six arranged around a seventh. For example in Room 7 at Bignor (Lysons iii, 1817, pl. vii and ix) with the central hexagon occupied by a *piscina*, at Spoonley Wood, (R.C.H.M. *Glos.* i pl. 14), and within a hexagonal-shaped room at Keynsham (Bulleid and Horn 1926, fig. 3.). All the schemes quoted are attributed to the fourth century.

It is also to Bignor, in the border of Room 26, that we must look for an example of open guilloche (Lysons iii, 1817, pl. xv); but like the same pattern in a corridor at the Greetwell villa, Lincoln,[3] its loops are broader, which provides more space for the insertion of larger motifs, e.g. guilloche knots and flowers.[4] The occurrence of two similar schemes at Bignor and the presence of open guilloche does not necessarily indicate work of the same *officina*. The Fullerton mosaic is far inferior to the Bignor pavements, which in the opinion of the writer are the best in Britain, and are most unlikely to be the work of the same contractor. The exceptional quality of the Bignor pavements could, however, have been the *inspiration* for Fullerton. There is no parallel for the central figure, but a reference of 1796 (*Gents. Mag.* 1796, 472) suggests that a pavement from Calne, Wilts, '. . . represents a Roman soldier or military officer of higher rank, of the natural size, armed with a spear . . .' He also may have been Mars.

References. Toynbee 1964, 258: Smith 1977, 38 and 80

[1]Interpreted by Toynbee as wreathed youths (Toynbee 1964, 259); but there is insufficient evidence for wreaths and since one wears a necklace they are more likely to be female.
[2]The break in part of this pattern is the result of modern relaying and not an error by the mosaicist.
[3]A plan and fragments of this pavement are preserved in Lincoln City Museum.
[4]The motif also occurs at Wigginton (No 78). Other examples are to be found at Lufton, Somerset (Hayward 1952, fig. 3), Lydney, Glos (Bathurst 1879, pl. xvi). The scheme of the Oulston mosaic, Yorks. (Clark 1935, 119) is a variation with two concentric bands of guilloche joined to one another by four large loops.

Mosaic 46. Fullerton. Pelta pattern

From a villa at Fullerton, Hants. Fourth century. Fragment 13 ft 5 in (4.10 m) long. Lifted and set in Fullerton Manor. Drawn and painted 1964. NPP.

This simple rectangular panel probably decorated a corridor and consists of all-over running peltae, in black and red, with cross points. Along the pattern is a break; this is not indicative of prefrabrication as has been suggested (Rainey 1973, 80) but merely an error in the relaying.

As we have seen in the description of the Bancroft mosaic (No 5), running peltae occur on a number of other corridor pavements. Unlike those at Bancroft, however, the peltae of the Fullerton pavement have crossed points, a feature at Box (Brakspear 1904, pl. i.2) where the mosaic is further elaborated by the introduction of small yellow and black centres, similar shading to the threshold separating panels A and B at Hinton St Mary (No 61). For another mosaic in the collection with peltae, see Thenford (No 72). The workmanship is coarse, Grade 3.

Mosaic 47, Fullerton. Ashlar pattern

From a villa at Fullerton, Hants. Fourth century. Fragment 6 ft 9 in by 4 ft 9 in (2.06 by 1.45 m). Lifted and set in Fullerton Manor. Drawn and painted 1964. NPP.

Like No. 46 this fragment probably also came from a corridor and is decorated with an ashlar pattern in dark grey against a white background.

Although simple, the pattern is unusual in Britain. It resembles some of the borders at Fishbourne, where squares are divided by rectangles and small squares to give a 'brickwork' or ashlar pattern similar to that on Nos 55 and 59 from Gloucester. The closest examples known to the writer are another mosaic from Gloucester illustrated in the collection (No 57) with two rows of ashlar in a panel alongside an octagonal scheme, and a mosaic from the forum at Cirencester (Wacher 1964, pl. XII b) dated to the fourth century. The Fishbourne and Gloucester examples, however, are dated to the first and second centuries respectively. The workmanship is coarse, Grade 3.

Mosaic 48a and b. Fullerton. Labyrinth

From a villa at Fullerton, Hants. Fourth century. Overall dimensions of mosaic and room approximately 18 ft 6 in (5.65 m) square. *In situ*, buried. Drawn and painted 1964. NPP.

During the excavation a hole was found in part of this mosaic which corresponded in size to a fragment, stylistically indentical, relaid in Fullerton Manor (No 48b). There can be little doubt that this fragment is from the same pavement and accordingly the drawing shows the missing section restored. The design comprises a crudely executed labyrinth in dark grey bands with a broad crenellated surround and bordered by plain dark grey and white bands. In contrast to the labyrinth mosaics[1] from Cirencester (Nos 21 and 27), Caerleon (FIG. 19), and Harpham (FIG. 20), the pavement is naively simple and clearly the work of an inexperienced mosaicist without recourse to a pattern-book. For all the naivety of the labyrinth, however, the bold crenellated border is unusual. It is perhaps, based on the 'city wall' crenellations seen e.g. at Rudston (No 69). Like the other mosaics from the site the workmanship is coarse, Grade 3.

[1]For discussion on the labyrinth mosaics listed above see p. 63.

Mosaic 49. Fullerton. Meander pattern.

From a villa at Fullerton, Hants. Fourth century. Dimensions of pavement and room 15 ft 8 in by 9 ft 9 in (4.80 by 2.97 m). *In situ*, buried. Drawn and painted 1964. NPP.

This strikingly effective design is based on a scheme of opposed and linked spaced swastika-meanders with a square in each space. Here the pattern comprises a single square flanked on either side and linked by swastika-meanders. The design is surrounded by broad white, dark grey and white bands. All the tesserae are coarse but the workmanship (Grade 2) is finer than pavements 46-8 and 50.

A very similar monochrome scheme (red on white) was found at Middle Brook Street, Winchester in 1953 (Bennet-Clark 1954, fig. 1). It occupied an equally narrow room, but longer; and consequently there was originally more than one square. The similarity and proximity between the two mosaics suggests they may possibly be products of the same contractor. No 28 from Cirencester is also very similar, but the square contains a guilloche-bordered square instead.

Mosaic 50. Fullerton. Geometric

From a villa at Fullerton, Hants. Fourth century. Dimensions; panel 11 ft (3.36 m) square, room 21 ft by 18 ft (6.40 by 5.49 m). *In situ*, buried. Drawn and painted 1964. NPP.

Only a series of dark grey and white right-angled lines and part of a square of guilloche remain, but these are sufficient to establish that the scheme consisted of an all-over spaced swastika-meander with double returns, the spaces staggered in a quincunx arrangement and containing guilloche knots. The latter are dark grey, red and white; but otherwise the mosaic is monochrome. The pavement has a broad white border. Other examples in the collection include No 5 from Bancroft and No 26 from Cirencester. In more complex forms it occurs at Chedworth, No 19 and Woodchester, No 87. The workmanship is coarse, Grade 3.

An interesting aspect of the pavements from Fullerton is the clear distinction between the figured polychrome mosaic (No 45), in what was obviously the principal room, and the essentially monochrome pavements in coarse tesserae throughout the rest of the house. It would appear that the owner was determined to have as many rooms as possible tessellated, but could afford only one of reasonable quality.

Mosaic 51. Gadebridge Park. Eight-lozenge stars

From the Roman villa in Gadebridge Park, Hemel Hempstead, Herts. Dated *c.* A.D. 325. Dimensions; 17 ft 4 in by 16 ft 4 in (5.30 by 4.99 m), room 23 ft (7.02 m) square. *In situ*, buried. Drawn 1966, painted 1967. Neal 1974, pl. XVI

The Roman villa at Gadebridge Park was discovered in 1962 during the construction of a by-pass road and subsequently excavated by the author between 1963 and 1968. The mosaic occupied a large heated room in the north-west corner. Although considerably damaged by the plough, sufficient survived to enable a reliable reconstruction to be made. Its scheme consists of a grid of spaced squares bordered in simple guilloche flanked by and tangent to smaller tilted squares also inscribed in guilloche. The interspaces are filled by large and colourful eight-lozenge stars. The surviving large square contains a square guilloche mat outlined in dark grey, with red, pale grey and creamy white braids. Occupying the tilted squares are small squares quartered diagonally to form two grey triangles set point to point. Each lozenge is bordered with concentric bands of various colours — red, pale grey, creamy white or pink, and contains a circle or spiralled motif with red-tipped leaves. Around the border are the remains of four rectangles — (half 'squares') filled with a guilloche strip, a guilloche knot, a pair of heart-shaped leaves with red tips and a guilloche knot in a chequered frame.

The mosaic is bordered with treble-strand guilloche in grey, red, pale grey and creamy white, and on one side by a strip of unusual 'open' guilloche. This lacks the conventional grey outline but is bordered instead by red bands. Its braids are cream, red and cream and the centres dark grey, red and pale grey alternating. It has a coarse red-brick surround of two phases: those adjacent to the pavement are contemporary with it but the larger outer tesserae belong to an earlier floor. Technically the floor is unusual. Unlike the other lozenged stars in the collection this is the only example with the lozenges outlined by a single fillet. Nor does the writer know of any other example in this style except for a second-century pavement from Caerwent (Ashby 1905, pl. LXVIII) where some of the lozenges are bordered by a double fillet and others by a single fillet. The effect of the single fillet at Gadebridge, probably intentionally, was to give greater emphasis to the multi-coloured lozenges and to suppress the star-like outline of the pattern. Another unusual aspect of the floor is that, apart from the grey stone used in the fillets, the remainder of the colours, including all the pale background tesserae, are tile. Frequent use of tile was also observed at Combley (No 42).

The scheme of the pavement is a common one. We have already observed it at Eccles (No 43) and noted examples of first-century date at Fishbourne. In the earlier mosaics the lozenges are either empty or contain small black rhomboids but, by the fourth century, there is a greater use of colour and a variety of filling motifs — as for instance on a mosaic at Barton Farm, Glos. (Buckman and Newmarch 1850, pl. VII), and at Stonesfield, Oxon. (Smith 1969, pl. 3.15), both products of the Corinian school (cf p. 19). However, it is in the villas in the Midlands — for example Great Staughton, Hunts. (Smith 1969, 3.25), Mansfield Woodhouse, Notts. (Smith 1969, 3.23), Medbourne, Leic. (V.C.H. *Leic.* i, pl. VII) and Nether Heyford, Northants. (V.C.H. *Northants,* fig. 24), where the greatest density of examples occur. The latter group may well be products of the same *officina* perhaps based at Durobrivae (cf p. 43). An outlying example from Winterton, Lincs. (No 86) should also be quoted. Although the mosaic has stylistic affinities with the pavements cited, there is insufficient evidence to suggest that it is related to either the Corinian or Durobrivan *officina*. Its workmanship is good (Grade 2), particularly the guilloche, which is finely worked and narrow (only 3½ in (9.0 cm) wide).

References. Neal 1974, 50: Neal 1976, 242.

The Gloucester Pavements. Nos 52-59

Gloucester City centre has over recent years seen major redevelopment, and since 1966 fragments of at least 13 mosaics have been found during emergency excavations in advance of construction.

Excavations by M. Hassall and J. Rhodes in 1966-7 revealed fragments of four mosaics (two are illustrated — Nos 52-3) on a site for the new Market Hall on the south-west side of Bell Lane, and another on a car-park at Longsmith Street (Hassall and Rhodes 1974). In 1969 excavations were carried out by H. Hurst in advance of the construction of the G.P.O. Telephone Exchange at Berkeley Street (Hurst 1972). He found a second-century courtyard house with fragments of two mosaics (Nos 54-5). Another major excavation in 1969, also by H. Hurst, was undertaken prior to the construction of a new Woolworth's Store off Eastgate Street, where fragments of five mosaics (four are illustrated, Nos 56-9) were found in a building occupying Insula V b. (Hurst 1974).[1]

The pavements are an interesting collection; they provide not only further evidence for the work of the Corinian *officina* in the fourth century, but also possibly evidence for an *officina* working in the city in the second century producing simple ashlar patterns of white on black. The mosaics will be described and illustrated in order of discovery.

[1] Of the 14 recorded floors in this building 12 had mosaics — mostly lost.

Mosaic 52. Gloucester. Bacchus and Leopard.

Found in the excavations at the New Market Hall in 1966. Fourth century. Dimensions excluding plain border 13 ft 7 in by 13 ft 2 in (4.15 by 4.02 m), room, 17 ft (5.19 m) square. Destroyed.[1] Drawn 1966, painted 1967. Hassall and Rhodes 1974, pls. II and III: Smith 1977, pl. 6.xvib.

This drawing was partly prepared on site and later completed from a series of vertical photographs and measured drawings of fragments found after the initial excavations in 1966. The reconstruction shows the scheme to be based on a regular grid of interlaced squares (FIG. 5A) at a 45° angle to the square frame. Consequently a single pair of interlaced squares occupies the centre of the pavement and 'quarter' interlaced squares occupy the four angles. The central interlaced squares enclose a fragmentary medallion outlined in dark grey. It is occupied by the right front paw and chest of a leopard in steel-grey and by red drapery interpreted as the dress of Bacchus, of whom only part of the left shoulder and right arm remain. A diagonal dark grey line across the side of the leopard indicates that Bacchus held a *thyrsus* in his left hand. It is likely that he held a wine cup in his right, as on the representations of Bacchus at Stonesfield, Oxon. (Smith 1965, fig. 15) and Thruxton, Hants. (Ingram 1849, pl. facing 241). In rectangular panels 'above' and 'below' the medallion are the remains of red and white gadrooned bowls with sprouting splayed grey and white leaves heavily outlined in dark grey, but terminating in delicate red and white heart-shaped petals.

A rectangular panel to the 'left' of Bacchus is occupied by a scroll with red and white leaves. The only surviving corner-panel contains a quadrant with a red and white pointed flower bordered in part with a band of dark grey waves. Each pair of lozenges is occupied by identical motifs which seem to have been repeated in the lozenges in the angles on the opposite side of the pavement. One pair has volutes with red-tipped leaves, another rhomboids quartered and shaded diagonally in purple, white and red bands (possibly imitating marble veneer); another has open rhomboids with strips of simple red and white guilloche; and the remaining pair has swastika lozenges with reverse returns.[2] The pavement is surrounded by a wide band of treble-strand guilloche in grey. red and local limestone.On one side only is a row of out-turned stepped triangles in Old Red Sandstone, and around the whole pavement lies a wide grey limestone border mixed with Old Red Sandstone.

The standard of workmanship is fairly good (Grade 2), but the mosaicist has been over ambitious with the simple guilloche. One of the interlaced boxes is in grey, steel-grey, red and white, and the other in the same colours but alternating with grey, red and white. This same treatment is to found in the angles — and in the outer frame. Where the guilloche is consistent throughout it is neat, but where it alternates it is 'loose' and untidy.

In the discussion of the mosaics at Caerwent (No 17) and Cirencester (Nos 25 and 36) we have already noted that schemes with interlaced squares are common (cf p. 52). These examples are not precise; but at Wigginton (No 78) we find traces of a virtually identical scheme, but larger. All the examples are fourth-century.

The similarity of the 'veneered' rhomboids to those on No 25 from Cirencester suggests it might be the work of the same contractor and possibly the work of the Corinian school. However, a problem here is the relationship to similar schemes at Bishopstone (V.C.H. *Hereford*, fig. 14) and Kenchester (Jack 1916, pl. 23) in Herefordshire, at Halstock, Dorset (Rainey 1971, figs. 10 and 11) and at Broad Street, London R.C.H.M., *Roman London*, pl. 48). To assume that all these pavements are the work of the Corinian *officina* may be pushing credulity too far. and it may be wiser to assume that they are the products of the same travelling contractor influenced by the Corinian school, not necessarily working from a centre, but moving on from job to job. A mosaicist only needs a workshop if prefabricated panels are to be assembled, and there is no evidence for this on any of the pavements cited.

In another room of the same building a fragment of 'perspective box pattern similar to that of the pavement described . . .' was found, and in another room a corner-panel occupied by a 'simple rosette where four heart-shaped petals alternate with pear-shaped leaves' (Hassall and Rhodes 1974, 26).

Reference. Hassall and Rhodes 1974, 26.

[1]Only the scrolled panel was lifted and is on display in the New Market Hall, Gloucester.
[2]Examples of swastika-meanders with reverse returns, but not in rhomboids, occur at Aldborough, Yorks. and Winterton, Lincs. (Nos 2 and 82).

Mosaic 53. Gloucester. Fragments.

From Longsmith Street Car-Park site. Second century. Dimensions uncertain. Destroyed. Drawn 1966, painted 1967. NPP.

The larger of the fragments has a coarse rectangular panel alongside a finer mosaic almost totally lost. The rectangular panel has a wide dark grey band bearing a row of large red squares, set lozengewise and tangent to one another, and surrounded by white, dark grey and red bands. The finer mosaic is also bordered in wide dark grey and white bands and bears a series of right-angled dark grey lines possibly belonging to a swastika-meander pattern and part of a wave border. Its place in an overall scheme is uncertain, but perhaps it is part of a nine-panel design similar to No 20 from Chichester. An isolated fragment has traces of a rosette within a linear circle, surrounded by a scroll with dark grey tendrils springing from red and white sheaths.

Its squares set lozengewise bear a similarity to the surround of No 54, also dated to the second century (cf p. 84). Workmanship, Grade 2.

Mosaic 54. Gloucester. Fragment

From the GPO Telephone Exchange site, 13–17 Berkeley Street. Second century. probably 11 ft 9 in (3.58 m) square. Destroyed. Drawn 1971, painted 1972. Hurst 1974, pl. IV.

This occupied a room on the south range of a Hadrianic courtyard house (Buildings I, 18) and although fragmentary, was sufficiently preserved to enable a tentative reconstruction to be made. Of the principal square scheme only a right-angled fragment of simple guilloche remains. It encloses part of a corner-panel with traces of a yellow and red leaf or petal. The colours in the guilloche alternate — blue, pale grey and white, red, yellow and white. Bordering it along two opposing sides are rectangular panels with thick black outlines enclosing a row of black squares, set lozengewise and tangent to one another. The black outlines turn the angles of the mosaic to enclose, on at least one side, a row of egg-and-dart motifs in black with twin-stalked heart-shaped leaves shaded white, yellow and with red tips. The darts are shaded white and pale grey and have blue tips. The workmanship, Grade 2, is very neat and the tesserae very tightly set.

All that can be said of the scheme is that it possibly had nine panels similar to No 73 from Verulamium (cf p. 101). The egg-and-dart motif with petals in the centres is a common pattern on second-century floors in Britain. We have already observed it in No 39 from Colchester; it also occurs at Colchester on at least three other pavements of approximately the same date. Another feature which appears to be fairly common in the second century is the row of squares set lozengewise. It appears on the pavement previously described (No 53) and on a nine-panel scheme from Building IV, 1 at Verulamium (Wheeler and Wheeler 1936, pl. XLIV).

References. Hurst 1972, 37 ff: Hurst 1974, 21, and pl. IV.

Mosaic 55. Gloucester. Border fragment.

From the GPO Telephone Exchange site, 13–17 Berkeley Street. Second century. Fragment 12 ft 6 in (3.80 m) long, room 24 ft by 19 ft (7.32 by 5.80 m). Destroyed. Painting prepared in 1978 from site records of 1969. NPP.

Also from Building I, 18, this fragment bordered a large room on the east side of the court-yard. Of the principal mosaic only part of its coloured guilloche surround remains, but its dark grey border has white four-oblong squares (or four equal oblongs arranged to enclose squares). The pattern is similar to the border of No 59 from Eastgate Street and also occurs at Fishbourne in a Flavian context in room N 12 and in a mid second-century context in room N 14 (Cunliffe 1971, pls. LXXVIII and LXXXVI). However, an important distinction between the pavements from the two sites is that the Fishbourne border decoration is black on white, whereas at Gloucester it is white on black. It would seem, from the similarity of the pattern to No 59 and to the ashlar border of No 57, that they may represent the work of the same mosaicist or at least the same *officina*.[1] It is very interesting to note that the precise pattern does not occur at Verulamium, Colchester, or Cirencester. The workmanship is fairly fine, Grade 2.

Reference. Hurst 1972, 37 ff. (shown on plan fig. 10 and pl. x a).

[1]Since this paper was written another mosaic with a white on black ashlar border has been discovered at Gloucester.

Mosaic 56. Gloucester. Acanthus scroll with human mask

From the Woolworth's basement site, 10–18 Eastgate Street. Probably second century. Fragment, dimensions uncertain. Lifted, in Gloucester Museum. Drawn by Henry Hurst 1969, painted by D.S.N. 1978. NPP.

This mosaic was found in Building V 17 and, although fragmentary, is an unusual pavement which bears two particularly interesting motifs. Its overall scheme is uncertain; but it was possibly square, with a square central panel (now lost) outlined in alternating three-strand guilloche, in red, yellow and white, and grey, pale grey and white, outlined in grey. On one side of the panel, but probably originally on the other sides also, is an elaborate plant-form based on the acanthus. Projecting from its rippled lip are two (originally three) pointed yellow and white leaves, outlines in dark red, behind which springs an ornate acanthus-scroll with red, yellow and white leaves terminating in a roundel containing a human mask with thick upturned lips, a flattened nose and tiny piercing eyes. It is shaded blue-grey, dark red, yellow and white. Bordering the scroll are alternating blue-grey and white bands, simple guilloche in grey, red and white, another white band and a wide blue-grey border. The workmanship is fine (Grade 2), particularly the rendering of the scroll. As with No 34 the borders are constructed with small tesserae. The pavement has no parallel on pavements dated to the second century, but its ornate acanthus-scroll is similar in style to that on a number of fourth-century pavements. The multi-coloured leaves bear a resemblance to the work of the Durnovarian *officina*, particularly the pavement from Hinton St Mary, Dorset (No 61). However, it is probable that its design has been influenced by wall-paintings. It is reminiscent of a second-century frieze from Insula XXI, 2 at Verulamium, with an acanthus scroll terminating in birds and leopard heads (Frere 1957, pl. v). The mask itself is not unique; examples can be found in the ornate foliage occupying trapezoidal panels on one of the Dewlish, Dorset, pavements (*Britannia* iv (1973), pl. XXXII B) at Thruxton, Hants. (Ingram 1849, pl. facing 241) and Room W at Keynsham (Bulleid and Horne 1924-6, pl. XVIII, 2).

Reference. Hurst 1972, pl. x b.

Mosaic 57. Gloucester. Scheme of octagons

From the Woolworth's basement site, 10-18 Eastgate Street. Probably mid second century. Very fragmentary but original dimensions of main panel approximately 14 ft (4.25 m) square. Destroyed. Drawing prepared from excavator's field-sketches made in 1969 and 1972. Painted 1978. NPP.

Although fragmentary, sufficient remains to reconstruct the main panel. It consisted of an overall pattern of octagons (four rows of four) forming tilted square interspaces, all outlined in simple guilloche in red, yellow and white and outlined in blue/grey. At least four octagons were occupied by eight petalled flowers each with a blue/grey centre surrounded by concentric white, yellow and red bands. The flowers are set in linear octagons bordered on three examples with an inturned band of right-angled triangles, on another with a band of wave pattern and on another with a circle of simple guilloche.

On the 'left' side of the mosaic is part of a second panel bordered in coarse three-strand guilloche in blue, red, yellow and white, surrounding a band of simple guilloche in similar colours. Too little survives to enable a reconstruction but the blue tesserae here are a shade different from the octagonal scheme, which may signify that the two parts are not contemporary. At least one side of the mosaic had an ashlar-pattern border in white on blue/grey, somewhat similar to the borders of No 55.

The writer has not seen any part of the pavement but the site drawings and photographs would suggest poor workmanship (Grade 3), particularly the wave-pattern which shows considerable distortion. As we have already seen (p. 44), with few exceptions the majority of octagonal schemes belong to the second century. The style of the border would also indicate a second-century date; but the crude workmanship suggests a late product, perhaps even as late as the early third century.

Reference. Hurst 1972, 50-51, pl. x c.

Mosaic 58. Gloucester. Interlaced squares

From the new Market Hall site, 12-36 Eastgate Street. Fourth century. Dimensions uncertain, at least 16 ft by 14 ft 3 in (4.95 by 4.35 m). Destroyed. Drawn and painted 1972. Hurst 1974, pl. v.

This pavement was found in a late second-century building occupying Insula V b. Although extremely fragmentary, it is possible to reconstruct its scheme which consisted of four pairs of interlaced squares within a square frame. This in turn was surrounded by a band of spaced swastika–meander, with a rectangular mat of three-strand guilloche in each space, and a broad Pennant stone border with a red strip.

The only surviving motif, occupying an interlaced square, is part of a flower with eight red-tipped petals and a red and pale grey centre. The missing interlaced squares were probably similarly ornamented and also had similarly inscribed guilloche borders — one square in grey, red and white and the other in grey, pale grey and white.

FIG. 22 Gloucester, No 58. Reconstruction

From the evidence available it is not possible to reconstruct the remainder of the design positively, but it is likely that the central, side and corner-interspaces contained a circle, semicircles and quadrants, as shown on FIG. 22, and similar to a mosaic discovered at Cirencester in 1808 (Lysons ii 1817, pl. v). On some pavements, e.g. at Bramdean (V.C.H. *Hants*, fig. 19), pairs of interlaced squares are tangent at the angles to form lozenge-shaped compartments, without a linear surround as on this example. A pavement from Caerwent (No 17) appears to have been similar. For further discussion on interlaced squares see comments on No 17; but they are all assigned to the fourth century. The few traces remaining indicate good-quality workmanship, Grade 2.

Reference. Hurst 1974, p. 27.

Mosaic 59. Gloucester. Fragment

From the Woolworth's basement site, 10–18 Eastgate Street. Mid second century. Fragment 9 ft 2 in (2.80 m) long, overall dimension of decorated area probably 7 ft 3 in (2.20 m) square. Lost. Painting prepared from field drawings made by H. Hurst in 1972. Painted 1978. NPP.

The pattern, worked in white tesserae against a grey background, consists of a series of squares divided into four oblongs arranged around smaller squares.

We have already seen the pattern used as a border on No 55 and compared it to first-century pavements from Fishbourne (p. 84). In room N19 at Fishbourne (Cunliffe 1971, pl. LXXX) is another pavement, dated to *c.* A.D. 75, where the pattern covers the entire floor. Our example is an almost exact copy, only smaller, and white on grey as opposed to grey on white. Since the decorated area is so small it is unlikely to have been merely a border. The similarity of the pattern to No 55 and the ashlar border of No 57 would suggest that it is possibly the work of the same contractor (see comments on No 55). Workmanship, Grade 2.

Reference. Hurst 1972, 50.

Mosaic 60. Gorhambury. Bands of guilloche and scroll

From a villa at Gorhambury, St. Albans, Herts. Possibly early fourth century. Dimensions: fragment 15 ft 6 in by 7 ft (4.70 by 2.15 m), decorated area originally 14 ft 2 in by approximately 16 ft (4.30 by 4.90 m), room 20 ft 10 in by 20 ft (6.35 by 7 m). Lifted.[1] NPP.

Gorhambury villa lies about ½ mile north-west of Verulamium and was partially excavated between 1956 and 1961 (Anthony 1961) — the year the pavement was discovered. New excavations by the writer from 1972 found that since 1961 much of the pavement had suffered plough damage. The drawing therefore shows the condition of the pavement in 1961 and has been prepared from oblique photographs taken at the time of its discovery and surveys made in 1973 and 1974.[2]

Unfortunately too little remains for a reliable reconstruction of its main scheme, which could have been either square or rectangular. The former is the more likely and will be assumed for the purposes of the description. From inside outwards its decoration consists of two concentric bands of simple guilloche in grey, red, yellow and white (the same colours are used throughout the pavement), perhaps originally bordering a square central panel. The simple guilloche is bordered in turn by a broad band of four-strand guilloche, and a voluted scroll terminating in red, yellow and white heart-shaped leaves. This is set within a linear frame. Along one side of the main scheme is a make-up panel of three-strand guilloche converting the square into a rectangle. A similar strip probably existed on the opposite side. It has a broad border of coarse grey limestone tesserae.

The workmanship is reasonably good (Grade 2), but the mosaicist has made an error 'completing' the guilloche at the end of the make-up panel. Together with mosaics from Combley (No 42) and Gadebridge Park (No 51) this is another example where a considerable quantity of fired-clay tesserae has been used — the red and yellow tesserae are brick.

Examples of this type of concentric scheme have already been discussed in relation to No 1 from Aldborough. The closest parallel known to the writer, however, is a pavement discovered in 1854 at Castle Hill Farm near Ipswich (Reid Moir and Maynard 1931-3, plan C) which on stylistic evidence is probably also of fourth-century date. This had a square central panel (lost), bordered by a succession of concentric bands of guilloche, running triangles and peltae, squares set corner to corner and a voluted scroll.

Our example is believed to be contemporary with additions made to the villa in the early fourth century: the villa was ruinous by the middle of the fourth century.

[1]In store with mosaic drawing collection, DOE, S. Ruislip.
[2]Excavations by the writer still in progress.

Mosaic 61. Hinton St Mary. Christian pavement

From a villa at Hinton St Mary, Dorset. Dated c. A.D. 350. Dimensions 26 ft 7 in by 17 ft 1 in (8.10 by 5.20 m), room 28 ft 3 in by 19 ft 3 in (8.60 by 5.85 m). Lifted, on display in the British Museum. Drawn and painted 1963. NPP.

This mosaic was discovered in 1963 at the rear of the village smithy when a post-hole was being dug. The blacksmith, Mr. W.J. White, invited members of the Dorchester Museum to excavate the pavement, which upon exposure proved to be perhaps the most important mosaic to have been found in Britain: in the central panel was a male bust superimposed over the Chi-Rho monogram and believed to represent Christ. The mosaic is in two parts — the larger Panel A, is 17 ft 1 in by 14 ft 10 in (5.22 by 4.53 m) and Panel B, 16 ft 6 in by 8 ft (5.04 by 2.44 m) each separated by a rectangular threshold 9 ft 2 in by 2 ft 11 in (2.80 by 0.89 m) internally.

Panel A

Its scheme is based on a grid of nine circles (FIG. 6 A). In this instance the central circle is tangent to four lateral semicircles and four quadrants in the angles, forming tilted cirvilinear squares as interspaces, each divided into two parts by a diagonal rod of guilloche linking the central circle to the quadrants in the angles: the visual effect is that of a large St Andrews Cross. The whole scheme is outlined in single guilloche edged in dark grey with red, buff and white braids. These colours are used in all the repeating patterns excepting the scrolls.

The central circle contains a series of concentric bands of right-angled Z-pattern, three-strand guilloche, waves and a single fillet and a double fillet, the latter forming the surround to a circular panel bearing a male bust with penetrating eyes and a cleft chin. His flesh is white and His hair yellow. He wears a white pallium across His right shoulder and has a Chi-Rho monogram, in yellow and white, behind His head, and a red and yellow pomegranate in the field on either side of Him. The figure is believed to represent Christ.

Depicted in three semicircular panels above and to the side of Him are vigorous hunting scenes with dogs wearing studded collars attacking stags, and in one example a hind. Behind the pursued are trees with blue and grey trunks and leaves. The 'bottom' semicircular panel is filled by a spreading tree, also in blue and grey and interpreted as symbolising the Tree of Life (Toynbee 1964 b, 10). In quarter-circles occupying the corners are busts, also with cleft chins, wearing red cloaks fastened by brooches on their right shoulders. Their right arms are bent at the elbow and tucked beneath their tunics. Their hair is in an upstanding and windswept style, and consequently the figures have been interpreted as representing Wind Personifications, rosettes and pomegranates on either side of them being emblems of life and immortality.

Panel B

Panel B, separated from Panel A by a rectangular threshold bearing running peltae shaded red, yellow and white with black centres, consists of a large circle of guilloche in a square flanked on either side by two large rectangles. The circle contains a scroll-pattern, with red and yellow leaves surrounding a charming portrayal of Bellerophon riding Pegasus and killing the three-headed Chimaera. Bellerophon is partly damaged, but wears a red cloak across his left shoulder and carries a red and white shield behind his back. He holds a spear in his right hand and the reins in his left; he is sitting on a red saddle edged in yellow. Pegasus is depicted in two tones of pale grey and has a flowing mane and feathery tail in black, yellow and white. The bridle is edged in red and speckled white and yellow. The three-headed Chimaera with a lion's head, a goat's head emerging from the centre of its back and serpent's head for its tail is shaded pale grey and bright yellow and is edged in red and dark grey. Its mane is portrayed as a lattice with red and yellow lozenges, and its serpent's tail in 'millefiori'. The tip of Bellerophon's spear touches the forehead of the goat and is joined at the top of the shaft to the linear surround of the panel. Occupying the four spandrels between the square and circular panels are open-mouthed canthari with gadrooned bowls and fluted necks. The S-shaped handles form into voluted trails, and sprouting from the base of one of the canthari is a stalk with a red leaf. The large rectangular panels on either side of Bellerophon both contain hunting scenes with stags pursued by dogs wearing studded collars. Behind the animals are trees, in blue, pale olive and deep red, in a style similar to the trees elsewhere on the pavement. Amongst the trees on one panel, looking over her shoulder towards her attacker, is a doe.

The quality of the workmanship and drawing is fine, particularly the figured subjects; but the setting of the guilloche is inferior. Many imperfections, the consequence of poor geometry, have occured where one guilloche band joins another, particularly around the Christ medallion. Here the semicircular panel 'below' Him is linked by five strands of guilloche, whereas the panel to the 'right' is linked by only one. The sizes of the rectangular panels flanking Bellerophon also vary and consequently the symmetry here and in the threshold is imperfect.

This same error occurs on a pavement from a villa at Frampton, Dorset (Lysons iii 1813, pl. v) which is so remarkably similar in its layout and motifs that it is almost certainly a product of the same contractor.[1] Furthermore it also bears a Chi-Rho monogram and has a panel with the same scheme and content[2] as Panel B. Another pavement from this villa has circular corner-panels, each occupied by similar windswept figures but each with a conch across the right shoulder and with wings on their temples.

The scheme of Panel A is unusual, but it can be compared to the fourth-century radial mosaics shown on FIGS. 10 and 11, e.g. Brantingham (No 12). The closest example, however, is No 16 from Caerwent which also has guilloche strips radiating from a central medallion towards the angles.

References. Toynbee 1964; Painter 1967.

[1]The mosaics from the two sites, and others, have been attributed to the Durnovarian school of mosaicists (Smith 1965, 99; Smith 1969, 109).
[2]Apart from the Frampton example the only other representation of Bellerophon killing the Chimaera is the fourth-century pavement from Lullingstone (Toynbee 1962, pl. 228-9). This is treated in a linear style and lacks the colour and vitality of the Dorset examples.

Mosaic 62. Hinton St Mary. Fragment

From a villa at Hinton St Mary, Dorset. Possibly second century. Fragment 11 ft (3.35 m) wide, overall dimensions not known. *In situ*, buried. Drawn and painted 1964. NPP.

This fragment was discovered in 1964 during an exploratory excavation by the British Museum (Painter 1967, fig. 4 (plan)). It has part of a band of simple guilloche in blue, red and white surrounded by a row of blue out-turned stepped triangles, bordered by blue, white, and blue bands. It has a white border.

The absence of samian from the site and the lack of coins earlier than *c.* 270 prompted the excavator to suggest that occupation of the villa did not begin until the third century (*op cit.*, 24). However, the style of the border with its blue and white bands and stepped triangles is common on pavements attributed to the second century, including mosaics from Boxmoor (Neal 1974-6, pl. 29) and Verulamium, Herts (Wheeler and Wheeler 1936, pl. XLIII). On stylistic evidence, therefore, late second-century or even an early third-century date is possible. The workmanship is inferior to that of No 61, Grade 3.

Mosaic 63. Kingscote. Venus mosaic

From a possible villa at Kingscote, Glos. Late third to early fourth century. Dimensions, Panel A, excluding coarse decorated border, 8 ft 2 in (2.50 m) square. Drawn 1976, painted 1978. NPP. Lifted, to be displayed in Corinium Museum.

This pavement occupies Room 1 of a possible winged villa occupying a site of at least 20 ha, and was discovered in 1975 during excavations by the Kingscote Archaeological Association under the direction of Mr. E.J. Swain. The mosaic had originally three adjoining panels but only parts of two survive.

Panel A

The scheme, drawn in simple guilloche, consists of two interlaced squares one in grey, red, yellow and white and the other in grey, blue, pale grey and white, within and tangent to a square frame with quadrants in the four angles. In the interlaced squares is a medallion occupied by a bust of Venus looking towards her right; she wears a yellow-ochre diadem and a colourful string of beads around her neck; above her left shoulder is a mirror. Her forehead and right shoulder are missing. The medallion is encircled by an elaborate ivy-scroll springing from a 'pelta'-like plant-form supported on a small triangular pedestal and intended to represent the foot of a bowl. The ivy leaves are heart-shaped and divided — one half is red and the other pale blue. Surrounding the scroll is a band of grey waves. Two of the opposing quadrants contain unique chains of heart-shaped petals with red tips and pale blue and white centres. The remaining quadrant has a cantharus with a gadrooned bowl, small triangular foot and S-shaped handles (a missing quadrant opposite was probably similarly ornamented). Around the design is a coarse border with a band of spaced swastika-meander with a strip of simple guilloche in each space.

Panel B

This is a threshold-panel between two larger areas of pavement. It is only half complete, but bears in its centre the fore-quarters of a beast, possibly a sea-panther, in pale greenish-grey. Its neck is looped and its head faces towards its back.[1] In front of the creature are two bulbous dolphins swimming in opposite directions. Their backs are greenish-blue and their bellies pale grey. Beaks, teeth, pectoral and dorsal fins are red. A dorsal fin survives beneath the sea-panther, so it is likely that another pair of dolphins existed in the damaged area. Along one side of the panel is a row of right-angled Z-pattern alternating in colour between pale blue-grey and white and red and white. At either end of each Z-form are three grey tesserae in a stepped arrangement similar to that on the Bancroft mosaic (No 7). Both the dolphin panel and the Z-pattern are enclosed by a guilloche chain.

The workmanship is fine (Grade 2) and the tesserae closely set. The use of colour, particularly the greenish blue, is not common but is most appropriate here and ideally suited to the aquatic forms. The head of Venus is very finely executed (Grade 1) with flesh-coloured tones and is of a workmanship superior to that of the rest of the floor. Perhaps it represents the work of the master mosaicist either laid by the direct method or as a prefabricated panel. An unusual feature of the construction is the exceedingly sparse use of white, which appears in limited quantities only in the central bust and the dolphins. The background tesserae are cream—coloured limestone throughout, unlike the backgrounds of all the other pavements in the collection which, excepting the borders, are white. However, at Woodchester (No 87) we find a similar technique employed encircling the central octagon and as background to many of the medallions and octagons occupied by rosettes and canthari in the outer ambulatory. Extensive use of this technique also occurs in Room 10 at Chedworth (Goodburn 1972, pl. 8) where the background is cream, and white is only used around the birds, voluted peltae and in the twin-petalled flowers. The confinement of this technique to a small geographical area would suggest possibly the work of the same contractor, and since both the Woodchester and Chedworth pavements are regarded as the products of the Corinian *officina* (Smith 1965, 105 ff) then perhaps the Kingscote pavement is likewise. The similarity of its meander-border to that in Chedworth, Room 10, would perhaps suggest this; but it must be said that neither the form of the dolphins, the chains of heart-shaped petals nor the voluted scroll appear on work assigned to the Corinian school. Its general scheme[2] is similar to No 36 from Cirencester.

Reference. Swain 1978.

[1] The writer knows of no parallel for the looped neck of this animal. Usually it is the tails of the marine creatures, whether of fish, equus or feline form that are spiralled. The presence of the front paws indicates conclusively that the remains are part of the fore and not the hind quarters of the beast.

[2] For further comments related to interlaced squares see No 17.

Mosaic 64. London. Cantharus

From a town-house at Milk Street, London. Second century. Overall dimensions 5 ft 5 in (1.65 m) square, room 10 ft 10 in by 6 ft 6 in (3.30 by 1.78 m). Lifted.[1] Drawn 1977, painted 1978. NPP.

Its scheme consists of a circle within a square, both drawn in simple guilloche — the braids in the circle are dark grey, grey, pale grey and white and in the square grey, red, yellow and white. The circle is occupied by a cantharus with a red, yellow and white gadrooned bowl, a cushion-shaped knop and a triangular yellow-ochre pedestal. Its voluted handle is red as is the body. This has a single black tessera which may have formed part of a swastika as seen on a number of second-century pavements including for example No 39 from Colchester and No 75 from Verulamium. In each angle is a red-tipped heart-shaped leaf or petal with a double stalk. Around the mosaic is a dark grey band, and on two sides a broad white limestone border. A single row of coarse red tesserae along the 'bottom' of the panel indicates possibly the position of a threshold here.

References. *London Archaeologist,* Autumn 1978, Vol 3, No. 8, pl. p 199. *Britannia* ix (1978), pl. xxvii, 452.

[1] In store, London Museum.

Mosaic 65. Rapsley. Geometric with L-shaped panels.

From a villa at Rapsley, Ewhurst, Surrey. Dated *c.* 220–280. Dimensions; panel; 10 ft 10 in by 9 ft 10 in (3.30 by 3 m), room 22 ft 6 in by 21 ft (6.86 by 6.40 m). *In situ*, buried. Drawn and painted 1967. Hanworth 1968, pl. VII; Smith 1975, pl. CXII.2.

This mosaic was found in 1961 and occupies Room 4 in Building 6 of a small villa partly engaged in the production of tile. Its scheme, based on an arrangement of squares, octagons and crosses (FIG. 4 B), consists of a central square panel bordered in three-strand guilloche, contiguous with four lateral octagons which are contiguous with four chevrons in a field of lozenges and lateral triangles. The central square is missing; but the lateral octagons contained medallions, bordered in simple guilloche and occupied by rosettes and eight-petalled flowers. The chevrons contain L-shaped strips of three-strand guilloche, and the field of lozenges and triangles contains linear rhomboids and open triangles. Along one edge, probably two, is a broad grey band, and surrounding the mosaic is a red-brick border.

The workmanship and the geometry is fairly crude (Grade 3) and certain aspects of the pavement are distinctly unusual — it appears that it did not have a white tessellated background and that its design was set into *opus signinum*. Apart from a simple mosaic with two tessellated roundels against an opus signinum background discovered in London in 1979, the writer knows of no parallel. Perhaps, as the excavator remarks (Hanworth 1968, 26), there might have been white chalk tesserae which a fire and subsequent weathering caused to decompose. If this is so, the floor could have been subsequently rendered with *opus signinum*, which may account for the surfaces of the *opus signinum* and the tesserae being flush.

We have already seen and discussed the general scheme of the Rapsley pavement in the commentary on the Bancroft mosaic (No 7) and have noted similarities to a second-century mosaic (No 38) from Colchester and to fourth-century examples at Woodchester (No 87) and Scampton (Illingworth 1808, pl. 6). However, as we have also seen (p. 31), the various examples either have the L-shapes contiguous with octagons, as on this example, or hexagons, as at Colchester (No 38). Although the pavements look similar, the basis for the pattern is very different (cf. p. 34). When L-shapes are separated by hexagons, the pattern has devolved from a grid of squares tangent to smaller tilted squares with eight-lozenge stars filling the interspaces. And on examples with L-shapes separated by octagons the basis of the scheme is a grid of squares tangent to octagons, the octagons tangent to cruciforms (FIG. 4 B). Mosaic 34 from Cirencester may appear very different, but in reality it is merely a larger area of the Rapsley scheme, without its cruciforms truncated into L-shapes.

Whereas schemes with L-shapes separated by hexagons occur in both the second and fourth centuries in Britain, the writer knows of *no* examples with L-shapes separated by octagons attributed to the second century. It would appear therefore that this adaptation was a later development and, if so, the Rapsley design was one of the earliest. This raises the question how early the Rapsley example is? Perhaps it is nearer to 280 than to 220.

References. Hanworth 1968, 26; Smith 1975, 274.

The Rudston Mosaics. Nos 66-70

Nos 66-8 were discovered during ploughing in 1933; they occupied the principal wing (House 1) of a substantial villa lying in an exposed position in the Yorkshire Wolds, six miles west of Bridlington Bay. Following the discovery the mosaics were displayed to the public; but because of deterioration they were transferred to Hull's Museum of Transport and Archaeology in 1962. At the same time a major excavation was undertaken by Dr. I.M. Stead for the then Ministry of Works. Further excavations by Dr. Stead in 1971 revealed another two mosaics (Nos 69-70) occupying House 2, situated on the north side of a courtyard. These also were lifted and presented to Hull Museums where they, together with the earlier finds, are displayed.

Mosaic 66. Rudston. Venus

Possibly mid fourth century — original dimensions 15 ft 4 in by 10 ft 6 in (4.67 by 3.20 m), room 19 ft by 15 ft 6 in (5.80 by 4.70 m). Drawn and painted 1962. Richmond 1963, pl. 1; Smith 1976, pl. IV; Smith 1977, pl. 6.XXIX a.

The scheme, based on a grid of circles (FIG. 6 A), is a square containing a central circle tangent to four lateral semicircles and four quadrants in the angles forming tilted curvilinear square interspaces. 'Above' and 'below' the square are rectangles.

In the central circle are two lively figures, the more dominant being a somewhat ungainly nude representing Venus at her toilet. She has broad hips, a flat narrow chest, outstretched arms and diminutive feet. Her sex is clearly apparent from a pronounced red pubic region and a mass of streaming hair. In her right hand is an apple, the golden apple won in a celebrated beauty-contest and, falling from her left hand, a grey mirror with a red handle. On each arm is a bracelet.

Apart from Venus' face, which is highlighted in white, the figure is treated in yellow ochre with a somewhat paler shade used for the lower legs, hands, nipples and shoulders. Her hair is brown and pale olive-green. Her glance is to the lower right where, below her outstretched arm, is a figure interpreted as a Triton or merman with a human torso and a fish's tail. He faces Venus, holds across his left arm a burning torch, and wears on his head a band. His body is olive-green, his tail red, and his right arm purple. Unusually, neither figure is outlined except for grey around the merman's tail and purple around his left arm.

The four semicircles each contain an animal and these, together with the figures in the curvilinear square interspaces, form an overall hunting scene progressing in a clockwise formation. In the panel 'below' Venus is a lion, facing left, with a spear piercing its belly and protruding from its back; the wound spurts blood. His head is missing (in the museum this part of the lion is shown as surviving, but it is a modern restoration probably carried out in the 1930s and deliberately omitted from the drawing) except for an ear and part of his mane. The body is in yellow ochre and outlined in grey, and the mane red. Beneath the animal is a tessellated inscription reading [LEO] F[R]AMEFER 'the spear-bearing lion' or 'the lion (called) spear-bearer'.

Clockwise, the next semicircular panel contains a stag, the stylized trees on either side and below the figure representing a wood. The stag is also in yellow ochre — a lighter tone being used for the belly and hind legs. The next panel at the 'top' contains a boldly drawn if somewhat stylized leopard in white, with red markings with black spots 'red paws and tail and a yellow and white collar'. He is looking across his shoulder where there is a large chequered disc, possibly a shield. In the remaining semicircular panel is a red bull running towards the left, beneath which is another tessellated inscription reading TAVRVS OMICIDA, 'the man-killing bull' or 'the bull (called) man-killer'. Over the bull is a rod terminating at one end with a crescent-shaped device and at the other end with a knob. Various interpretations of its purpose have been suggested — an ox-goad or a yoke or a form of spear or axe. The OMICIDA inscription would possibly suggest the implement to be a weapon.

The three hunters (a fourth is missing) occupying the curvilinear square interspaces are all naked and shown with prancing gaits and are shaded yellow ochre without an outline. One figure holds a net, which to judge from the man's glance, is about to be thrown over the wounded lion. Another figure, a spearman, waits hand on hip possibly for the approaching stag to emerge from the wood, whilst another hunter is looking towards the bull with his arms in a position which might suggest that he has just thrown (? two handed) the axe towards the bull. In each of the quadrants is a ? peahen pecking a fruit, perhaps a pomegranate. (This same scene is represented in four rectangular panels in No 64, also from Rudston, an earlier floor and perhaps the inspiration for the birds on the mosaic under discussion).

In the rectangular panel at the 'top' of the scheme is a bust of Mercury identified from a caduceus to his right. On either side of him is a leafless vine bearing large bunches of grapes, growing from a cantharus. The main stem of the vine is formed from two narrow tendrils, not sprouting from the mouth of the vessel which has a conical lid, but springing from both sides of the vessel's bowl where it joins a triangular pedestal. The two tendrils sprout S-shaped 'handles' duplicating handles on the actual vessel. Damage has resulted in the opposite cantharus being only partly preserved, but it was probably of similar form. A vine, perhaps also flanking a bust, filled another panel at the 'bottom' of the pavement. The absence of any association between Mercury and the vine has led Dr. Smith (Smith 1976, 14) to conclude that the bust is possibly a misrepresentation of a portrayal of Bacchus crowned with grapes and vine leaves, and accompanied by or bearing a thyrsus — the staff entwined with vine and ivy.

The workmanship is poor (Grade 2) and the tesserae fairly coarse (12-15 mm) and laid without attempt at following the profile of the forms so that, sometimes, they run at right angles to the actual pattern.[1] The central roundel, in grey edged in red, is irregular as is the guilloche (which is grey, white, red and white only — it lacks yellow). However, although technically imperfect, the boldness of the figures and the varied use of at least 12 colours make the pavement one of the most colourful and charming in Britain. Its classical subject influenced by Celtic taste, clearly represents the work of a Romano-British craftsman.

Schemes with tangent circles are common. We have already seen examples of them in an adapted form on fourth-century mosaics from Caerwent (No 16) and Hinton St Mary (No 61); but the scheme can be found on second-century pavements at Dyer Street (Buckman and Newmarch 1850, pl. VI) and Victoria Road (Smith 1975, pl. CXI 2), Cirencester, in Room N7 at Fishbourne (Cunliffe 1971, pl. XLVII), and at Vine Street, Leicester (Smith 1975, pl. CXIX. 2.) In the fourth century the scheme was equally popular. For example we find it at Dorchester (R.C.H.M., *Dorset* pl. 220), and Fifehead Neville (Smith 1965, fig. 9), Dorset, at Ilchester Mead (Hayward 1974, fig. 1), Lufton (Hayward 1952, fig. 3), and Yatton (V.C.H. *Somerset,* fig. 67) — all with knots or panels of guilloche in the curvilinear square interspaces, suggesting perhaps the products of the same contractor. It appears at Brook Street, Winchester (Butcher 1955, pl. I) and further north on a possible fourth-century floor from the Exchequer Gate, Lincoln (Morgan 1886, fig. facing p. 138). There is no common theme or motif to these various examples, but five of them have aquatic creatures in the semicircles. Rudston is alone in its subject-matter and is one of only one of three examples where Venus is portrayed full-length — the other pavements are Hemsworth, Dorset (Hinks 1955, pl. XXX) and Low Ham, Somerset (Toynbee 1962, pl. 235).

References. Richmond 1963; Toynbee 1964, 287, Smith 1976, 11 ff.

[1]This same technique of laying tesserae is to be found in the Wolf and Twins pavement from Aldborough in Leeds City Museum (Toynbee 1962, pl. 220). Their naïvity may suggest that they are the work of the same mosaicist.

Mosaic 67. Rudston. Aquatic scene

Possibly mid fourth century. Original dimensions 10 ft 6 in by 8 ft (3.20 by 2.45 m), room 16 ft 3 in by 12 ft (4.95 by 3.66 m). Drawn and painted 1962. Richmond 1963, pl. 3; Smith 1976, pl. VI: Smith 1977, pl. 6 XXVIII a.

No 62 occupied the *apodyterium* of a bath-suite situated at the south end of House 1. Its scheme consists of a square flanked on four sides by narrow oblongs and at the 'top' and 'bottom' by rectangles.

The principal panel, a lively and colourful aquarium, contains a variety of sea-creatures including a dolphin and an open bivalve, swirling around what was once a centrally-placed feature which is neither a fish nor sea-monster but possibly part of a bust of Neptune: its rippled edge being hair, its L-shaped projections stylized crabs' legs and a lobed feature possibly a beard or even a shoulder (see below). In the rectangular panels surrounding the aquarium is an undulating line bearing lotuses turned inwards and outwards alternately. The oblong panels at the 'top' and 'bottom' are only partially complete, but sufficient remains of a handle to establish the presence, originally, of a centrally-placed cantharus flanked by birds and highly stylized trees edged in grey and with orange trunks.

The workmanship (Grade 2), although slightly coarse, is better than the Venus pavement but without so many colours — at least 8 compared to 12. Stylistically and technically there is no evidence to suggest that they are contemporary. There is little similarity between the trees on the two pavements, and the background tesserae on the aquatic mosaic are slightly finer. The method of setting the white background-tesserae also varies — on this example the tesserae follow the contours of the figures, technically more correct. It is the only mosaic in the north of England with a representation of Neptune and, as far as the writer is aware, the only one in Britain where Neptune is encircled by fishes. On a mosaic from Ashcroft Villas, Cirencester (Smith 1977, pl. 6 X a), Neptune is flanked by fishes and set in a rectangular panel just as at Withington, Glos. (Lysons ii, 1817, pl. XX), where he is shown holding a trident and sprouting large pincers from the top of his head. On either side of him are two bulbous dolphins depicted as swimming out of his mouth. This same treatment is to be found on a frieze from Frampton, Dorset (Lysons 1813, pt. iii, pl. V): indeed, so closely similar are the two in this and other aspects, that they may well be the work of the same contractor — the Durnovarian *officina*. A bust of Neptune, without fishes, is represented on a pavement dated 160–90 from Building IV, 8, at Verulamium (Wheeler and Wheeler 1936, pl. XLI) which also has large lobster-claws sprouting from his head; but only the tops of his shoulders are portrayed and consequently look awkward. The same applies to the shoulders of the bust of Neptune from Hemsworth, Dorset (Toynbee 1964, pl. LIX a) which has three crabs' legs sprouting from either side of the head. It is the Hemsworth bust which is the closest parallel, for not only does it explain the L-shaped projections, or crabs' legs, on the Rudston example but it also provides a clue to the possible 'beard' which, when compared to Hemsworth and Verulamium, is more likely a shoulder. Although the interpretation of the fragmentary 'handle' as being part of a cantharus is questionable, affinities with birds flanking canthari can be found for example on No 25 from Cirencester. In the description of No 25 affinities and variations of the motif have already been discussed, but it is interesting to note the frequency with which birds appear on the Rudston pavements. We have already noted them pecking pomegranates in the quadrants of the Venus pavement and will also observe them again on No 69.

References. Richmond 1963; Smith 1976, 15.

Mosaic 68. Rudston. Geometric

Possibly mid fourth century. Overall dimensions of main panel excluding border, 9 ft (2.75 m) square; room 15 ft 6 in (4.72 m) square. Drawn 1962, painted 1964. NPP.

The floor occupied the central room of House 1, a room flanked on two sides by corridors.

The room's axial arrangement to a building central to the courtyard may possibly suggest it to have been a hall, or less likely a *triclinium*. The mosaic has a large square central panel, bordered by a row of red inturned stepped triangles, containing four very bold swastika-peltae in grey, red, brown and white. Surrounding the panel is a wide band of running swastika-meander, in grey, and two broad grey bands.

Although the mosaic is boldly drawn, the workmanship is very coarse (Grade 3) and the tesserae large. The setting of the meander is poor and at two places, to the 'right' of the design, the mosaicist has mistakenly continued the outer band where two breaks should occur.

The swastika-pelta is a common motif. It first appears in Britain in a second-century context, for example at Boxmoor (Neal 1974-6, fig. XXXII A) and Silchester (Hope and Fox 1896, pl. XII), but in the third and fourth centuries the motif becomes increasingly popular particularly in the Midlands and Lincolnshire, e.g. at Castor, Northants. (Artis 1828, pl. XVIII), at Great Staughton, Hunts (Smith 1969, pl. 3.25), Great Weldon, Northants. (Lysons i, 1813, pt. IV, pl. VII), Medbourne, Leics. (VCH *Leic.* i, pl. VII), Roxby (Fowler 1796-1818, No 3), and at Scampton, Lincs. (Illingworth 1808, pl. 6). It also appears in the Somerset and Gloucestershire areas, but less frequently, although at Woodchester it occurs on three pavements, No 87, Room 15 and Corridor 2 (Lysons 1797, pls. XVIII and XI respectively), where a group of four swastika-peltae, identical to those at Rudston, occupy three panels. Frequently the motif is used singly, but at Roxby and Medbourne, for example, rows of swastika-peltae are used as borders.

References. Richmond 1963; Smith 1976, 15.

Mosaic 69. Rudston. The Charioteer mosaic

Probably early fourth century. Room 30 ft by 14 ft 3 in (9.15 by 4.35 m). Panel A, 9 ft 10 in (3.0 m) square; Panel B, 7 ft 9 in by 3 ft 6 in (2.37 by 1.07 m); Panel C originally 9 ft 3 in (2.82 m) square. Drawn 1972, painted 1976. NPP.

No 69 occupied a large room divided into two areas by responds, possibly for an arch. It has three adjoining schemes, two square panels (A and C) separated by a rectangle (B). In the north wall of the room, 'below' the charioteer, is a shallow recess 8 ft wide by 7 in deep (2.45 by 0.18 m), possibly once containing a relief or a mural. The width of the border here may suggest this end of the room was the *triclinium* where diners could recline on their couches with the charioteer scene spread out before them.

Panel A: The Charioteer

Its scheme consists of a large central circle tangent to four rectangles and four circles in the angles. Its central circle portrays a finely drawn and executed victorious charioteer holding aloft in his right hand a wreath — the winner's crown — and in his left hand a palm-frond — both symbols of victory. He is dressed in a red tunic with a laced corselet around his waist and bindings around his wrists and arms; he wears a rounded grey cap. The chariot is drawn by four horses, shown frontally, with the central pair reddish brown, the right horse grey and the left horse yellow with a white chest; the bridles are red. Between the ears of each horse is a plume — their manes are bound with ribbons. The chariot is in yellow ochre with grey beading and has a red diagonal cross on the front. Beneath the cross is a vertical white line possibly representing the chariot's shaft. The artist has made no attempt to depict the chariot's wheels nor to show the hind legs of the outer horses. By omitting these he has skilfully avoided the scene becoming too cluttered. Surrounding the panel is a band of treble-strand guilloche in grey, red, yellow and white — the same colours used in the guilloche throughout the three schemes. The four rectangular panels each contain a stylized bird accompanied by fruit — one piece is round and the other pear-shaped. The birds are rather clumsily portrayed with small heads and thick tails curving upwards towards the corners of the panel. Three of the birds face to the left while a fourth, that to the right of the chariot panel, faces right. The feet of the birds are shaded to suggest perspective; in the foreground they are yellow but in the background dark red. Birds pecking at fruit also occur on the Venus mosaic (No 61), where they are more skilfully portrayed and less wooden. More skilfully drawn, however, are busts of The Seasons with Spring, Summer and Winter (Autumn is missing) occupying circular panels in the corners. Spring (top right) is expertly drawn and is looking across her right shoulder where a swallow is perched. Her hair is grey with touches of dark red and her face and chest are in white and two shades of pink: she is outlined on one side only in dark red. She is set within a circle outlined with a shaded cable in white, yellow, pink, red, dark red and grey, with tesserae set in a reticulated technique. Summer (lower right) is more colourfully portrayed and wears three red poppies in her yellow hair. She is looking across her left shoulder which is outlined in dark red and shaded yellow and two tones of pink, and she occupies a circle bordered with a band of right-angled Z-pattern in grey, white, yellow and red. The figure bottom left of the chariot scene is only partially complete, but sufficient survives to show that she is facing towards her right and has yellow hair with red curls. Unlike the busts of Spring and Summer her shoulders are inelegantly drawn and are represented by a straight grey line suggesting, possibly, that she is dressed. Above her shoulder is a yellow rake — an attribute of Winter usually portrayed wearing a hooded cloak (it is unlikely that she represents Autumn, for she is not wearing a garland of grapes). The circular panel is framed similarly to that around the figure of Spring — a shaded cable. Part of this cable and the figure's chest has an ancient patch which neglected to copy the original work. The remaining panel, top left, is lost except for part of another patch; but it is likely to have been occupied by Autumn. It has a right-angled Z-pattern border similar to that around Summer.

The mosaic is surrounded by a band of four-strand guilloche, and by a coarse outer border of red bands on either side of a row of red T-shapes with alternating red and white tesserae across the top and bottom of the 'T'. The pattern is a form of border depicting a city wall with crenellated parapet and towers. This same pattern borders Panels B and C. At the 'bottom' of the pavement the wide border has a band of squares, outlined in red, with small red squares in the centres, and a separate broad red band.

The writer knows of no exact parallel for the design in Britain but it is a composite of a scheme with squares or circles tangent to similarly proportioned semicircles or rectangles with quadrants or 'quarter' squares in the angles (FIGS. 2 B and 6 A). Here, however, the central panel has been enlarged at the expense of the side panels, which has allowed more space in the angles — occupied by the Four Seasons. An unusual feature is the use of solid dark grey spandrels and triangles filling interspaces between the panels. It has given the mosaic a very heavy appearance: it is more common to fill interspaces the size of these with linear motifs. Shaded cables are also a motif rarely used, occurring only on five mosaics in the South and West of England.[1]

Panel B. The Leopards Panel

This is viewed from the reverse direction to the Charioteer and contains a centrally-placed cantharus flanked by leopards. The body and S-shaped handles of the cantharus are outlined dark red; its mouth is grey. Its neck is pale yellow and has 'vertical' red lines depicting gadrooning. The bowl is shaded buff and has alternating red and white gadroons, and is mounted on a circular yellow stem on a triangular pedestal (missing).

The leopards face the cantharus and spring towards its neck. They are similarly drawn (but not as a mirror image) with olive-green bodies, grey spots and white bellies. They are outlined in grey and have red tongues. Unlike on the charioteer panel no attempt has been made to show the animals in relief, and consequently they lack vitality and a feeling of movement.

Panel C

Although virtually the whole of this panel is lost, two small areas of mosaic and traces of guide-lines in the underlining bedding-mortar are sufficient to permit a reconstruction. Its scheme originally consisted of a linear square containing a linear circle around a large octagon, drawn in simple guilloche and divided by radial spokes into eight trapezoidal compartments. In the centre was a circular panel. Unfortunately the content of these panels is not known, but fragments of two spandrels in the 'lower' corners indicate the decoration to have been human figures. The 'bottom left' spandrel has the lower remains of three tiny figures each wearing black boots and standing on an undulating grey line. Two wear baggy calf-length dresses, one with red and black vertical stripes and the other with yellow and red vertical stripes. The head and body of another tiny figure survive in the opposite spandrel. Adjacent to the figure, but set within an interspace between the linear circle and the octagon, is part of a red ellipse with two small circles at one end. Projecting from the circles is a yellow triangle. Dr. Smith has interpreted this motif as a conventionalized *phallus* (Smith 1976, 5) which, apart from a possible representation on a corner-panel from Gayton Thorpe (Atkinson 1926-8, pl. 1 facing p. 166), is unique on British mosaic.

Radial schemes (see FIGS. 10 and 11) dated to the fourth century[2] are not uncommon in the North of England and occur at Winterton (No 83) and Horkstow (Smith 1976, 23) for example. Mosaics here depict Orpheus in a central 'hub', charming animals parading within the surrounding panels; there is no evidence, however, to suggest that the pavement under discussion was similarly illustrated. Indeed there is a distinction between it and the parallels just quoted — these examples have circles divided radially and not octagons: at Winterton the 'hub' is octagonal and at Horkstow circular. The radial scheme at Brantingham (No 12) is based on an octagon, but the design is adapted by the introduction of semicircles. A close parallel, however, is to be found at Bramdean, Hants. (FIG. 10 C), where an octagonal scheme is divided into eight radial compartments depicting the gods of the days (VCH *Hants*, fig. 18, facing p. 308). Here the 'hub' is circular and contains a head of Medusa. At Room 5, Chedworth (FIG. 10 D), the radial divisions are less dominant because the borders of each trapezoidal panel alternate between simple guilloche and waves. It has an octagonal 'hub'. Pavement 1 at Pitney, Somerset (FIG. 11 H) may also be quoted.

The quality of workmanship of the charioteer and The Seasons is good, but elsewhere the geometry and setting of the tesserae is relatively poor, especially in the repeating elements. The four-strand guilloche bordering Panel A is neatly executed and the pattern regular, but that bordering the charioteer and leopards panel is very 'loose' and rather untidy. It may represent the work of two mosaicists. At least ten colours have been employed, a higher number than in many pavements but still fewer than the Venus mosaic (No 66).

Reference. Smith 1976, 6.

[1]Shaded cables with tesserae set in a reticulated formation also occur for example at Colliton Park, Dorchester, Dorset (R.C.H.M. *Dorset*, pl. 218), Lufton (Hayward 1972, pl. v), Keynsham (Bulleid and Horne 1924-6, pl. xviii, 2), and Combe St. Nicholas (drawing by R. Walter preserved in Somerset County Museum, Taunton) Somerset, and Silchester, Hants (Fox Coll, Box 5, 13).
[2]At Chester there is an unusual parallel to No 69 (see footnote 1 following discussion on No 12 from Brantingham) possibly of an earlier date.

Mosaic 70. Rudston. Interlaced circles.

Fourth century. 10 ft 9 in (3.28 m) square, room 13 ft (3.97 m) square. *In situ*, buried. NPP.

This mosaic occupied a room on the west side of Building 2, north of the courtyard, and lay adjacent to No 69. Its scheme consists of a square (7 ft 2 in (2.18 m) wide) bordered in simple guilloche in grey, white and red, containing a linear square infilled with large grey interlaced circles. The concave-sided squares formed in the pattern are filled with rows of red, brown and white tesserae set in a reticulated formation, and in the ellipsoid intersects there are red and brown ellipsoids. The panel is surrounded by a coarse chequered border of large red and white squares. At the 'left' side and at the 'bottom' right corner brown squares instead of red are used. They are contemporary with the rest of the work and are not a later patch; the remainder of the floor is paved with coarse white limestone tesserae.

Although the reticulated infilling is an unusual technique, the standard of workmanship is fairly poor (Grade 3). The guilloche border lacks a third colour (cf. the Venus mosaic, No 66) and is poorly laid, especially at the angles. The use of brown instead of red squares along one side shows disregard for symmetry and standards.[1]

On Nos 5 and 6 from Bancroft we have already seen that interlaced circles are a common motif, but one of the closest examples is a fourth-century pavement from Newton St Loe (Rainey 1973, pl. 12 B). This has a square panel occupied by interlaced circles and having a chequered border. It does however have a square central panel containing a swastika-pelta.

Reference. Smith 1976, fig. 2 (plan).

[1]Various standards of workmanship, clearly of contemporary date, are found on a number of pavements; it can be seen at Cirencester (No 34) for example. The practice is curious since it reflects the attitude of some mosaicists towards their work. It would appear that some made no attempt at perfection in the pattern, let alone quality of setting. The same applies to tessellated patches (e.g. No 69). It also raises the question why the owner of the property was prepared to accept such work. The mosaicist could have run out of tesserae of the appropriate colour or even have failed to complete the commission. If that was so the owner would have had to get another contractor to complete the task.

General Note

The quality of the Rudston pavements is variable and nowhere can we see evidence for the same mosaicist at work. The primitive Venus pavement has a background infilling technique not observed on other pavements from the site, It has already been noted that the fish mosaic has smaller tesserae than the Venus mosaic; this and variations in the tones of colour are likely to preclude their being contemporary. The variations in workmanship between the Charioteer and interlaced Circles pavements suggests that they too are by different mosaicists.

Mosaic 71. Sparsholt. Flower

From Sparsholt villa, Hants. Fourth century. Dimensions 10 ft 6 in (3.20 m) square. Room 19 ft by 14 ft (5.80 m). Lifted, on display in Winchester Museum. Drawn and painted 1967. NPP.

Sparsholt Roman villa lies on a slight spur of chalky land (now forested) about four miles west of Winchester and was excavated between 1965 and 1972 by D.E. Johnston. The mosaic occupied Room 7 of a corridor-building situated opposite a gatehouse on the west side of a courtyard. Barn-like buildings flanked the north and south sides of the court. Room 7 was placed axially to the building, which suggests it to have been the *triclinium* or principal room.

Its scheme comprises a square, bordered by a wide band of four-strand guilloche, occupied by a linear square contiguous with a linear circle. Within this circle is another, outlined in simple guilloche, containing concentric bands of swastika-meander, waves, and red and grey bands. In the centre is an eight-petalled flower with white, yellow and red pointed leaves and with a 'millefiori' centre. In two opposing spandrels formed at the interspaces between the linear square and circle is a calix with red-tipped voluted petals. Across its body is a red and white chequered line which, together with a diminutive triangular pedestal, indicates the motif to be a stylized cantharus. In the remaining opposing spandrels are scallop or fan-shaped motifs in dark red, pale red, pale grey and white. They radiate from the angle of the linear square; the central scallop is pointed. Surrounding the pavement is a finely worked band of right-angled Z-pattern in red, grey and white and a coarse plain red-brick border.

The geometry and setting is good (Grade 2), but an unusual aspect is the limited use of yellow tesserae — only featuring in the central flower. Pale grey has been used as a substitute and occurs in the guilloche, the calyx and shell-motifs and the right-angled Z-border. The reason for this is not understood, but it is more likely to have been the difficulty of obtaining yellow stone, rather than whim. Limited use of yellow is also to be found in a late third- to early fourth-century pavement from Upper Brook Street, Winchester (Butcher 1955, pl. 1), an inferior product compared with the mosaic under discussion, but also with scallops or fans occupying two quadrants. The writer knows of no parallel for the scheme but the calyx is similar to an example at Chilgrove (Down 1979, pl. 7) and could be a product of the same contractor.

References. Johnston 1972; *JRS* lvii (1967), pl. xvi.

Mosaic 72. Thenford. Portrait medallion.

From a villa at Thenford near Banbury, Northants. Dated *c.* 350-60. Dimensions; 15 ft 2 in by 5 ft 2 in (4.63 by 1.59 m), room 19 ft 3 in by 8 ft 7 in (5.87 by 2.62 m). Lifted, preserved in Thenford House. Drawn 1971, painted 1972. NPP.

The Thenford mosaic was excavated in June 1971, following a chance discovery during casual exploration. Larger-scale excavations were carried out in 1971 and 1972 by the late I.F. Sanders for the Oxford University Archaeological Society on behalf of the landowner, Sir Gerald Spencer Summers. The building was constructed at the beginning of the fourth century but converted and enlarged *c.* 350-60 to include a bath-suite, and it was at this time that the mosaic was inserted.[1] A house of earlier construction lay to the south. The mosaic's long rectangular scheme is divided into three panels — a central rectangle with squares at either end, all outlined in simple guilloche in white and red only, with a blue edge. The same colours are employed in all the repeating patterns. The central rectangle contains a medallion, bordered in chain guilloche with yellow centres, occupied by a female bust with finely-worked staring eyes, a pink face and a very pale grey chin. Her neck is white and shaded on one side in yellow. She is wearing a very pale grey diaphonous bodice with short sleeves patterned around the hem and, on her head, a red cap. Her yellow hair has a central parting and is arranged in two plaited locks tied with red ribbons which fall on her breasts. Across her left shoulder is a branch, apparently not being held, with three red leaves and behind, a red cloak. Her arms are truncated above the elbows by the margin of the panel. At the 'top' and 'bottom' of the medallion are panels filled with four-strand guilloche and in the remaining interspaces tiny shield-motifs within quadrants. Of the square panels in the scheme, one contains a large guilloche mat and the other a mat of running peltae. The pavement has a coarse cream-coloured limestone border.

The identification of the bust is not known. A branch is a common attribute of Winter, but here the branch is leafed and not bare. Diaphanous dress also is not indicative of Winter, who is normally dressed more appropriately for the season in a hooded cloak. The absence of a cornucopia precludes her being either Fortuna or Ceres and it is unlikely that she represents Venus who is often portrayed with a mirror (e.g. at Kingscote, No 63, and Rudston No 66) but never with a branch. At Winterton, the central medallions of Nos 84 and 85 are also occupied by busts: of interest stylistically is that No 84 has a very similar scheme, but larger. That the two pavements represent the work of the same contractor is a possibility. Their date and standard of workmanship (Grade 3) is comparable, and both employ a limited range of colour. However, the Thenford bust is superior in execution (Grade 2) to the Winterton examples and superior to the remainder of the work; is likely therefore to be the work of the master mosaicist.

References. *Britannia* v (1973), 294.

[1]The writer is grateful to A.S. Esmonde Cleary for providing the date for this pavement and construction details.

The Verulamium pavements. Nos 73-76

In 1954 it became known that plans existed for a new road across Verulamium, St. Albans, Herts, following the line of Bluehouse Hill and across the fields to the A5 at Batchwood Drive. Consequently a programme of excavations was mounted in advance of the threat and carried out by Professor S.S.Frere between 1955 and 1961. He revealed a complex sequence of buildings dated from the mid first to the late fourth centuries. Initially, the buildings were constructed in timber and wattle and daub and their floors paved with clay, thin mortar or, more substantially, *opus signinum*, but in the second century dwarf masonry footings bearing clay walls were introduced together with tessellated pavements and mosaics. The 1955-61 excavations revealed remains of seven mosaics, some complete, other very fragmentary. These together with the pavements excavated by Wheeler (Wheeler and Wheeler 1936), and another found during excavations directed by C. Saunders of Verulamium Museum, brings the number of known pavements to 24. Half are attributed to the second century and half to the fourth century. The lack of pavements dated to the third century may merely reflect our lack of knowledge in the period generally, but the evidence does suggest that the town was suffering from serious neglect and it was not until the early fourth-century that many of the town houses were refurbished.

Mosaic 73. Verulamium. Dolphins and fountain

From Building XXVIII, 3., room 9. Dated *c.* 145-50. Dimensions; 7 ft 7 in (2.30 m) square, room about 17 ft (5.20 m) square. Lifted, on display in Verulamium Museum. NPP.

Discovered in 1958, this mosaic adorned a half-timbered house destroyed in the Antonine fire of *c.* 155-60 (Frere 1959, 13) and lay off-centre in a large room paved in coarse red-brick tesserae. A damaged corner is patched with clay, which prompted the excavator to suggest the break possibly having been the intentional emplacement of an altar (Frere, *op. cit.*)[1] Its scheme consists of nine panels — a central square flanked by four lateral rectangles and tangent to four squares at the angles — all drawn in simple guilloche outlined in dark grey with the colours of each braid alternating, pale grey, very pale grey and white, and red, yellow and white. The central panel is occupied by a yellow-ochre cantharus spurting two jets of water indicating it to be a fountain. It is outlined in black and portrayed as if the interior is visible. It has a rounded stem and a yellow-ochre triangular pedestal with a white highlight. The body has a black right-angled Z-motif with a 7-shaped patch of white above. On the inside of the rim is a series of alternating white and black tesserae intended, possibly, to represent gadrooning, and on the lower part of the body, outlined in black, three adjoining Λ-shaped features each coloured red, yellow and white. Its handles are entwined with the tail fins of two dolphins which dip towards the bottom corners of the panel. The dolphins are outlined in black and infilled with pale grey and white, their snouts being yellow and outlined in red — the same colour as their fins. The jets of water are pale grey. In rectangular panels above and below are two lozenges of simple guilloche, and in panels to the right and left, simple scrolls each with two heart-shaped and one forked leaf. In diagonally opposed corner-panels is a chequer-pattern of grey rectangles and a grey square set lozengewise containing a white curvilinear square. The pavement is surrounded by narrow bands of white, grey and red tesserae and a coarse red-brick border (not shown on the published illustration but featured on the original painting).

Although the scene in the central panel is drawn in a lively style, the standard of workmanship is mediocre (Grade 2) and many errors have occurred in the guilloche. A curious feature of the guilloche, not observed by the writer elsewhere, is that on either side of the central 'eye' between the braids are black triangular tesserae possibly intended as registration-pieces.

The scheme of the pavement is a common one in the second century. It is based simply on a grid of nine squares, but with the outer squares truncated by the margin (p. 23 and FIG. 2B). We have already seen variants at Colchester (Nos 39 and 40), where the grid is superimposed over concentric circles; but it also appears at Colchester on three other examples closely related stylistically to the pavement under discussion and probably also of the second century. The first to be discovered was at the Three Cups Inn (Hull 1958, pl. XXIII A) in 1763; this also has two opposing panels occupied by lozenges of simple guilloche, and also has a 'squared rosette' in one of its angles. The same decoration is found on a second mosaic found at North Hill in 1922 (Gurney Benham 1923, pl. facing p. 251). The third example was found at Bury Field in 1923 (Hull 1958, pl. XXXIV). This also has rosettes in the angles but the rectangular panels contain fabulous marine creatures. A single example of this scheme known to the writer from Ashcroft Road, Cirencester, discovered in 1950, has the angles of the central square 'cut' by diagonals to form an octagon which contains a guilloche-bordered medallion occupied by a cantharus. An opposed pair of rectangles contains lozenges of simple guilloche whilst the others have rectangular mats of guilloche. A squared rosette in two of the angles would suggest a second-century date for its construction. Other examples include pavements from Wadfield, Glos. (Dent 1877, pl. facing p. 13), but with linear lozenges in the rectangles, and from Castor, Northants. (Artis 1828, pl. 12). This example also has lozenges of guilloche in the rectangles but the presence of a large multi-petalled flower centrepiece. (cf. p. 66) and the linear composition of its nine-panel grid raises the possibility that this is a later example — third or even fourth-century. A probable fourth-century example was found in the villa at Gayton Thorpe, Norfolk (Atkinson 1926-8, pl. facing p. 166). Again its rectangular panels also contain lozenges of guilloche and like the other corner-panels also contain flowers. The central panel is occupied by a guilloche-roundel with its centrepiece lost. Around the mosaic is a broad band of four-strand guilloche and chequered border.

The cantharus and dolphins on our example are very similar to those on fragments discovered in Building IV, 10, at Verulamium (Wheeler and Wheeler 1936, pl. XLVII): the cantharus has identical Λ-shaped decoration on the bowl and is almost certainly the product of the same mosaicist. The scene is not uncommon. We have already seen variants of it at Caerwent (No 16) where an isolated cantharus is associated with dolphins, and also at Cirencester (No 34). A closer parallel, however, dated to the early fourth century occurs at Downton, Wilts. (Rahtz 1963, pl. 1), but in a more severe style with the dolphins intended to represent the handles rather than being entwined with them.

References. Frere 1959, 13, pl. IV *a*: Toynbee 1962, Cat No. 180, pl. 209. Frere, *Verulamium Excavations* ii (forthcoming), pl. XXXVI.

[1]This hypothesis, in the opinion of the writer, is untenable. He knows of no parallel in Britain for a pavement cut by an altar. A household shrine is more likely to have been set against a wall.

Mosaic 74. Verulamium. Bacchus mosaic

From Building XXVII, 2, room 8. Dated after *c*. 380. Dimensions; Panel A, 15 ft 3 in (4.65 m) square. Panel B, uncertain, room 19 ft (5.80 m) by at least 21 ft (6.41 m) but probably double that length. Lifted, fragments in Verulamium Museum. Drawn and painted 1959. Frere 1960, pl. V.

This pavement, of *c*. 380–400, is one of the latest dated pavements in Britain and occupied a large heated room on the north angle of a town-house.[1] It had at least two panels (A and B), both considerably damaged, but sufficient in extent to permit a partial reconstruction.

Panel A is a square drawn in four-strand guilloche in grey, red, yellow and white and containing a grey all-over spaced running swastika-meander pattern developing 25 squares in a staggered arrangement. Each square is occupied by a simple motif except the central square, which has the partial remains of a male bust with a large head and somewhat truncated shoulders. The figure faces forwards and is shaded in pale yellow ochre with white high-lights to the lips and nose. Across his right shoulder is a Z-shaped line which is likely to be part of his dress but possibly, although less likely, an attribute. Around his forehead is a brown head-band and above his temple a cluster of green glass tesserae possibly representing a bunch of grapes, an attribute of Bacchus. The four squares in the corners each contain a guilloche mat whilst other squares contain eight and four-petalled flowers, an arrangement of four grey peltae forming a flower, interlaced circles forming quatrefoils, a cantharus, and in a square below Bacchus a concave-sided octagon in a linear circle. The octagon is divided radially; each division is coloured yellow, white, black, red and white.[2]

Panel B to the north consists of part of an eight-lozenged star (filling interspaces between an arrangement of large squares and small tilted squares). A large square is occupied by an open square of guilloche, and in two triangles (squares cut diagonally by the margin of the design) appears a flower with pointed white, yellow and red leaves and a calix. Along its external edge is a rectangle divided into at least two parts; one with a large open lozenge with its pointed ends terminating in peltae, and the other traces of a band of three-strand guilloche or a knot.

For its late date the design of Panels A and B is unusual. Spaced running swastika-meanders and eight-lozenge stars with monochrome solid rhomboids more frequently adorn mosaics dated to the first and second centuries. Both patterns for example occur at Fishbourne in a context dated c. 75-80 (Cunliffe 1971, pls. LXXV and LXXVII a). The writer knows of no other example with monochrome rhomboids of such a late date — they do not appear at Great Casterton, Rutland (Corder 1951-61), Denton (Smith 1974), Hucclecote (Clifford 1933) or Lydney (Wheeler and Wheeler 1932), all sites with pavements dated later than c. 360; and it raises the question what region the mosaicist came from to construct it, for apart from another fragment from the same building it has no parallel in Verulamium nor affinities with any of the pavements assigned to the various schools of mosaic (p. 19), many of which by c. 380 may have been disbanded. In the fourth century eight-lozenge stars are usually infilled with colourful centrepieces or a colourful alternating pattern such as at Gadebridge (No 51) dated to c. 325 and Barton Farm (Buckman and Newmarch pl. VII) which is also no later than c. 320. The style and late date of the pavement may suggest a reversion away from the highly-coloured technique back to the more formal style of the earlier centuries, but until more late pavements are identified this must remain supposition.

References. Frere 1960, 19. Frere, *Verulamium Excavations* ii (forthcoming), pls. XXVI B, XXVII.

[1]A contemporary room (15/16) on the western side of the house had a fragment of mosaic, with a lozenge and peltae pattern similar to Panel B (Frere 1960, 19-21; Frere, *Verulamium Excavations* ii (forthcoming), pl. XXIX B.)
[2]The motif is probably a scallop-pattern, normally represented as semi or quarter circles, but there is a very similar motif at Grately, Hants. (Rainey 1973, pl. 1 B), in this instance with a handle and clearly a fan.

Mosaic 75. Verulamium. Lion mosaic

Building XXI, 2, Room 4. Late second century. Dimensions; 11 ft 9 in (3.58 m) square, room 24 ft 6 in by 19 ft 6 in (7.47 by 5.95 m). Lifted, on display in Verulamium Museum. Drawn 1959, painted 1960. NPP.

This mosaic came from the south-west wing of a courtyard-house first discovered and partially excavated in 1956. It was set towards the south side of the room, nearest the door, with a wider border on its north side possibly for couches. Its scene, however, was viewed on entry into the room and not from the wider border.

Its scheme (see p. 26), based on a central square tangent to four lateral semicircles in a square (FIG. 6 A), is further elaborated by the elimination of the outer margin of the 'semicircles', resulting in the formation of a large curvilinear saltire. This is drawn in chain guilloche and the central square in four-strand guilloche both outlined in grey with braids alternating dark red, brown and white, and red, yellow ochre and white. The central panel is occupied by a lion, portrayed striding towards the left, holding the severed head of a stag with blood dripping from its neck. The lion has a long tail, chopped short by a linear border, a shaggy mane and pointed tufts of hair on the backs of his forelegs. The body is vigorously drawn and depicted in five colours — umber, yellow ochre, pale yellow, dark red and black — modelled to show muscle contours and highlighted white. His head and face are less successfully illustrated owing to the introduction of too many colours: all of those listed and in addition grey and yellow. Over-detail has resulted in the lion's head being indistinct from the stag's head, which is depicted in brown with a black lower jaw and a black left antler, shown superimposed across the lion's shoulder. The right antler is dark red. Grey lines beneath the lion's feet indicate shadow.

In the four curvilinear chevron-shaped interspaces in the arms of the saltire are canthari with gadrooned bodies in red, yellow ochre, and white. The slender necks of the canthari are decorated with swastika-meander devices worked in grey, with background spaces in red and yellow ochre. They have S-shaped handles with red grips and lower spirals, cushion-shaped stems and triangular pedestals.

The 'semicircles' 'above' and 'below' the lion enclose semicircular panels drawn in simple guilloche bearing 'half' flowers with pointed petals. The semicircles on either side of the lion panel are bordered with bands of waves and each contain two calices joined together by undulating stems.

The figured emblema is a dramatic piece of work and clearly by a skilled mosaicist, no doubt using a copy-book for detail. It may have been prefabricated, because the lion's tail is cut short and the figure unbalanced in its panel. There is no reason however to asume that the remainder of the pavement (Grade 1) is by a different mosaicist; considerable skill is shown in the geometry, and its chain-guilloche is of exceptional compactness. Swastika-meanders on canthari are not uncommon and occur for example on No 39 from Colchester. Its scheme is remarkably similar to a figured pavement found in 1978 at Middlesborough, Colchester (*Catalogue* No 4, p. 6), a mosaic of comparable quality and conceivably by the same mosaicist.

References. Frere 1960, pl. 1, 16–18 (for first report on Building XXI, 2, see Frere 1957, 13–14): Toynbee 1962, Cat No. 179, pl. 208. Frere *Verulamium Excavations* ii (forthcoming), pl. XVIII.

Mosaic 76. Verulamium. Hunting scene

Building XIV, 5, room 3. Late third to early fourth century. Dimensions; originally *c.* 6 ft 6 in by *c.* 4 ft 6 in (2.0 by 1.39 m), room 17 ft (5.20 m) by at least 14 ft (4.28 m). Lifted, on display in Verulamium Museum. Drawn and painted 1974. NPP.

No 76 was situated at the rear of a shop facing Watling Street (Frere 1972, 102–3). It was only 2 ft (0.60 m) from a wall, the direction from which the fragment was observed, which would suggest possibly that it marked the proximity of a door. Unfortunately the mosaic was seriously damaged by its subsidence into an underlying pit, so seriously that some of its original surface was almost vertical when found. The drawing was prepared after relaying and shows the true position of the fragments.

The scene depicts a deer fleeing towards the right and pursued by a lion which is about to spring upon the deer's back. Only the deer's forequarters, right leg, tail and lower hind legs survive; they are outlined in dark grey and shaded in two tones of grey. The flank and legs are highlighted white. Under the right fore-hoof is a grey line indicating shadow. The lion is more complete, except for his head, belly and tail. He has a tufted mane portrayed in a lively style, outlined in dark grey and shaded yellow and dull orange. A single tuft of orange hair to the right is likely to be the lion's beard. The body also is shaded dull orange and has grey and yellow lines to indicate leg muscles and his rib-cage; the hind legs are heavily burnt and their original colour is uncertain. Beneath is an undulating grey band running from the right front paw to the hind leg and which, like the grey line beneath the deer's hoof, is likely to represent shadow. The scene is bordered with a wide grey band and the remainder of the floor paved with coarse red-brick tesserae.

It is dated no earlier than *c*. 275 but was considered to be possibly contemporary with another fragmentary pavement nearby sealing a coin of Constantine Caesar (A.D. 330-5) (Frere 1972, 103). Hunting scenes in Britain are rare and it is interesting that this is the second example from Verulamium, the other example having just been described (No 75). Another example with a feline on the back of a hind or gazelle was found in the Dewlish villa, Dorset, in 1972 (Puttenham 1972, fig. 8) and is likely to be fourth-century. This, however, is only part of a much larger pavement, and as far as the writer is aware the pavement under discussion is the only mosaic in Britain where the hunt occupies the whole area: it is also unusual in not having a guilloche surround. The dramatic and vigorous movement of the animals indicates the mosaicist to have had considerable talent, further indicated by the gradation of colour and the bold high-lights to the limbs. Although the workmanship (Grade 2) is technically inferior to that of No 75, there can be little doubt that it shows more vitality and personal expression.

References. Frere 1972, 102-3, pl. xxxiv *a* and *b*.

Mosaic 77. Widford. Geometric

From a villa at Widford, Oxfordshire. Fourth century. Fragment 3 ft 9 in by 3 ft 6 in (1.16 by 1.08 m); overall dimensions not known. *In situ*, preserved in the chancel of St. Oswald's Church. Drawn and painted 1966. Neal 1967, pl. xx *a*.

In 1904, during the restoration of St. Oswald's Church, tessellated paving was exposed in the chancel where it remains on view. The fragment in the north-west corner of the chancel is part of a plain border, but the fragment in the south-west corner has a scheme of interlaced octagons forming squares flanked by irregular hexagons. Each square is occupied by an open square and each hexagon by solid red oblong hexagons. The pavement has a coarse white border with a band of grey inturned stepped triangles. The scheme is not uncommon. It occurs for example at Dorchester, Dorset (R.C.H.M. *Dorset*, pl. 222), Wellow, Somerset (*Vet. Mon.* 1738, i, 48, No. iii). and Withington, Glos. (Lysons ii, 1817, pl. xix A). Further north it is found at Great Weldon, Northants. (Lysons i, 1813, pt. 4, pl. vii), Norfolk Street, Leicester (*Gents. Mag.,* 1786, 56, ii pl. i facing p. 825) and Denton (Fowler Col. i, 10) and Haceby, Lincs. (Fowler Col. iii, 22). Another example comes from Ipswich (Reid Moir and Maynard 1931-3, pl. facing p. 247). Apart from this example and those from Haceby and Leicester, which comprise solely interlaced irregular octagons without any other infilling to the pattern, the remainder all contain oblong hexagons, some multi-coloured. The concentration of the pattern in the Midlands and Lincolnshire may suggest that these examples are the products of a single *officina,* possibly the Durobrivan school. All the examples quoted can be attributed to the fourth century and it is likely that our example is likewise.

Reference. Neal 1967.

Scale

Metres

12 Brantingham, N Humberside. Tyche and Nymphs

Scale

61   Hinton St Mary, Dorset. Christian pavement

0   1   M   DSN

63   Kingscote, Glos. Venus mosaic

69 Rudston, Yorks. The Charioteer mosaic

73 Verulamium, Herts. Dolphins and fountain

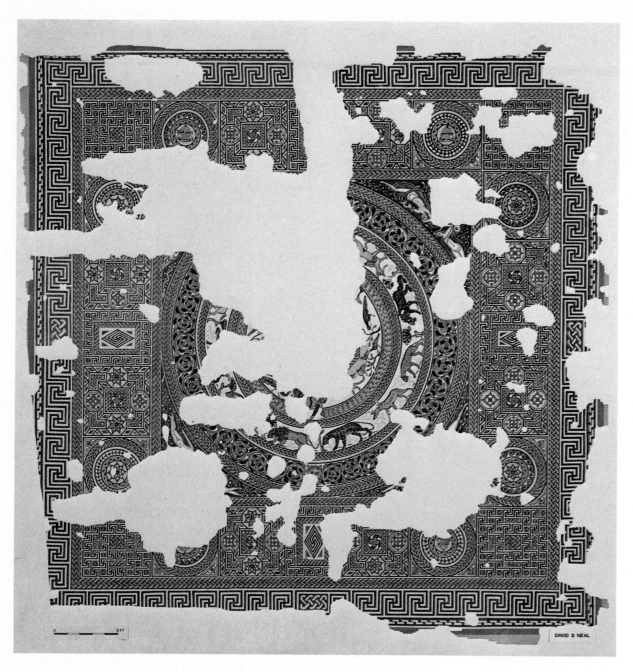

87 Woodchester, Glos. The Great Pavement

The Wigginton Mosaics. Nos 78–80

Wigginton Roman villa, Oxon, lies about six miles south-west of Banbury and was discovered in 1824. In 1841 a plan of a hypocausted room with an apsed mosaic (republished here, FIG. 23) was published in Beesley's *History of Banbury* (Beesley 1841,[1] pl. XI). Excavation by E. Greenfield between 1965 and 1967 confirmed the survival of this pavement, sealed beneath protecting slabs, and the existence of at least four others including a corridor-pavement (not illustrated). They were drawn by the writer in 1965 and 1966. Loose fragments of mosaic with geometric patterns were also found in the filling of hypocaust-channels in Rooms 4 and 16.

FIG. 23 Wigginton, Oxon. Mosaic found in 1824. Copy of an engraving in Beesley's *History of Banbury*

Mosaic 78, Wigginton. Interlaced squares

From Room 1. Fourth century. Dimensions; excluding coarse decorated border originally 20 ft 5 in (6.23 m) square, room; 27 ft (8.23 m) square. *In situ*, buried. Drawn and painted 1965. NPP.

Although very broken and distorted, sufficient fragments remain to attempt a reconstruction of its scheme, which is based on an overall grid of interlaced squares (see p. 25 for discussion on variations) set tangent to one another, with interspaces forming half saltires (FIG. 24). The missing central area originally contained two very large interlaced squares tangent to squares in the angles intersected by diagonals — really 'quarter' units of the lost central squares. The interspaces between panels are subdivided by linear rectangles and large lozenges. The dimensions of the latter are inconsistent: the reason is that the diagonal guilloche-bands across the corners of the mosaic are shorter than the width of the missing interlaced squares in the centre. Consequently the lozenges bordering the corner-squares are smaller than the lozenges around the central squares. A further consequence of this irregularity is that each rectangular panel has unusual angular projections on its internal corners.

In two corner-panels are large gadrooned canthari, one with a red, yellow and white fluted

105

FIG. 24 Wigginton, No 78 Reconstruction

neck and the other with its neck in the form of a lotus with red and white voluted petals. They are both set in a linear quadrant. Only two lozenges survive; the smaller contains concentric circles with pointed red-tipped excrescences and the larger a pair of red-tipped heart-shaped motifs with spirals. Fragments of two rectangular panels survive; one is infilled with a row of guilloche knots with peltae in their angles and the other, a row of interlocking lotus-buds facing alternate directions in red, yellow and white, with the end bud terminating in a volute. Surrounding the pavement is a crudely-worked border in coarse tesserae: along one side it has an uncommon band of open guilloche forming small circles, and designed possibly to make an otherwise square scheme rectangular. It is bordered by a band of spaced swastika-meanders with a rectangular strip of guilloche in each space, and a crudely-worked band of mauve tesserae.

The pavement's scheme, with its probably central interlaced squares, saltire pattern, spiralled motifs and swastika-meander borders, is typical of a number of mosaics attributed to the Corinian school (Brown *et. al.*, 1969) — namely Tockington Park, Glos. (MacLean 1887-8, pl. VII), Gloucester (No 52,) Halstock, Dorset (Rainey 1971, figs. 10-11), Bishopstone (VCH, *Hereford* fig. 14) and Kenchester, Hereford (Jack 1916, pl. 23) and Broad Street, London, R.C.H.M. *Roman London*, pl. 48). However, on none of these examples has the mosaicist made serious errors in the geometry, and although there are stylistic similarities their standard of workmanship is superior to our example, which is Grade 3. It would appear, therefore, that either two mosaicists or *officinae* were laying similar schemes, or the Wigginton mosaic is a late and degenerate product perhaps later than *c.* 350. The band of open guilloche forming small circles along a border is an uncommon pattern. We have already seen a parallel for it at Fullerton (No 45) and quoted other examples. It is interesting that it does not occur on any other pavements attributed to the Corinian School — further evidence perhaps that the work is by a different *officina*.

Reference. Smith 1969, 97 (footnote 1).

[1]Both Smith (Smith 1969) and Rainey (Rainey 1973) quote Beesley's work as dated 1848. This is incorrect: error has occurred because the copy now in the S.A.L. library was split in 1848 into two volumes and a new title-page printed with a new date. Hence the caption on the illustration in the *Gents. Mag.* of 1842 (Vol. xvii, May) reading 'From Beesleys History of Banbury'.

Mosaic 79, Wigginton. Meander border fragment

From Room 3, fourth century. Dimensions; originally 17 ft (5.18 m) square, room 25 ft (7.62 m) square. *In situ*, buried. Drawn and painted 1965. NPP.

The principal panel is lost, and all that remains are fragments of border-decoration with a spaced swastika–meander pattern in blue/grey, with rectangles in each space, two rectangles on each side of the pavement. Of four rectangles surviving two contain pelta motifs. One has a row of three pairs of confronting peltae, flanked by a pelta at either end of the row, and the other (fragmentary) a row of linked peltae facing alternate directions. A third rectangle has a border of small triangles and originally contained a chequered arrangement of T and L shapes enclosing small red squares set point-to-point. A fourth, almost totally lost, probably contained a volute.

Swastika–meander borders with rectangular spaces are typical of many pavements attributed to the Corinian school, and it is likely that this mosaic is one of their products. Its workmanship is superior to that of No 78 (Grade 2), and its geometry more accurate: it is likely therefore to be the work of a different mosaicist and to be earlier in date, probably early fourth-century. This is perhaps reinforced by the presence of a wall built across the pavement, clearly indicating a rearrangement of the internal layout of the villa.

Mosaic 80, Wigginton. Fragment.

Fourth century. Dimensions uncertain, fragment *c.* 4 ft by 3 ft (1.23 by 0.92 m). *In situ*, buried. Drawn 1965, painted 1978. NPP.

The remains originally consisted of a scheme of large squares tangent to smaller tilted squares with the interspaces containing lozenges forming eight-lozenge stars. The motifs in the large squares are lost, but each lozenge is occupied by a solid grey rhomboid. The border is divided into squares and rectangles — the square contains a solid square with a diagonal row of three small red squares set corner-to-corner (forming L-shapes), and the rectangle (possibly an L-shape if it turned the corner of the mosaic) contains a strip of guilloche in grey, red and cream. Bordering the pavement is a grey band and a broad border of cream-coloured limestone — both worked in coarse tesserae. The similarity of the patterned square to the border of No 79, and the similarity of workmanship and colour would suggest it was by the same mosaicist. The reconstruction shows a square panel in the centre, but it could have been an eight-lozenged star. Both designs occur on a corridor from Woodchester (Lysons 1797, pl. XI) and the latter occurs in three instances on mosaics B and C from Stonesfield, Oxon (Smith 1969, pl. 3.15), all products of the Corinian school. An early fourth-century date is probable for this pavement.

The Winterton Mosaics. Nos 81-86

Winterton Roman Villa, South Humberside, lies about ½ mile west of Winterton village on the west-facing slope of the Lincolnshire Limestone belt. The site was first mentioned in a letter as long ago as 1699,[1] but it was not until August 1747 that remains were first excavated. In that year two mosaics (Nos 84 and 85) were recorded by Charles Mitley of York, and were subsequently transcribed into engravings by George Vertue in 1751 and published the following year.[2] In 1798 William Fowler, a native of Winterton, published copies (Fowler Col. i, pl. i) of the earlier engravings with additional details of the guilloche borders, indicating that the pavements had again been exposed to view. Fowler is likely to have made these additions in 1797 when he also drew and engraved the newly-discovered Providentia pavement (No 85). He was later to become famous for his drawings of these and pavements from other sites. Further chance-discoveries were made in about the middle of the 18th century, but it was not until 1958 that systematic excavation began in advance of opencast ironstone mining. Dr. I.M. Stead directed this work for the Inspectorate until 1967[3] during which time fragments of another three mosaics were unearthed and two of the earlier discoveries lifted for display. No 84 is housed on the foyer of Scunthorpe Civic Centre, and No 85 in Scunthorpe Museum.[4]

Although late Iron-Age and early Roman occupation in the form of circular buildings has been discovered at Winterton, sophisticated buildings with pavements were not erected until c. 180. The principal house (Building G) then consisted of a long single corridor (with a central porch), terminating at both ends in a group of rooms. Aisled houses skirted the north and south sides of an eastern courtyard. In this period mosaic pavements were confined to the main house, but in the middle of the fourth century the aisled building (Building D) on the north side of the courtyard became pre-eminent. Additional rooms were built into the south aisle and four mosaics laid. The earlier house was truncated and may have ceased to be used as living apartments, although a *triclinium* was built on its east side. No new mosaics was laid here.

The earliest pavements will be described first.

[1]*Surtees Society*, liv (1869), 212.
[2]It was subsequently included in *Vetusta Monumenta* (1789), pl. IX.
[3]Further excavation by R. Goodburn has continued from 1968 onwards (Goodburn 1978).
[4]Nos 84 and 85 have been incorrectly re-laid. The central panel in No 84 has been rotated through 90°, so that it is now viewed from the side of the mosaic; and the bust in the central panel of No 85 has been raised so that there is now less space between it and the internal edge of the medallion.

Mosaic 81. Winterton. Scroll pattern.

From Room 13, Building G. Dated *c*. 180. Fragment 13 ft 6 in (4.11 m) long by about 2 ft 8 in (81 cm) wide. Room 16 ft 6 in by 14 ft 6 in (5.02 by 4.42 m). *In situ*, buried. Drawn 1964, painted 1966. Stead 1976, pl. XIXb.

This mosaic adjoined the east wall of the room and comprised a voluted pattern springing from either side of an undulating tendril sprouting red leaves. The volutes terminate in rounded buds, drawn out to a point, shaded white, brown and with red tips. In each alternate space between the volutes and the tendril is a red-tipped sheath bearing a red stepped triangular motif around its girth. The pattern is bordered along one side by a grey double fillet and at one end by a fragment of grey band. Parallel to the double fillet, and separated from it by a broad white margin, is a fragment of simple guilloche in red, brown and white.

The scroll pattern is almost certainly a border and to have been part of a make-up panel making an otherwise square scheme rectangular. All that remains of the principal scheme is the fragment of guilloche. The workmanship is mediocre (Grade 3) and the tesserae fairly coarse, but its date of *c*. 180 makes it particularly interesting since, like No 82, it is one of the few second-century pavements from a villa[1] and one of the few dated archaeologically.

Reference. Stead 1976, pl. xx (for discussion on the mosaic by D.J. Smith see *ibid.*, Mosaic E, p. 253).

[1]For a survey of Roman mosaics before the fourth century see Smith 1975 (for further additions see also *ibid.*, p. 287, footnote 81).

Mosaic 82, Winterton. Swastika-meander.

From Room 15, Building G. Dated *c*. 180. Fragment 9 ft 4 in by 3 ft 3 in (2.86 by 1.00 m), room 9 ft 6 in by 12 ft (2.91 by 3.67 m). *In situ*, buried. Drawn 1968, painted 1970. Stead 1976, pl. xixa.

The fragment, possibly part of a surround, has a swastika-meander pattern worked in grey tesserae with the arms of the swastika developing a reverse return. How the motif related to other right-angled lines to the 'left' is not understood, but it is possible that it was repeated but with the meander turned through 90° anti-clockwise. The right-angled pattern may have been inserted between two sets of meanders following an error in the setting.

Along one margin is a grey band terminating just beyond the outer edge of the meander. Running diagonally between them are two intentionally-placed dark grey tesserae, an unusual feature not observed elsewhere by the writer but recalling the treatment of the angles of the stepped-triangle border around the central flower on No 2 from Aldborough, for example. The same pavement is also the only example[1] with swastika-meanders developing reverse returns.

The workmanship is fairly precise (Grade 2) and superior to that of No 81, the other early pavement from the villa.

Reference. Stead 1976 (for discussion on the mosaic by D.J. Smith see *ibid.*, Mosaic F, p. 253).

[1]A variation of the design can be found on a fourth-century pavement from Gloucester (No 52), but in a staggered arrangement within a lozenge.

Mosaic 83, Winterton. Orpheus mosaic.

Room 3. Building D. Dated *c*. 350. Dimensions, excluding coarse decorated border, originally 24 ft 6 in by 15 ft (7.47 by 4.57 m): room excluding ante-chamber, 28 ft by 20 ft 6 in (8.54 by 6.25 m). *In situ*, buried. Drawn and painted in 1963 from excavator's field-sketches, notes and vertical photographs. Stead 1976, pl. xxiv.

Vertue's engraving of 1751 (*Vetusta Monumenta* (1789), pl. ix) and Fowler's copy of 1796 (Fowler Coll, i, pl. 1) show the Orpheus pavement intact, but unfortunately ploughing and exposure has since caused considerable damage particularly to the central area and the west end. Damage was also caused in the 18th century when a pit was dug into the Orpheus panel and a chamber-pot inserted — perhaps an unsavoury joke by a local vandal.

The early engravings show at the west end fragmentary remains of another pavement (FIG. 25) comprising a circular medallion in a rectangle and in another rectangle a stag. Excavation has established this mosaic to be contemporary with the Orpheus mosaic and to have occupied an ante-chamber 10 ft by about 16 ft 6 in (3.05 by 5.03 m) at the west end of the room. The early engravings place the fragment 'below' the seated figure of Orpheus, but in reality it is 'above' and therefore at the 'top' of the published illustration. Another fault with the engravings, apart from misrepresentations of the motifs (Fowler was aware of these errors and

FIG. 25 Winterton. Fragmentary remains of a Pavement occupying an ante-chamber west of Mosaic 83

attempted to compensate for them by adding detailed drawings of the guilloche), is that the animals in the eight panels around the figure are misplaced. An elephant appears in one panel instead of a she-wolf and other animals misrepresented. Descriptions of the missing animals are based on Fowler's engravings.

Description

The scheme comprises a square with four triangles in the angles forming an irregular octagon. It is drawn in treble-strand guilloche (outlined in blue and coloured red and white only — no third colour, e.g. yellow, appears in any of the guilloche throughout the pavement), and contains a large circle of chain guilloche. 'Above' and 'below' the square, are rectangles.

The central circle is occupied by a yellow linear circle divided radially by yellow 'spokes' into eight trapezoid compartments around an octagonal hub. Within this is another linear octagon in red and blue, with red circles placed outside its angles, and containing part of what appears to be a linear square. The Vertue/Fowler engravings show this central panel, now totally lost, to have been occupied by a seated, mis-shapen figure of Orpheus (poorly drawn by Mitley and subsequently copied by the engravers) set against a square 'frame' and holding a fan-shaped object intended to represent a lyre. The surrounding trapezoid panels each contain an animal, enchanted by the music of Orpheus and proceeding in an anti-clockwise direction around him. Of the animals, two are lost and only parts of six remain. In the first panel (descriptions of the animals will begin with the stag in the 'top' right-hand panel (Panel 1) and follow clockwise) is the neck and fore-quarters of a stag with his right hoof folded back as though he is leaping. His body is orange and outlined in blue. The remainder of the panel is filled with the branches of a tree; its trunk is missing, but the position of the branches to one side of the panel would suggest it to have been to the rear of and not behind the stag as shown by Fowler. Its leaves are red.

Fowler correctly places the stag in the 'first' panel and shows the animal with a fine set of antlers. The second panel is lost but is shown by Fowler as containing a lion superimposed against a tree.

A third panel bears all but the head of a leopard, outlined in blue and shaded olive-green with a long tail and claws. Its body is covered with red and white spots and is superimposed against a stylized tree with a red trunk, outlined in blue and with straight blue leafless branches terminating in blue roundels. Fowler fails to show a leopard here but instead a fox with a circular motif.

The fourth panel is the best-preserved and depicts an animal, possibly a she-wolf, with a somewhat over-large head with a white eye and a black pupil giving a piercing gaze. Its body is yellow ochre and outlined in pale red — the same colour for her tail, the muscles on her right haunch, and claws. She has four teats on her belly. Beneath, rising from the border of the panel, is a tree-trunk in a style similar to the tree behind the leopard. Its trunk is red and outlined in blue. In the right corner of the panel, beneath the creature's open jaw is a circle divided into four red ellipses and with a white concave-sided square centre. This motif has been interpreted as a textile '*orbiculus*' (Stead 1976, 262) but more likely the motif was inserted merely to fill an empty space. Early engravings incorrectly show an elephant here. Of the animal in the fifth panel, only part of its front paws and a head with a pointed nose and red tongue are preserved. It is outlined in dark grey and shaded in pale yellow ochre. In front of the nose is a short line of red, white, brown and grey tesserae extending an imaginary line from the tongue. It is perhaps intended to represent drooling spittle. From this evidence and the presence of a dog on Fowler's engraving, there can be little doubt that the animal is a running hound. A fragment of a tree-trunk and branches are preserved below and above the animal.

In the sixth panel the engravings show the mythical gryphon, and its presence is confirmed by a small fragment showing a wing, neck and back outlined in blue and shaded black. To its rear, against the side of the panel, is part of a tree-trunk in red and outlined in blue. Its curving branches overhang the gryphon and each bear a single red leaf. Contrary to the other panels, except perhaps that with the stag, the tree is likely to have been placed to the rear of the gryphon because the area above the animal was filled by his wings. It is the only mythical animal depicted.[1]

The seventh panel is lost. Fowler shows it incorrectly with a boar, but fragments of this animal have been found in Panel 8. It is probable therefore that it once contained an elephant, misplaced by Fowler in Panel 4.

The remaining panel (8) preserved the body, hind legs and part of the fore-quarters of a boar with a row of bristles along its spine. He is outlined in blue and shaded medium brown. A tree, also with a red trunk and red leaves, occupies the spaces beneath and above the animal. Unlike the two other tree-trunks preserved, this is shown with a bulbous swelling on its left side. Fowler's engraving shows panel 8 with an animal looking more like a bear. The interpretation of it as a boar, however, is suggested by the presence of a boar on the Horkstow Orpheus mosaic (Smith 1976, pl. XI) which also has a bristled back.

The rest of the scheme is uninspiring and nowhere is colour, other than blue and red, employed. In a direction outwards from the central panel, wing-shaped interspaces between the inscribed circles and the octagon contain a red line (running around the octagon) with blue tendrils sprouting from either side of a red semicircle. Only one of the triangles is preserved and is occupied by an inelegant red cantharus with an unusual flared rim considerably wider than its neck, which is shown fluted or gadrooned. Its bowl also projects beyond the neck and is shown with a white band divided into square inadequately depicting jewels or 'millefiori'.

The bowl has sketchily-portrayed gadrooning and curves sharply down to meet a small pedestal. The cantharus has two simple S-shaped handles. The remains of a bowl and pedestal in another triangular panel would suggest that they were similarly ornamented.

Of the rectangles on either side of the square one is substantially lost, but they both contain a highly-complicated geometric pattern of guilloche. It has a simple guilloche border with inward-projecting crenellations and contains a smaller panel with outward-projecting crenellations interlocking with the first. In the smaller panel are two red bands with grey super-

posed triangles with white centres. Between the two bands is a tiny cantharus. Bordering the
pavement are long narrow linear panels subdivided into large and small rectangles. The larger
contain linear red lozenges with blue rhomboids with red centres, and the smaller contain red
and white chequers. The workmanship is decidedly poor (Grade 3). Apart from a lack of
colour, which makes the pavement dull by comparison to others, the guilloche is irregularly
spaced and poorly finished. For instance the number of crenellations in the rectangle differs on
opposite sides. The animals are also poorly drawn in a naive style, in some cases barely looking
like the animals they are meant to represent. Clearly the mosaicist has worked from memory;
for had he used a copy-book the animals would surely have been more accurately portrayed.
The same criticism can be made about the large inelegant canthari and perhaps also about the
missing figure of Orpheus. Had his human form been well drawn his representation on the
early engravings may have been less 'bear'-like.

The closest representation, geographically, of Orpheus playing to and charming the beasts
occurs on the mosaic at Horkstow, (FIG. 10, J) only about five miles east. Other representations
are confined to the south and south-west of England.[2] At Horkstow also Orpheus is contained in
the centre of a wheel-like scheme divided into eight trapezoid compartments by radial spokes of
guilloche. Unlike at Winterton, however, these compartments are subdivided into three smaller
zones by concentric arcs. The larger outer zones contain the larger beasts, the middle zones pairs
of confronting birds pecking at bunches of grapes and the small zones, nearest the central panel,
smaller animals such as a hare and a hound. On the same pavement is another large wheel
pattern, this time divided into four trapezoid compartments. At Woodchester (No 87), Barton
Farm (FIG. 10, A; Buckman and Newmarch, 1850, pl. VII) and Withington (FIG. 11, U: Lysons ii
1817, pl. XX) Orpheus occupies a central panel but the animals progress around him within
uninterrupted concentric circles. Dr. David Smith has attributed the work of the Winterton
pavement to the Petuarian school of mosaicists (Smith 1969, 103), and has suggested that the
same workshop laid the Horkstow and the Brantingham Tyche mosaics (No 12). This may be
so, but although the subject and scheme of the Winterton and Horkstow pavements is similar,
the Horkstow pavement is technically superior and more imaginative in its content and colour.
In the writer's opinion it is doubtful whether they can both be the work of the same *mosaicist*. The
animals at Horkstow are more skilfully portrayed, and although only two and part of a third
survive, showing an elephant, a bear, and the head of a boar, they have a greater vitality. The
Brantingham pavement also uses a greater range of colour and it is difficult to equate its fine
portraits with a product of the same mosaicist. It is more likely, perhaps, both on the technical
evidence and on the use of flat areas of background colour, such as those used behind the central
œgure of Tyche and on the 'painted ceiling' panel at Horkstow, that the Brantingham and
Horkstow pavements are by the same *mosaicist* and that Winterton is not.

The similarity of subject and scheme with other pavements in the south-west of England has
led Dr. Smith to suggest that craftsmen from the Corinian school 'were attracted by prospects
of employment elsewhere . . . and that one or more of them found a niche for a time in
Petuaria' (Stead 1976, 271).

References. Stead 1976, pls. xxv a and b (for discussion on the mosaic by D.J. Smith see *ibid.*, Mosaic A, p. 259):
           Smith 1969, 102: Toynbee 1964, 282.

[1]The animal was believed to represent Pegasus, but since a winged gryphon is shown at Woodchester (No 87) the
previous interpretation is now believed to be incorrect.
[2]For a list of all known representations of Orpheus on Romano-British mosaic see Smith 1977, 125-8.

Mosaic 84. Winterton. Fortuna

From Room 6, Building D. Dated *c*. 350. Original dimensions excluding coarse decorated
border 30 ft by 7 ft 2 in (9.16 by 2.20 m), room 35 ft by 12 ft (10.68 by 3.66 m). Lifted, on
display in Scunthorpe Civic Centre. Drawn and painted in 1963 from excavator's field-
drawings and vertical photographs. Stead 1976, pl. XXIIIa.

Since Vertue's engravings of 1751 and Fowler's copy of 1796 the west end of the mosaic has been considerably damaged by ploughing, but sufficient is preserved to establish the engravings as reasonably accurate.

Its very long oblong scheme is divided longitudinally into three approximately equal rectangles. The end rectangles contain overall repeating patterns, but the central rectangle is further subdivided into three by a linear square containing a circle of chain guilloche. It is flanked by oblongs with a scale-pattern. Apart from the central bust, the only colours throughout are blue, red and white, the same as in the Orpheus mosaic.

The central circle is occupied by two interlaced squares, one blue and the other white, forming an eight-pointed star. The interspaces within and at the angles of the squares are shaded red and the eight spaces between the squares and the outer circle are each halved radially and coloured blue and white. Inside the boxes is a medallion, bordered in simple guilloche, containing the fragmentary remains of a female head in pale buff, with dark red tesserae used to accentuate the cheek-bones, the cleft of the chin, the upper lip and the brow. Her hair is also pale buff and is outlined in dark red and parted down the centre. She has white piercing eyes with circular blue pupils. The engravings show her draped. To her right is a cluster of blue tesserae in a pointed formation believed to be the end of an attribute, shown on the engravings as being held across her right shoulder and interpreted as a sheaf of corn. The figure was believed to represent Ceres. However, Dr. Smith has suggested (Stead 1976, 259) that grey tesserae are unlikely to have been used to portray corn; and he has tentatively suggested they might be grapes and the figure Bacchus. A possibly better interpretation is that the attribute was a cornucopia or a torch. It may have terminated in three flame-like projections similar to those on No 85 and on the cornucopia held by Tyche on the mosaic from Whatley, Som. (Smith 1977, pl. 6. xxxb). Our figure lacks a mural crown and cannot be similarly identified; but personifications of either Abundantia, Fecunditas, Felicitas, Fortuna, or Providentia may all be possibilities. Normally they would hold their attribute across their left shoulder, not their right; but as we are dealing with fairly primitive work the mosaicist may not have paid too much attention to detail.

The four spandrels between the circle and the red linear square each contain red spandrel-shaped panels with a white central area bearing a cantharus. Each cantharus has two red-tipped stalks bending downwards from either side of its rim. Minor variations occur in the gadrooning on each one, and that to the 'lower right' has a less globular body. Their bun-shaped pedestals 'break' into the outline of the panels, as do some motifs at Brantingham (No 12), indicating that they were made a little too large and laid before the spandrels were infilled. Oblong panels 'above' and 'below' the square each contain an identical scale-pattern outlined in blue with red centres. The repeating intersecting-circle patterns in the remaining rectangles are not quite identical. The 'lower' panel has blue circles, white ellipsoids and red concave-sided squares with blue centres, but on the 'upper' panel the blue centres in the red concave-sided squares are each outlined in white. Bordering the scheme in large coarse tesserae are nine coloured bands in (from the outside inwards) white, blue and red, the same repeating, followed by white, red and white. There can be little doubt that the mosaicist of the Orpheus pavement also laid this one. It is of slightly better quality, probably because the artist confined himself mainly to repeating motifs which have been laid with reasonable skill and without error. When one looks at the figure, however, we find that, like the animals surrounding Orpheus, it too lacks imagination. Other than the accentuation of facial features with red tesserae, no attempt has been made to show relief by shading or highlighting. The same colour for the flesh has also been used for the hair. Again it is difficult to equate the mosaicist with the maker of either the Horkstow or Brantingham pavements.

The scheme of the pavement, but much smaller, occurs at Thenford, Northants. (No 72) in a mosaic of comparable date. This also has chain guilloche around the central bust and shows the same restraint in the use of colour — only blue and red, except in the central medallion. The scheme, without the end rectangles, is the same as No 85, also from Winterton.

Reference. Stead 1976, pl. xxiiib (for discussion on the mosaic by D.J. Smith see *ibid.*, Mosaic B, p. 258).

Mosaic 85. Winterton. Providentia

Room 13, Building D. Dated *c*. 350. Panel 7 ft 9 in by 4 ft 11 in (2.37 by 1.50 m) room 12 ft by 9 ft 4 in (3.66 by 2.85 m). Lifted, on display in Scunthorpe Museum. Drawn and painted in 1963 from excavator's field-drawings, notes and vertical photographs. Stead 1976, pl. xxi.

In 1797, while William Fowler was recording details of the previous two pavements (Nos 83–4), schoolboys discovered the remains of another in the side of a ditch-cutting (Fowler 1907, 8–21). The mosaic was promptly excavated and recorded by Fowler and published by him as an engraving in 1799 (Fowler Coll. i, pl. 5). This drawing was probably his first of a mosaic *in situ*, for previously he had copied the work of Mitley. Fowler shows the pavement complete, but its situation by the side of a ditch and the circumstances of its discovery would perhaps rule this out. Certainly he made no attempt to indicate a large ancient patch: it is likely therefore that the pavement was damaged, but shown in restored form on his drawing.

Its scheme comprises a rectangle divided into three parts — a central square flanked by oblongs. The central square is occupied by a medallion, inscribed in simple guilloche and containing a bust, possibly Providentia holding a cornucopia. Her face, outlined in blue, is ovoid and shaded cream. She has rounded staring eyes beneath linear eye-brows which curve downwards to form the nose. Her cheek-bones, chin-cleft and forehead are picked out in blue and the right side of her face highlighted white. She has dark red hair arranged tightly about the scalp and cut short at the nape of the neck — which is white. About her shoulders is a white garment, perhaps a tunic, indicated by simple linear folds. On her left shoulder is a dark grey area perhaps representing shadow. Fowler's engraving shows, uncoloured, a fibula or possibly a pendant hanging from the collar, but there is no evidence for this on the pavement. The cornucopia is horn-shaped and rests across her right shoulder, apparently without support. It is outlined in blue and shaded cream, and has two thin red lines, perhaps intended to indicate joints. The top of the vessel has a broad blue rim or collar and contains three red semicircles, perhaps fruit. In four spandrels between the medallion and its red frame are bipartite peltae, one half blue, the other red. They have long drawn-out tails slightly flared at the ends. The flanking oblongs at the 'top' and 'bottom' of the scheme both contain mats of guilloche, in blue, red and white and, bordering the mosaic, a series of plain white and blue bands, a row of red inturned stepped triangles and a row of small alternating red and white squares. The pavement has been patched in the 'top left' corner with a jumble of various coloured tesserae — perhaps marking a threshold.

The workmanship is variable. Providentia is not unskilfully drawn and, as has been noted, includes highlights. However, as with the Orpheus pavement the mosaicist has shown his inexperience, or lack of application, by his errors in the mats of guilloche.

Winterton is the only site where two mosaics are occupied by portrait medallions. We have already seen another example from Humberside, at Brantingham; but two others occur in the general area. One comes from the Bailgate, Lincoln,[1] and is occupied by a female holding a cornucopia across her left shoulder and adorned with leaves or possibly corn. The other was discovered in 1974 at the Ebor Brewery site, York and shows a female bust, damaged, with long shoulder-length hair. Another example in the collection comes from Thenford (No 79), a pavement remarkably similar to the mosaic under discussion with a central medallion filling a square flanked by oblongs, also containing guilloche. The bust displays greater skill in its execution with detailed facial features and locks of hair, but there is a surprising similarity in the poor workmanship and lack of colour. It is not impossible that the two mosaics, excluding the Thenford portrait, are the work of the same *officina*. The Thenford mosaic is dated *c*. 350-60 — a date similar to that of the Winterton pavement.

Reference. Stead 1976, pl. xxii (for discussion on the mosaic by D.J. Smith see *ibid*., Mosaic C, p. 256).

[1]Unpublished. Panel preserved in Lincoln Museum.

Mosaic 86, Winterton. Geometric

Room 5, Building D. Dated *c.* 350. Three loose fragments from a room 18 ft by 12 ft (5.49 by 3.66 m). Preserved in Scunthorpe Museum. Painting prepared in 1970 from field-drawings. Stead 1976, pl. xxb.

These three fragments were not found *in situ*, so their relationship to one another is uncertain and they may come from different sides of the same floor. However, as the scheme is based on an overall grid of spaced squares tangent to smaller tilted squares, forming eight-lozenged stars, their relative position within the general arrangement can be reconstructed with a degree of reliability. They all come from the edge of the design for here the tilted squares have been adapted into gable-shaped panels to fit the frame.

The eight lozenges within each star are not all outlined in grey; the larger squares are joined diagonally but the tilted squares are not linked apex to apex. The result is that on either side of each tilted square is a chevron which is shaded white in one half and red in the other. It is by alternating these colours within a group of four chevrons that the eight-pointed star-pattern is formed. Of the larger squares, parts of two are preserved — both are quartered in a red and white chequered arrangement. Two tilted squares are also preserved. One contains a small solid grey square with red stepped triangles on each if its sides and a row of tesserae, set lozengewise, across the angles. The other probably also had a grey solid but with red squares against its sides and also rows of tesserae set lozengewise running into the angles. Of the three gable-shaped panels, two are filled with concentric white, red and grey bands, while the third and most complete has a red and white millefiori surround to another grey gable-shaped form with a red 'pediment' and white and grey chequers separated by thin red lines.

The work is of good quality (Grade 2) and constructed in small (10-13 mm) tesserae and not large ones as previously recorded (Stead 1976, 255). It is superior to the other pavements of *c.* 350 from Winterton and would appear to be the work of a different mosaicist — possibly the work of the Durobrivan School. Its eight-lozenged star-patterns can be matched on many pavements in the East Midlands, the nearest being Roxby only one mile south. However, all the other eight-lozenge stars attributed to this workshop[1] are outlined and divided by grey lines and contain smaller lozenges with white surrounds. This is the only example where the star-patterns are completely filled, and partially formed, by colour.

Reference. Stead 1976, pl. iva (for discussions on the mosaic by D.J. Smith see *ibid.*, Mosaic D, p. 254).

[1]For Dr. Smith's list of these mosaics, with a suggestion of their course of evolution, see Stead 1976, 255.

Mosaic 87. Woodchester. 'The Great Pavement'

From a villa at Woodchester, Glos. Dated *c.* 300-325. Dimensions, excluding coarse decorated border, 39 ft square (11.86 m), including decorated border 45 ft 9 in by 45 ft 3 in (13.91 by 13.76 m), room 47 ft square (14.86 m). Drawn 1973, painted 1974–5. Neal 1976b, pl. xli.

Woodchester Roman Villa lies 1½ miles south of Stroud on a hill-side overlooking a tributary of the River Frome. It is one of the largest villas discovered in Britain, and lies partly beneath the old churchyard, occupying an area at least 600 ft long by 350 ft wide (182.00 by 106 m); moreover the building-complex has yet to be fully explored. Its plan (Lysons 1797, pl. vi) shows at least two courtyards (and possibly a third to the south), the outer being about twice the size of the inner. The outer court was entered on its south side via a gatehouse linked by a long garden-wall to two barn-like buildings with verandahs and central porches on the east and west sides. On the opposite side of the courtyard, between two large buildings, was another entrance leading into the inner courtyard, this being completely enclosed by buildings. On its far side, away from the entrance, was the main domestic range dominated mid-way along its axis by an *oecus* or chief reception-room — a large square room heated by a hypocaust and possibly partially two-storeyed. The range had a verandah along its front which turned south at the east and west ends to front two wings both containing living apartments. At least 19 rooms had mosaics of various degrees of quality, but the grandest occupied the hall. Not only is this mosaic the largest at Woodchester, but it is the largest discovered north of the Alps. It therefore deserves its title, first adopted by Samuel Lysons in 1797, of the Great Pavement.

The earliest recorded mention of the Great Pavement is in the *Additions* to Camden's *Britannia* (p. 247) published in 1695, where two sources are quoted which show it to be already known. One describes 'Woodchester, famous for its *tesseraick* work of painted beasts and flowers, which appears in the churchyard two or three ft deep in making the graves'. Antiquarian interest in the Great Pavement continued throughout the 18th century. In the second volume of *Recueil d'Antiquités,* printed in Paris in 1756, part of the pavement is represented including circular borders and the figures of a lion, lioness and peacock. This plate was engraved from a drawing by a Richard Bradley. Several other drawings by Bradley still survive; one shows the centre-piece missing; but according to a memorandum by Bradley on one of them it was 'said to be fish and a star about the centre'. This note appears to have been written in 1722. Another drawing of part of the pavement was made about the same date by Edmond Brown, at whose expense the mosaic is said to have been exposed.

FIG. 26   Woodchester, No 87. The lost elephant drawn in about 1787. Copy of an engraving in
Vetusta Momumenta ii

In about 1787 a small part was again unearthed to show the figures of an elephant and several birds (FIG. 26).[1] Unfortunately 'though much care was taken by the rector for its preservation, the wet and frost have long since entirely destroyed it'.[2] The pavement continued to be damaged by burials, and in 1789 another commentator concluded despairingly that a great number of graves having been dug through parts of it, further discovery was improbable. Fortunately he was wrong. Following the excavation of a vault in 1793, Samuel Lysons, a leading antiquarian, took an interest in the site and in that and the following year a 'considerable a portion of the same pavement was laid open . . .', which enabled him to ascertain its form and dimensions. Then, with the help of a local resident, George Hawker, he explored the remainder of the villa and made meticulous plans of it and other mosaics paving the surrounding rooms and corridors. His first published results appeared in 1796 in the form of a hand-tinted engraving showing the pavement restored. The following year he produced a lavish volume entitled *An Account of Roman Antiquities Discovered at Woodchester in the County of Gloucestershire* with detailed colour-engravings of the Great Pavement and other newly-discovered mosaics, showing their condition at the time of his survey. Since Lysons's excavations, burials over the Great Pavement have ceased. The pavement has been re-exposed to public view seven times, the latest in 1973, the date of the new survey. At the same time limited repairs were carried out by Carter Contracting Limited, London. The new survey, the largest drawing in the collection, took about three weeks to plan on site and almost one year to complete.

Before a description of the mosaic is given, it is necessary to understand its scheme in relationship to the architecture. Excluding the outer geometric panels, it consists of a large square (33 ft (10.06 m) square) containing a circle with a small octagon in the centre. Between the circle and the octagon are three concentric zones separated by bands of guilloche and laurel patterns. Bordering the square are 24 panels, 20 of them square (5 ft 6 in (1.68 m) square) and four rectangular. The rectangles are each situated at the axis of the mosaic opposite doorways in the east and west walls, and a possible principal entrance in the south wall.[3] These 24 panels form an ambulatory around the main area, for set in the four spandrels in the angles of the square were four stone column-bases, one of which is *in situ*. On the top of the surviving base is a circular mortise, suggesting the emplacement of a wooden column perhaps designed to support an upstairs gallery built over and following the plan of the ambulatory and also, possibly, a domed plaster roof — a reflection of the shape of the pavement (or *vice versa*).

Description. (Descriptions of missing parts are based on drawings by Lysons and others).

The theme of the design is Orpheus, seen on entry from the south side of the room, the quasi-divine musician and singer of Greek mythology whose music had the power to move trees and subdue the wild creatures — illustrated here entranced and encircling Orpheus.

The Central Zone

Apart from a border of guilloche in grey, buff and red only, the central octagon is lost, but in Lysons's time sufficient survived to demonstrate that its south side was unenclosed in order to allow the head of Orpheus to project into the panel. The contents were already lost as early as 1772, but as indicated above it is likely to have contained 'fish and a star'. Speculation as to the form of the star has suggested either a flower or an interlaced square, but the latter motif perhaps leaves insufficient room for Orpheus's head and therefore an eight-petalled flower is the more likely.

Regrettably the figure of Orpheus is also extensively damaged but sufficient survives to show him seated and holding on his left knee a lyre, presumably grasped in his left hand and played with his right. He wears a pale grey tunic, highlighted white and with grey folds, with a dark red zig-zag band down the front and a hem draped and folded across his knee. His right leg is dark red and his foot pink: the colour of his leg may suggest an attempt to represent trousers, yet his other leg is not similarly coloured, and therefore an attempt at shading to depict the leg folded back may be the explanation. His lyre has a semicircular sound-box and 'millefiori' decoration on the arms. Orpheus is accompanied by a fox to his left and a peacock to his right. The fox is very simply worked in pale buff with a grey outline, but the peacock is superbly rendered with a magnificent multi-coloured plume, in contrast to his head and neck which are in plain grey only broken by small squares of 'millefiori'.

The remainder of the zone is filled by a clockwise procession of birds, one of which, perhaps unintentionally on the part of the mosaicist, is standing on the fox's tail. In all examples the birds are outlined in grey and have 'millefiori' on their wings: their legs are red. The fifth bird to the rear of the fox is a cock. Its head is twisted upside-down to enable it to scratch its comb. Beneath the birds at the head of the procession is a grey tree with yellow-ochre leaves. Similar trees thereafter were placed between the birds. The white background is not consistent; along the top of the zone, bordering the octagon, buff tesserae and not white have been used. The reason is not understood (it is not a patch), but perhaps from this point onwards an attempt was made to distinguish between the sky (white) and clouds (buff).

Around the zone is a thin grey band followed by a broad band of laurel-wreath pattern in pink with pale grey leaves having olive-green centres. Around its margin is a row of grey spurs. Again, like the inscribed octagon, this band too stops (or starts) either side of Orpheus. The next concentric band is of three-strand guilloche in grey, red, yellow and white (apart from the octagon, the guilloche throughout the pavement has these colours) edged on its outside by two thin lines, one pale grey and the other grey. This forms the inner margin to a middle zone, bordered on its outside by three-strand guilloche.

The Middle Zone

This contains a clockwise procession of magnificently drawn animals all mesmerised by Orpheus's music and giving the impression of harmonious, unhurried movement. Only six complete animals and parts of three survive; they are, in order of progression (from the top right), a gryphon, a bear, a leopard, a stag, a tigress, a lion, a lioness (fragmentary), a boar (fragmentary) and a horse (fragmentary). The next animal was the elephant (FIG. 26), preserved until 1787. Between the animals, except the leopard and the staff and the tigress, are stylized trees. Where trees are absent the spaces are filled with conventionalised trailing plants in very pale grey. Similar plants fill the interspaces beneath the bodies and necks of all the surviving animals. To the right of each animal's foot is a red undulating line indicating shadow and movement. Each animal is outlined in grey.

As a result of Lysons's reconstruction it has been assumed that there were 12 animals; but this is not possible because there is insufficient space to fit three animals (including the elephant) in the break. The reason for the misconception is that Lysons placed the horse too far south with the tree behind it, mid-way along the west side of the mosaic. In reality this position is held by the trotter of the boar. No account has been left to indicate the species of the unknown animal — a wolf or dog is a possibility but a bull is perhaps more likely, for a bull occurs on the Orpheus pavements at Littlecote Park, Newton St Loe and Withington (Smith 1969 pls. 3.16, 3.10 and 3.11).

Description of the animals

The Gryphon

This is the only mythical animal in the procession. It has an unusual rounded head with a protruding snout bearing two trailing 'beards' one grey, the other red. Its ears are pointed forwards and, like the body, are shaded yellow ochre. On its shoulders are wings, also yellow ochre, but broken by grey lines to represent feathers and by red and pale grey 'millefiori'. Along the body and hind legs are very pale grey diagonal bands.

The Bear

This great animal, head downwards and in a shuffling movement, has thick back legs with large clawed paws. His front legs are thinner and without such exaggerated pads, and his body is shaded very deep red with broad diagonal grey bands. tipped in orange, depicting a shaggy coat. His head is rather feline in character (compare his head with the felines) and has red 'whiskers'. At the top and bottom of his spine are tufts of hair.

The Leopard

Like the rest of the animals the leopard is walking with head and neck arched downwards. Its body is very pale grey and covered in yellow spots encircled with grey. The long tail curls up at the tip to avoid a tree. Like the bear and other felines he has dark red whiskers.

The Stag

The stag is not so well drawn as the felines: his head and nose are too long and his body more like that of a dog. He has an intense forward gaze with his right ear cocked forward and pale red antlers which not only break into the grey inner margin, but also extend into the guilloche border. His body is yellow ochre with a very pale grey belly.

The Tigress

This figure is one of the most striking in the group. Its body is yellow ochre but has a mass of broad, very deep red, red and grey stripes along its body and legs. Its tail starts rather too high up the back, but swirls around to cross the left foot. She has four teats outlined in orange and shaded very pale grey. Like the bear and other felines, she too has deep red whiskers and tufts of hair on the inside of her front legs.

The Lion

The lion is not so well-drawn as the tiger: his head projects a little too far from the mane, but nevertheless the rendering is striking with a boldly-drawn tousled mane in yellow ochre and deep red to indicate shadow. His body is also in yellow ochre and has diagonal pale grey lines similar to those on the stag and gryphon.

The Lioness

Of the lioness only the head, part of the shoulder, and tip of the tail are preserved. Dr Smith has suggested (Smith 1973, 3) that the figure may be a female panther; but too little is preserved and the face too stereotyped to be positive. Its head is similar to the tigress and leopard, and shaded yellow ochre.

The Boar

This is also fragmentary, and all that remains is part of its head, a front trotter, a curly tail and a hind leg. Its head and legs are predominantly very deep red, and its tail is pink and grey.

The Horse

Only its back legs and tail survive, but sufficient to tell that it was very pale grey with pale yellow diagonal lines along its body and rump. Its tail is yellow ochre and juts out awkwardly without the graceful flowing movement of the tails of the other beasts. This animal is unlikely to have been completely exposed in Lysons's time, for he shows it as a dog.

The Elephant (FIG. 26)

The elephant is lost, but the engraving shows a short-legged animal with an exaggerated trunk trailing along the ground, and a rippled left ear. Its right ear is shown in profile projecting above the animal's head, its feet are rounded and its tail short. The body is covered with latticed and criss-crossed lines. It could be questioned whether this is artistic licence on the part of the copyist; but the tree behind the elephant, the birds, and other patterns are very similar to surviving examples and therefore we must assume the engraving is a fairly faithful rendering. Perhaps it is not surprising that an elephant was incorrectly portrayed, for it is likely that to the Romano-British the animal was almost mythical and its form known only from drawings and travellers' tales.

The Outer Zone

Between the outer guilloche margin of the middle zone and the outer chain-guilloche circle is an acanthus-scroll springing from the ears of a bearded Oceanus mask (situated below Orpheus), with the red claws and legs of sea-creatures protruding from his hair. He has white staring eyes, outlined in grey with round pupils, and pink cheeks and forehead on which is a pale yellow square, set lozengewise. Also on his forehead is a 'bump' or central parting. The scroll is finely-worked and heavily foliated with leaves alternating in yellow ochre and greenish-brown. The undulating stalk forming the structure of the scroll is red and very pale grey. Because the scroll runs away in opposite directions from Oceanus it is not possible for it to join at the top of the pavement (where it is unfortunately damaged). The scroll therefore must either have been 'broken' here or have sprouted from a bowl such as at Chedworth.

The Spandrels

As already mentioned, the angles of the four spandrels each contained a square column-base; but the remaining area was filled by a pair of reclining naiads or water-nymphs. Only in one (the top right spandrel) are the figures near complete; they recline in opposite directions with their arms resting on rounded objects, one with white radial lines and the other with a red and white striped feature, both intended to represent water pouring from the mouths of overturned urns. About their bodies are cloaks, in yellow ochre and deep red, with red hems and folds. Their bodies are white and outlined in red and yellow ochre. One has curly hair with a top-knot while the other has her hair cut short. None of the figures is identical; the nymph to the left of Orpheus appears to be completely nude, yet her companion wears a cloak and short ankle-length boots. The figure top left of Orpheus also wears boots and seems to have been more heavily draped. The nymphs are superimposed on a dark grey background, a most unusual technique more akin to painting, on which white trailing bushes or perhaps water-weeds are represented. Technically, an interesting detail is that an attempt has been made to show the rounded form of the arms and legs (on some only) by setting the tesserae in a reticulated formation. This method of setting also occurs on the Satyrs and Maenads at Chedworth, a mosaic probably laid by the same mosaicist.

The Ambulatory

The ambulatory is made up of 20 square and four rectangular panels (the latter in the middle of each side) measuring in extent 132 ft (40.27 m). Although at first glance the panels appear varied there are only four schemes. The three panels on one side of a rectangle are mirrored on the opposite side. However, minor variations occur in the details, and these will be described following the description of each scheme. The framework of the schemes and repeating borders is grey.

Scheme 1

This occupies the four corners of the ambulatory and comprises an all-over spaced swastika-meander with the spaces staggered and containing a small square. Further elaboration of the pattern has been produced by making three of the quarters mirror-images of the first, with the result that a large guilloche square (equivalent to four small squares) and four rectangles (each equivalent to two small squares) occur in the centre and at the axis of the pattern. The small squares contain four stepped triangles, two red and two grey, and the large squares and rectangles contain guilloche.

Scheme 2

Two panels occur on each side of the pavement, next to Scheme 1, and consist of a circle of chain guilloche, within a linear square, containing concentric bands of ornament around a central medallion each of them bordered in right-angled Z-pattern in red, yellow and white. In the north and south ambulatories the medallions each contain a cantharus set against a pale yellow background, with a gadrooned neck and bowl, S-shaped handles and diminutive foot. In the east and west ambulatories the medallions are filled with red-tipped eight-petalled flowers on a pale yellow background. On the east side the intermediate zone between the inner and outer inscribed circles is filled with a band of waves, and on the west side with a band of thorns. The spandrels between the circle and the linear square contain heart-shaped red-tipped buds, some voluted.

Scheme 3

These schemes, based on a distribution of squares, octagons and crosses (see FIG. 4 B and discussion of this type, p. 30), two on each side of the mosaic on either side of the central rectangle, comprise visually a square with four lateral octagons contiguous with four chevrons in a field of lozenges and lateral triangles. The central panel of each is bordered with simple guilloche and contains a swastika-pelta with a central knot, each chevron an L-shaped strip of guilloche, and each lozenge a smaller rhomboid outlined in red and infilled with black (or *vice versa*). Some lozenges are quartered with a yellow line and opposing areas shaded red on grey. In each octagon is a flower. Opposing octagons either contain red-tipped eight-petalled flowers or, alternatively, conventionalised roses set in linear circles. The only deviation is in the east ambulatory, where four-petalled flowers with pointed excrescences occur.

Scheme 4

This rectangular scheme, one on each side of the pavement at its axis, comprises a rectangular panel of guilloche bordered by swastika-meander developing small squares at the angles containing red and black stepped triangles (similar to those in Scheme 1). Inside the panel is a linear lozenge containing a swastika-meander with double returns. The four interspaces contain solid grey (or red, see the south panel) triangles bordered in yellow.

The Outer Border

The ambulatory is surrounded by a band of three-strand guilloche followed by a coarse decorated border. This has a grey swastika-meander pattern on a pale yellow background with a small rectangular space containing a guilloche mat midway along each side. Around the meander is a right-angled Z-pattern in grey, red and yellow, followed by a thin band of yellow, a broad band of red and finally, skirting the wall, a band of yellow ochre.

Discussion and the Workmanship

The subject of Orpheus playing to and subduing the wild beasts is protrayed on 10 Romano-British mosaics, possibly 12. The other mosaics are, Barton Farm, Glos (FIG. 10, A) (Buckman and Newmarch 1850, pl. VII); Brading, IOW (Price and Price 1880-1; pl. facing p. 134); Dyer Street, Cirencester (Beecham 1886; pl. facing p. 266); Horkstow, S. Humberside (FIG. 10.J) (Hinks 1933, figs. 112-124); Littlecote Park, Wilts. (FIG. 10, L) (Smith 1969, pl. 3.16); Newton St Loe (FIG. 10, M) (Smith 1969, pl. 3.10); Whatley, Somerset, (Smith 1977, pl. 6 xxxb); Winterton, S. Humberside (No 83 and FIG. 11, T); and Withington, Glos. (FIG. 11, U) (Lysons ii, 1817, pl. xx). The two other possible mosaics are at Caerwent (Gwent) where a description (Strange 1779, 58) records 'the Reverend Mr. Thomas, curate of Caerwent, assured me that he remembered the figures of a lion, a tiger and a stag' and Pit Mead, Wilts. (Hoare 1821 pl. facing p. 113, fig. 4), where a very fragmentary roundel contains figured subjects. Except Whatley, where Orpheus was probably in a square, all the examples show Orpheus in a circle, at Brading and perhaps Pit Meads actually with his subjugated beasts, but elsewhere either alone, as at Littlecote Park and Winterton, or accompanied by a fox. At Barton Farm and Dyer Street, Cirencester, and at Woodchester Orpheus is encircled by two concentric zones, the inner containing birds, the outer zone large quadrupeds. At Newton St Loe and Withington Orpheus is surrounded by only one zone, with quadrupeds only and no birds — at Withington the birds have been placed in side-panels bordering the mosaic. At Horkstow, Littlecote Park and Winterton, however, he is surrounded by radial compartments in a 'wheel'-formation, each compartment containing an animal progressing anti-clockwise.

Littlecote Park has four compartments (and therefore four animals), and Horkstow and Winterton eight compartments (and eight animals). At Horkstow a combination of the two styles is introduced by dividing each panel into three zones by arcuated lines, the large quadrupeds in the outer zone, birds in the middle zone and small quadrupeds in the centre zone.

Of the pavements cited there can be little doubt that those at Barton Farm and probably Dyer Street are not only the work of the Corinian school to which Woodchester has been attributed, but also the work of the same mosaicist. Apart from the similar concentric schemes, many of the animals and patterns are almost identical. Other almost identical features include the birds, the laurel-wreath, the trees between the animals, the very pale grey trailing plants beneath and in between the animals, and similar foliation and borders. Reticulated setting also occurs at Barton Farm, on the lion. Other mosaics not merely attributed to the Corinian School but possibly products of the same mosaicist are at Chedworth (Room 5) and perhaps the Bacchus pavement from Stonesfield. In terms of quality the Chedworth pavement is superior (Grade 1) with smaller tesserae; but this may be partly explained by the fact that it is a considerably smaller mosaic. If the mosaicist had chosen to attempt the Woodchester pavement using the same-sized tesserae, the work would have taken considerably longer and perhaps been more expensive. Far more tesserae would have been required than the 753,000 (640,000 small tesserae, and 113,000 large coarse tesserae) calculated by the writer to have been used.

Smith considers the Newton St Loe, Pits Mead and Withinton pavements also to be the work of the Corinian school and to have been laid in that order — a theory based on the criteria of typological progression with a gradual increase of elaboration. He believes that the work at these sites was then followed by the Orpheus pavements at Barton Farm, Dyer Street and Woodchester. However, as Dr. Smith himself admits, there is a number of differences between the two groups which, in the opinion of the writer, bring into question whether all the Orpheus pavements attributed to the Corinian school are in fact products of the same *officina*. Admittedly all the animals on the pavements are separated by trees, but at Newton St Loe and Withington the trees are very different in style. At the former site there are two types, one with the branches splayed and the other with a clump of foliage more like a bush. At Withington all the trees are similar and each branch terminates in a large flower in the form of a calyx. The animals too are different. They do not parade in rhythm but prance about and lack the heavy muscular treatment of Woodchester and Barton Farm. One of the most striking differences between Withington and Woodchester and Barton Farm, however, is in the technique of construction.

At Withington the tesserae are loosely set and the faces and feet of the animals laid mainly in thin rectangular tesserae — a technique not used at Woodchester or Barton Farm, except for a V-shaped arrangement of tesserae in the red undulating line forming the scroll. At Withington the guilloche is also poorly worked in grey, red and off-white only. No yellow is employed.

Another reason given in the past for the attribution of the Newton St Loe and Withington pavements to the Corinian *officina* is the use of motifs occuring at Woodchester such as swastika-meander borders, eight-lozenged stars and intersecting circles. These patterns are found extensively elsewhere, however, and should not perhaps be taken as major criteria in assessing authorship. Degenerate patterns and workmanship in mosaics attributed to the Corinian school have been argued elsewhere by Smith to be later products, and therefore on account of the inferior workmanship at Newton St Loe and Withington we should perhaps even consider them as copies — mosaics influenced by the creative and original work of the Corinian school. Dating evidence for the mosaics discussed is meagre, but two coins discovered during the lifting of the Barton Farm pavement include one of Allectus (AD 293-6) in mint condition which could indicate a date of *c*. 300-20. A similar date-range for the Woodchester and Dyer Street pavements could be argued therefore rather than 325-50 as has been proposed, and it may be suggested that the other pavements discussed are later and not earlier. Whether they are the work of a Corinian *officina* is doubted, but they could be products of another *officina* based at Ilchester, evidence for which is growing. Perhaps the Whatley pavement is their work also.

The Woodchester mosaic is expertly laid and very neat and regular (Grade 2). The tesserae are closely set and laid with little error; the guilloche, so often a pointer to lazy work, is also expertly worked. Coloured backgrounds, such as fill the spandrels, is a technique not observed in the south of England, but it does occur at Horkstow, Lincs., in the mosaic of the painted ceiling', a panel adjacent to the Orpheus pavement (FIG. 10, J, right). The figure of Tyche at Brantingham (No 12) may also be quoted — she is set against a red roundel.

References. Toynbee 1962, 198, pl. 222: Toynbee 1964, 272, pl. LXI: Smith 1973.

[1] *Vetusta Monumenta* ii (1789), pl. XLIV, No. ii. A coloured pencil-drawing, possibly a copy by S. Lysons and the source of the engraving, is preserved in the Library of the Society of Antiquaries.

[2] Lysons 1797, p. 2.

[3] The presence of a rectangle on the north side raises the possibility of there having been a door here too.

APPENDIX 1

Mosaic drawings by the writer awaiting completion.[1]

1. Brantingham, N. Humberside. Mosaic discovered in 1941 and stolen in 1948 during lifting operations (see Slack 1948-51, 515). The working drawing shown on pl. 88 has recently been prepared by the writer using photographs taken in 1941.

2. Chedworth, Glos, Room 10. Saltire scheme with central medallion occupied by cantharus. *In situ*, drawn 1978.

3. Chedworth, Glos, Room 11. Rectangular panel with interlaced circles. *In situ*, drawn 1978.

4. Cirencester, Glos. Large mosaic discovered at Watermoor in 1958. (Rennie 1971, fig.4) with scheme of spaced octagons and rectangles. Buried. Drawn from photographs.

5. Cirencester, Glos. Building XII, i. Mosaic 4. Solid red oblong surrounded by broad white and red bands. Buried, drawn 1972.

6. Cirencester, Glos. Building XII, i. Mosaic 5. Solid red oblong against limestone background. Buried, drawn 1972.

7. Dorchester, Dorset. Fragmentary pavement from circular laconicum of thermae. Lifted, drawn 1978.

8. Dorchester, Dorset. Fragment with lozenge pattern from thermae. *In situ*, drawn 1978.

9. Foxcote villa, Bucks. Panel of guilloche preserved in Queens Temple, Stowe School. Drawn 1979.

10. Leicester, St. Nicholas Street. Repeating patterns with L-shapes and squares forming chequers. In Leicester Museums store. Drawn 1979.

11. Leicester, St. Nicholas Street. Fragment with dark grey background with patterns of small white cruciforms. In Leicester Museums store. Drawn 1979.

12. Leicester. Fragment with parallel red lines. In Leicester Museums store provenance uncertain. Drawn 1979.

13. Leicester. Fragment with white criss-cross lines against red background. In museum store no accession number, provenance uncertain, possibly Ruding Street. Drawn 1979.

14. Leicester. Fragment with lozenge pattern. In museum store. Acc. No. VIII. Drawn 1979.

15. Leicester, Norfolk Street (Cherry Orchard). Fragment with bands of simple and treble-strand guilloche. In museum store. Drawn 1979.

16. Leicester, Norfolk Street (Cherry Orchard). Corridor pavement with red criss-cross lines against grey background. Excavated and drawn 1979.

17. Leicester, Norfolk Street (Cherry Orchard). Red interlaced circles against grey background. Excavated and drawn 1979.

18. Roxby, S. Humberside. Large mosaic originally recorded by W. Fowler (Fowler Col. I.3) with central flower and swastika–peltae surround. *In situ,* drawn 1972.

19. Roxby, S. Humberside. Mosaic with two square panels; one with a swastika–meander developing squares in a quincunx arrangement and the other with red crissed-crossed lines. *In situ,* drawn 1972.

20. Wigginton, Oxon. Fragmentary corridor mosaic. *In situ,* drawn 1965.

[1] Since this monograph was submitted for publication the writer has added five more drawings to the collection: two mosaic fragments from Norfolk Street (Cherry Orchard), Leicester, two new mosaics from Chedworth, Glos. (Drawn 1980) and a mosaic from the Ebor brewery site at York.

APPENDIX 2

Mosaics with grids of octagons

Site	References	No: of Octagons (rows of)
1. Bath, Somerset. Bridewell Lane	Cunliffe 1969, pl. LXXXII	?
2. Bancroft, Bucks.	No. 8	5 × 3?
3. Cirencester, Glos. Dyer Street.	Buckman & Newmarch 1850, pl. II	3 × 3
4. Cirencester, Glos. Dyer Street.	No. 37	?
5. Cirencester, Glos. Victoria Road.	Clifford 1946-8, pl. III	4 × 3
6. Crondall, Hants.	Smith 1975, pl. CXXIII, 1	3 × 3
7. Dorchester, Dorset. Colliton Park	R.C.H.M. *Dorset* 1970, Vol ii, Pt. 3, pl. 220	4 × 3
8. Dorchester, Dorset. Fordington.	R.C.H.M. *Dorset* 1970, Vol ii, Pt. 3, Frontispiece	3 × 3
9. Gloucester. Eastgate Street.	No. 57	4 × 4
10. Kenchester, Hereford.	Jack 1916, Frontispiece	1 × 2
11. Keynsham, Somerset. Room H.	Bulleid & Horne 1926, pl. XII	2 × 3
12. Leicester. Jewry Wall Street.	V.C.H. *Leicestershire* i, pl. III	3 × 3
13. Leicester. St. Nicholas Street.	V.C.H. *Leicestershire* i, pl. I	3 × 3
14. Silchester, Hants.	Hope and Fox 1896, pl. XI (plan)	4 × 4
15. Southwell, Notts.★	Daniels 1966, fig. 13.	4 × 5?
16. Wellow, Somerset.	Brown Port. Somerset 87.	2 × 4
17. Witcombe, Glos.	Smith 1975, pl. CXXV	3 × 3
18. Woodchester, Glos.	Lysons 1797, pl. XIX	3 × 3 rotated

★ A small linear pattern and not a scheme drawn in guilloche.

INDEX

PLATES

1 Aldborough, Yorks. Lion beneath a tree

0   1   3 Ft

0   1 M

DSN

2   Aldborough, Yorks. Eight-petalled flower

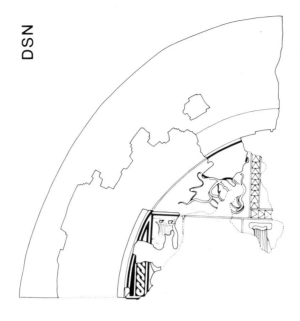

DSN

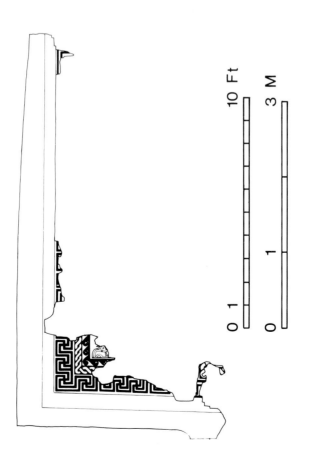

10 Ft

3 M

0 1

0 1

1

3 Aldborough, Yorks. The Muses mosaic

0   1   3 Ft

0   1 M

4 Aldborough, Yorks. Guilloche mat

DSN

5   Bancroft, Bucks.   Corridor pavement

0   5   10 Ft

0   1   4 M

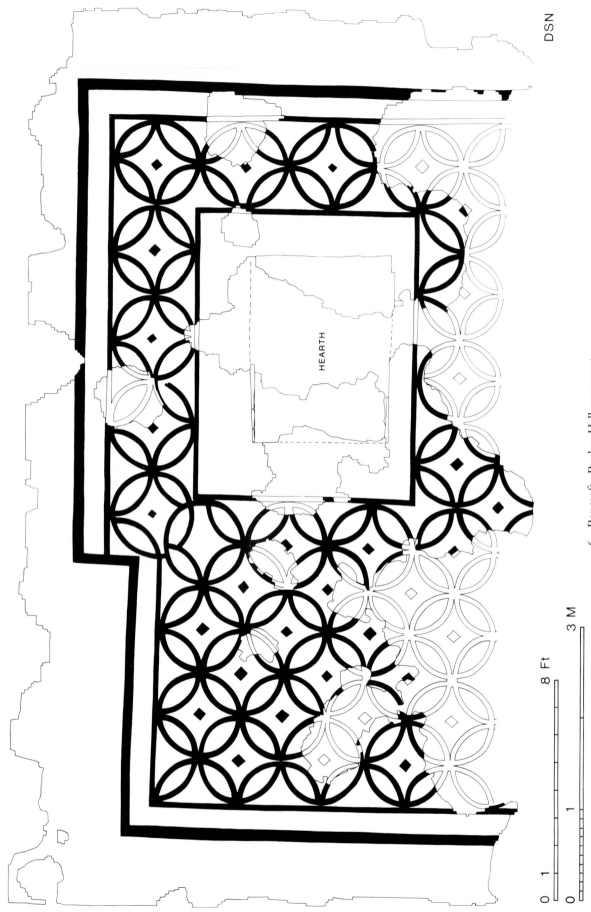

DSN

HEARTH

6 Bancroft, Bucks. Hall pavement

8 Ft

3 M

0 1

0

0   1   3 Ft

0   1 M

DSN

7   Bancroft, Bucks. Geometric square

DSN

8 Bancroft, Bucks. Grid of octagons

DSN

9 Beadlam, Yorks. Geometric

3 Ft

1 M

0 1   6 Ft

0 1   2 M

12   Brantingham, N. Humberside, Tyche and Nymphs
(See colour plates between pp. 104-5.)

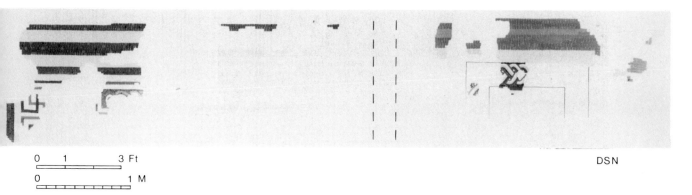

10 and 11   Bishopstone Down, Wilts. Fragments

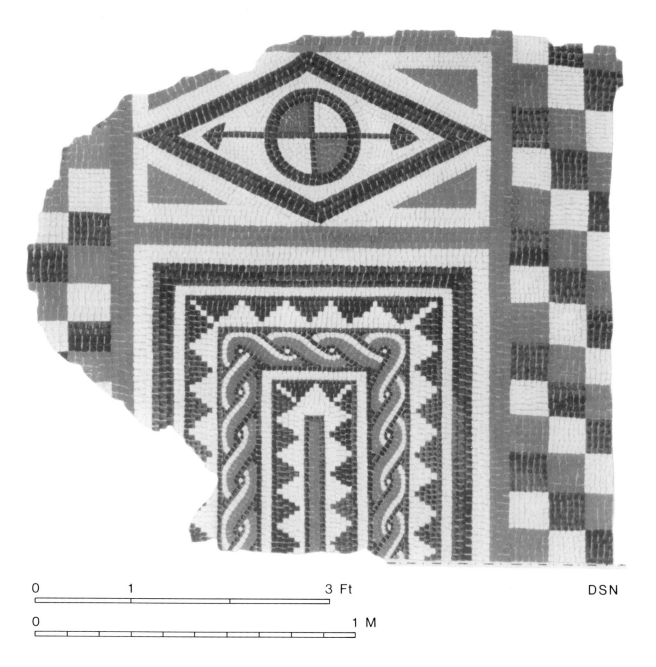

13   Brantingham, N Humberside. Corridor pavement

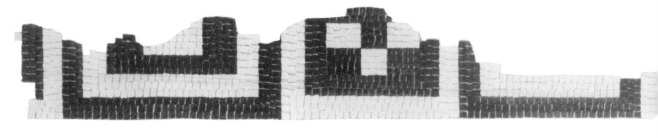

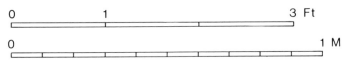

0   1   3 Ft

0   1 M

DSN

14   Brantingham, N Humberside. Fragment

0   1   6 Ins

0 1   25 Cms

DSN

15   Brantingham, N Humberside. Fragment

0   1   3 Ft   DSN

0   1 M

16 Caerwent, Gwent. Cantharus and Dolphins

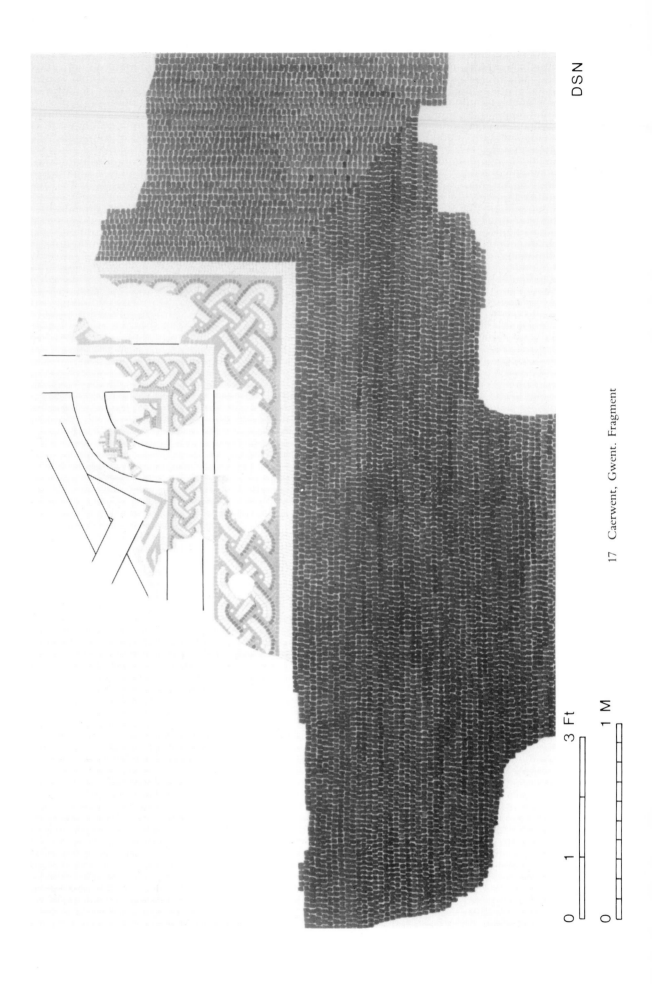

DSN

17 Caerwent, Gwent. Fragment

3 Ft

1 M

0   1

0

0   1   3 Ft   DSN

0   1 M

18   Carisbrooke, Isle of Wight. Fragment

DSN

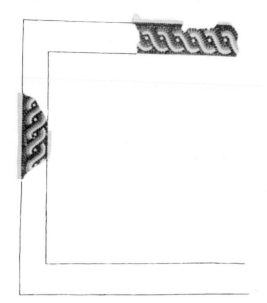

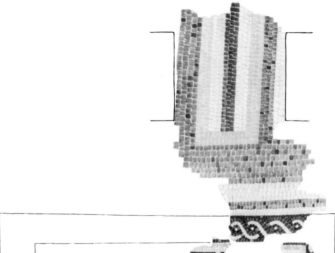

19   Chedworth, Glos. Meander pattern

0   1   3 Ft

0   1 M

0 1 3 Ft

0 1 M

DSN

20 Chichester, Sussex. Squared rosette

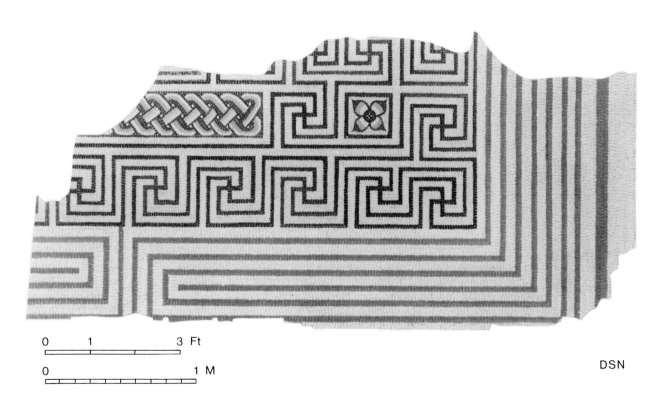

0 1 3 Ft

0 1 M

DSN

21 Cirencester, Glos. Meander and Labyrinth

22 Cirencester, Glos. Saltire pattern

0   1   3 Ft

0   1 M

23 Cirencester, Glos. Corridor pavement

0   1   3 Ft

0   1 M   DSN

24 Cirencester, Glos. Corridor mosaic

0   1   3 Ft

DSN   0   1 M

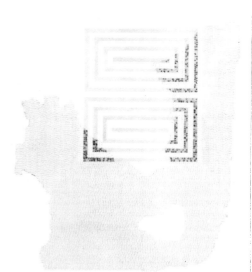

0 1 3 Ft

0 1 M

DSN

25a Cirencester, Glos. Hare mosaic (overall)

DSN

25b Cirencester, Glos. Hare mosaic (panel A)

3 Ft

0   1

1 M

0

0   1   3 Ft

0   1 M

DSN

25c   Cirencester, Glos. Hare mosaic (panel B)

0   1   3 Ft

0   1 M

DSN

26 Cirencester, Glos. Meander pattern

DSN

27 Cirencester, Glos. Labyrinth mosaic

0 ————————————— 1
0 ———————————— 1
6 Ft
2 M

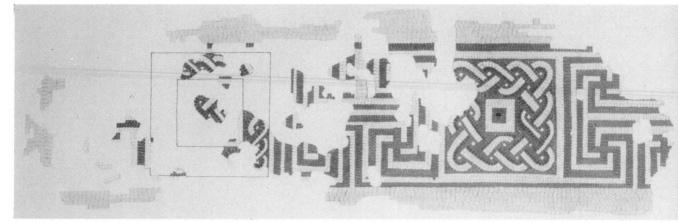

0   1   3 Ft

0   1 M

28 Cirencester, Glos. Meander

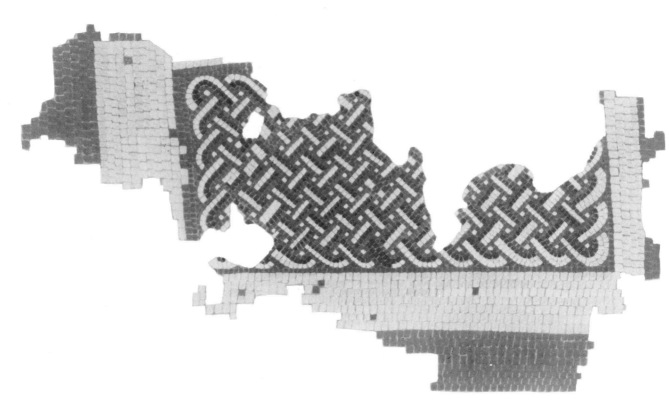

0   1   3 Ft

0   1 M

29 Cirencester, Glos. Guilloche mat

0   1   3 Ft

0   1 M

30   Cirencester, Glos. Roundle with flower

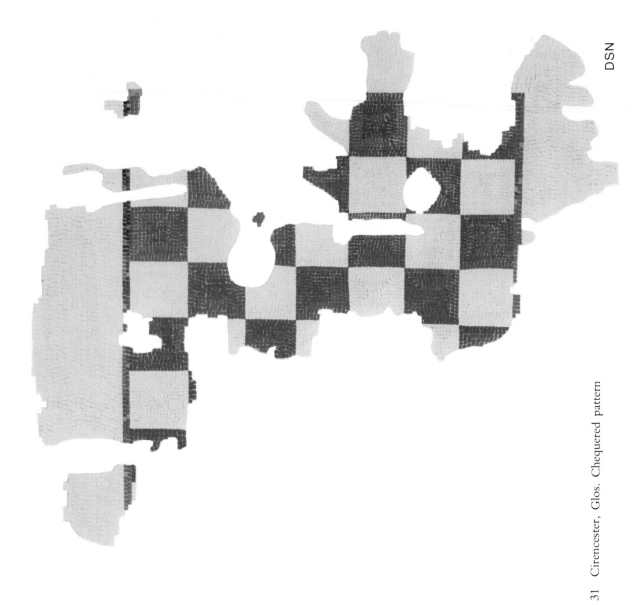

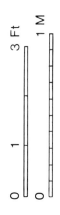

DSN

31 Cirencester, Glos. Chequered pattern

3 Ft

1 M

1

1

0

0

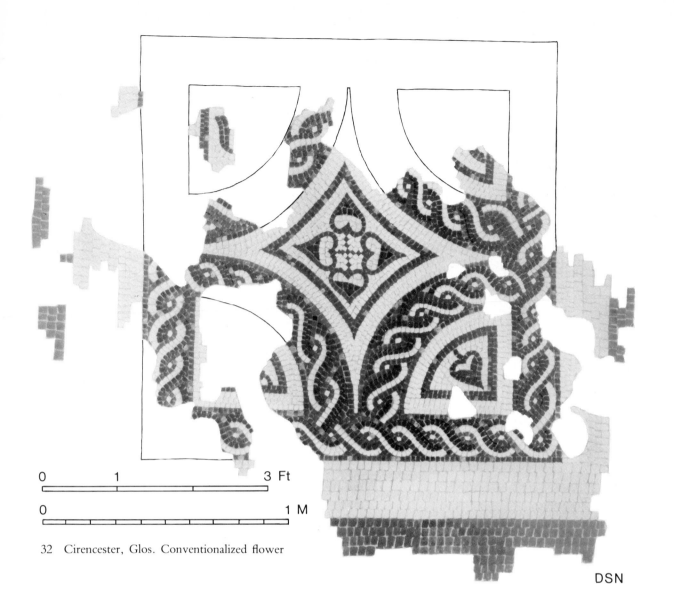

0   1   3 Ft

0   1 M

32   Cirencester, Glos. Conventionalized flower

DSN

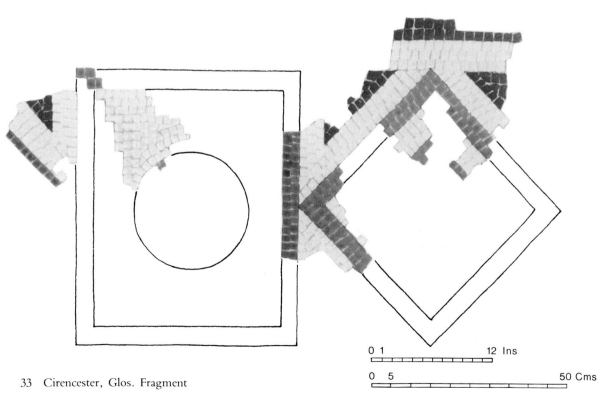

33   Cirencester, Glos. Fragment

0 1   12 Ins

0   5   50 Cms

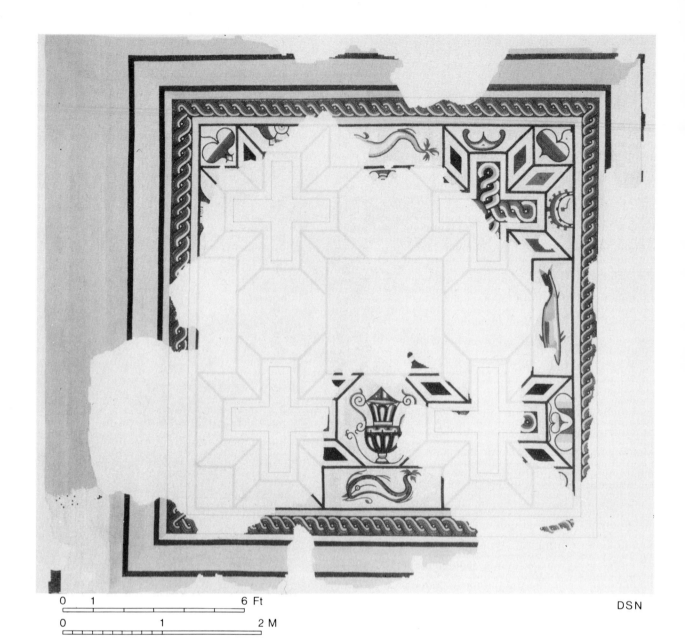

0 1   6 Ft

0   1   2 M

DSN

34 Cirencester, Glos. Dolphins and Canthari

0 1   12 Ins

0 5   50 Cms

DSN

35 Cirencester, Glos. Corridor fragment

0   1   3 Ft

0   1 M

DSN

36   Cirencester, Glos. Interlaced squares

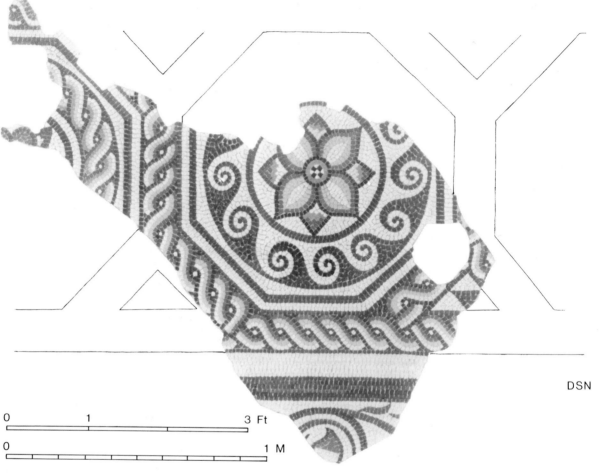

DSN

0   1   3 Ft

0   1 M

37   Cirencester, Glos. Octagons with flowers

0 1   3 Ft

0   1 M

DSN

38 Colchester, Essex. Four-petalled flower

0 1   3 Ft

0   1 M

39 Colchester, Essex. Cantharus

0   1   3 Ft

0   1 M

DSN

40   Colchester, Essex. Dahlia flower

0   1   3 Ft

0   1 M

DSN

41   Colchester, Essex. Radial mosaic

DSN

42 Combley, Isle of Wight. Octagon and peltae mosaic

3 Ft

1 M

0   1

0   1

0   1   3 Ft

0   1 M

DSN

43 Eccles, Kent. Gladiator mosaic

DSN

3 Ft

1 M

1

1

0

0

44 Fishbourne, Sussex. Amphorae and fishes

0 1 3 Ft

0 1 M

DSN

45 Fullerton, Hants. Mars

0   1   3 Ft

0   1 M

DSN

46   Fullerton, Hants. Pelta pattern

DSN

0   1   3 Ft

0   1 M

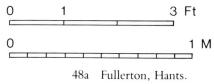

47   Fullerton, Hants. Ashlar pattern

48a   Fullerton, Hants.

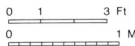

0   1   3 Ft

0   1 M

DSN

48b Fullerton, Hants. Labyrinth

0   1   3 Ft

0   1 M

DSN

49   Fullerton, Hants. Meander patterns

0   1   3 Ft

0   1 M

DSN

50   Fullerton, Hants. Geometric

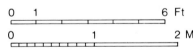

DSN

51 Gadebridge Park, Herts. Eight lozenge stars

0   1   3 Ft

0   1 M

DSN

52   Gloucester, Glos. Bacchus and Leopard

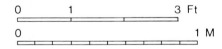

0   1   3 Ft

0   1 M

DSN

53   Gloucester, Glos. Fragments

0   1   3 Ft

0   1 M

54   Gloucester, Glos. Fragment

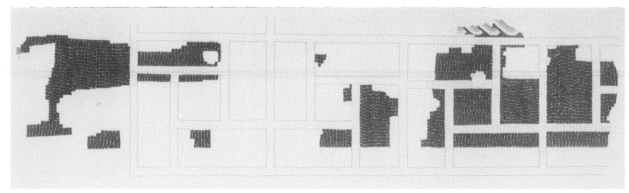

0 1 3 Ft

0 1 M

DSN

55 Gloucester, Glos. Border fragments

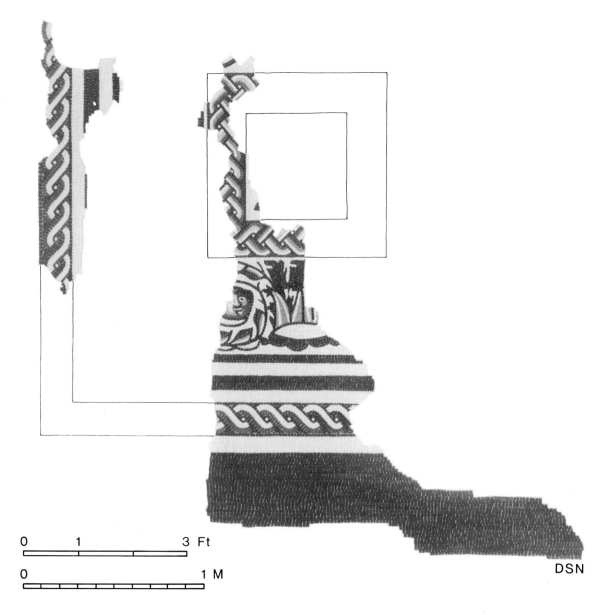

0 1 3 Ft

0 1 M

DSN

56 Gloucester, Glos. Acanthus Scroll and human mask

DSN

57 Gloucester, Glos. Scheme of octagons

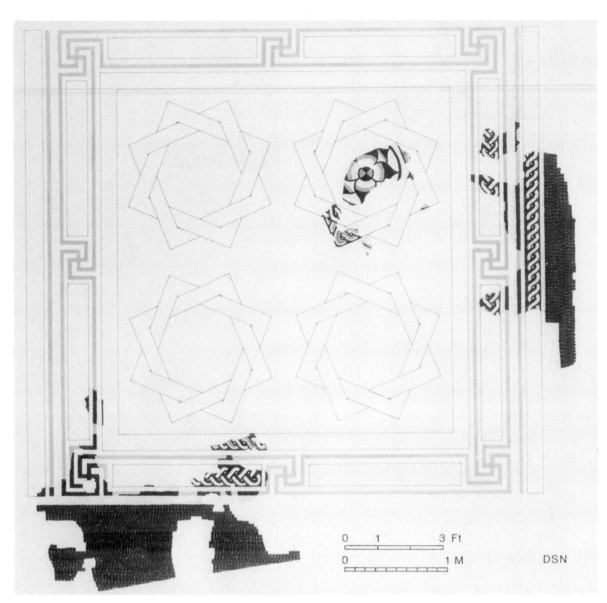

58   Gloucester, Glos. Interlaced squares

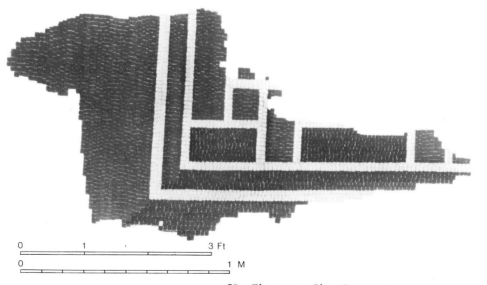

59   Gloucester, Glos. Fragment

DSN

60 Gorhambury, Herts. Bands of guilloche and scroll

3 Ft

1 M

0   1

0

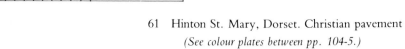

61   Hinton St. Mary, Dorset. Christian pavement
(See colour plates between pp. 104-5.)

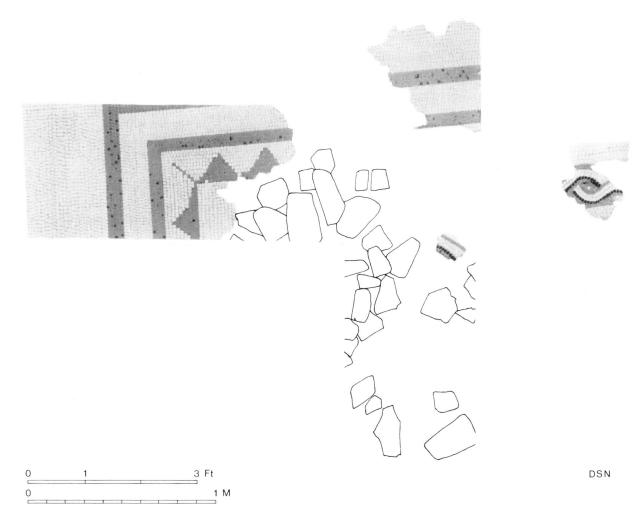

0   1   3 Ft

0   1 M

DSN

62   Hinton St Mary, Dorset. Fragment

0   1   3 Ft

0   1 M

63   Kingscote, Glos. Venus mosaic
(See colour plates between pp. 104-5.)

64 London. Cantharus

DSN

3 Ft

1 M

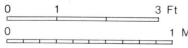

0   1   3 Ft

0   1 M

65   Rapsley, Surrey. Geometric with L-shaped panels

0   1   3 Ft

0   1 M

DSN

66   Rudston, Yorks. Venus

0   1   3 Ft

0   1 M

67   Rudston, Yorks. Aquatic scene

0   1   3 Ft

0   1 M

68   Rudston, Yorks. Geometric

0 1   3 Ft

0   1 M

69 Rudston, Yorks. The Charioteer mosaic
(See colour plates between pp. 104-5.)

0   1   3 Ft

0   1 M

DSN

70 Rudston, Yorks. Interlaced circles

0   1   3 Ft

0   1 M

71 Sparsholt, Hants. Flower

0   1   3 Ft

0   1 M

DSN

72   Thenford, Northants. Portrait medallion

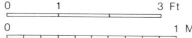

0   1   3 Ft

0   1 M

DSN

73   Verulamium, Herts.   Dolphins and fountain
(See colour plates between pp. 104-5.)

0   1   6 Ft

0   1   2 M

74   Verulamium, Herts. Bacchus mosaic

0   1   6 Ft

0   1   2 M

75 Verulamium, Herts. Lion mosaic

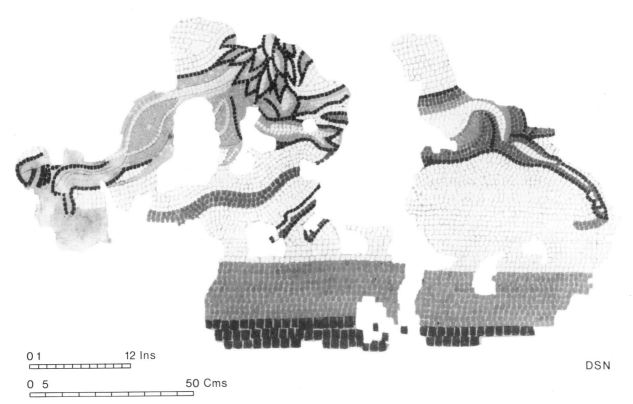

0 1   12 Ins

0 5   50 Cms

76 Verulamium, Herts. Hunting scene

0 1   12 Ins

0 5   50 Cms

77 Wideford, Oxon. Geometric

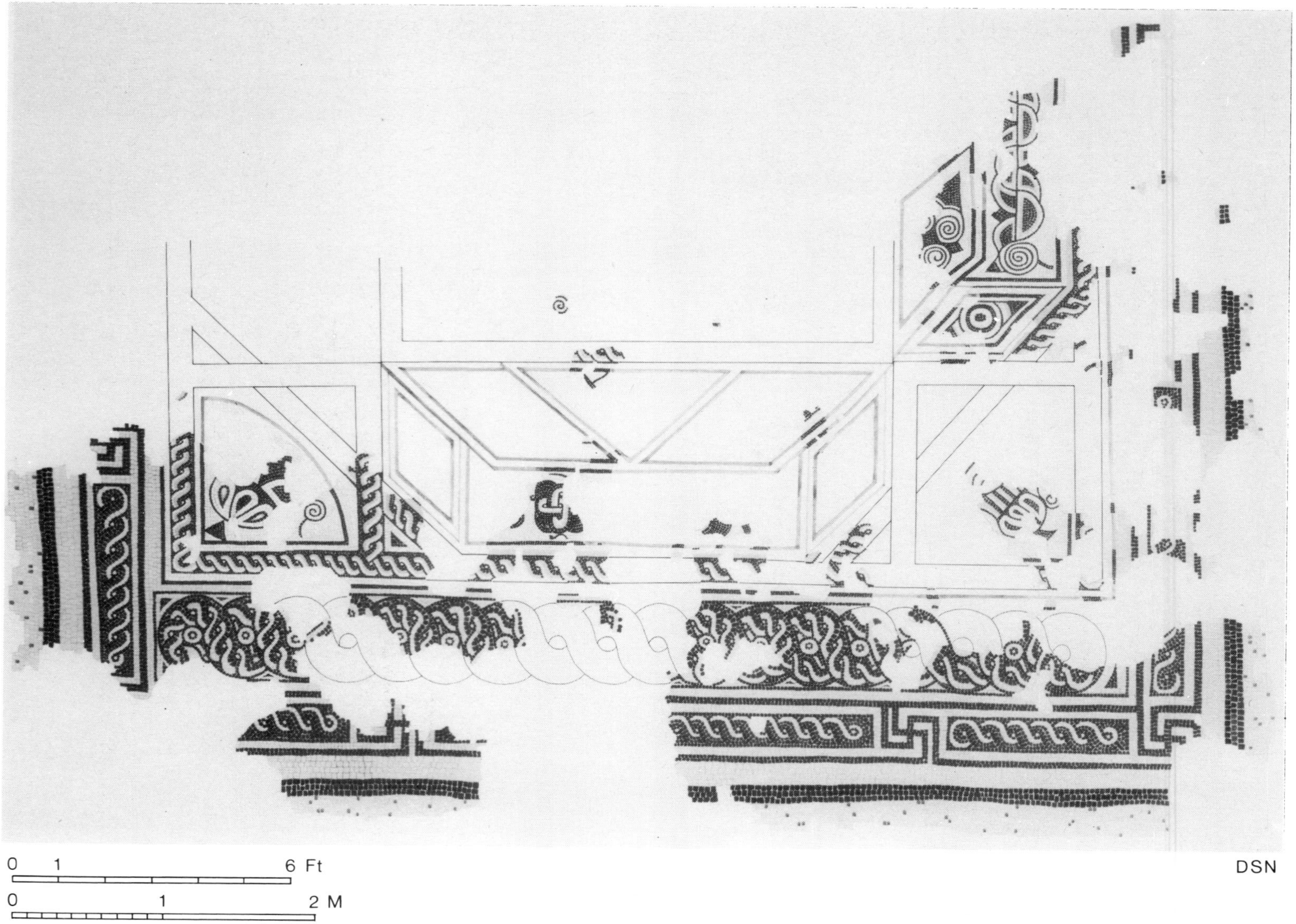

78 Wigginton, Oxon. Interlaced squares

0 ____ 1 ____ 6 Ft

0 ____ 1 ____ 2 M

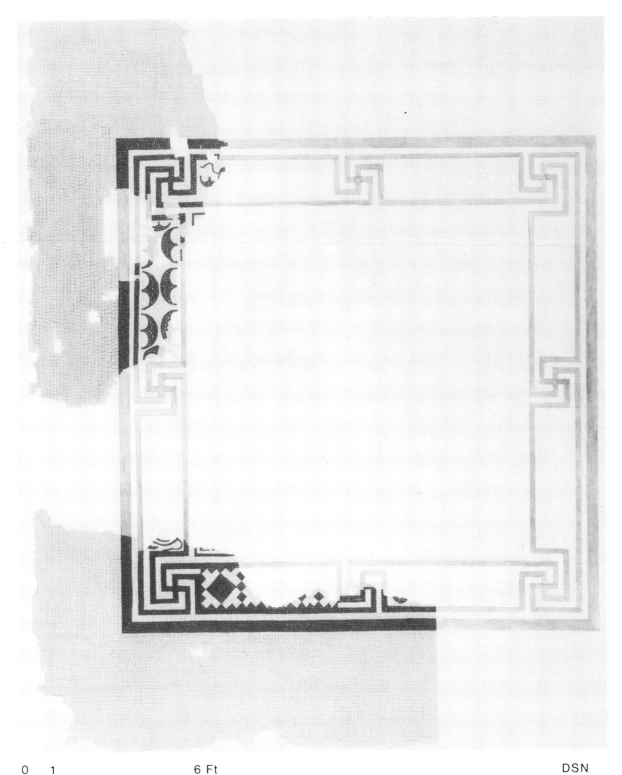

0 1   6 Ft

0   1   2 M

DSN

79 Wigginton, Oxon. Meander border fragment

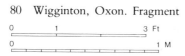

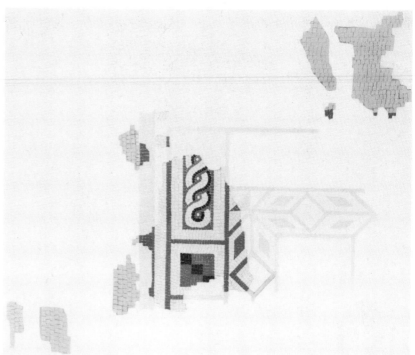

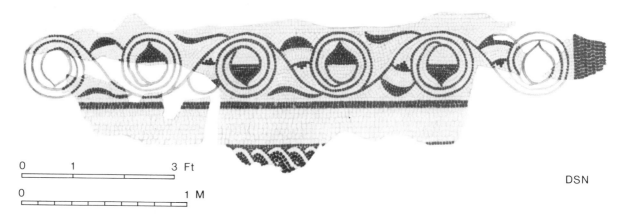

DSN

81 Winterton, S Humberside. Scroll pattern

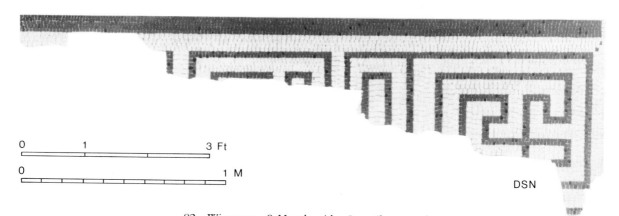

DSN

82 Winterton, S Humberside. Swastika-meander

0 1   6 Ft

0   1   2 M

DSN

83   Winterton, S Humberside. Orpheus mosaic

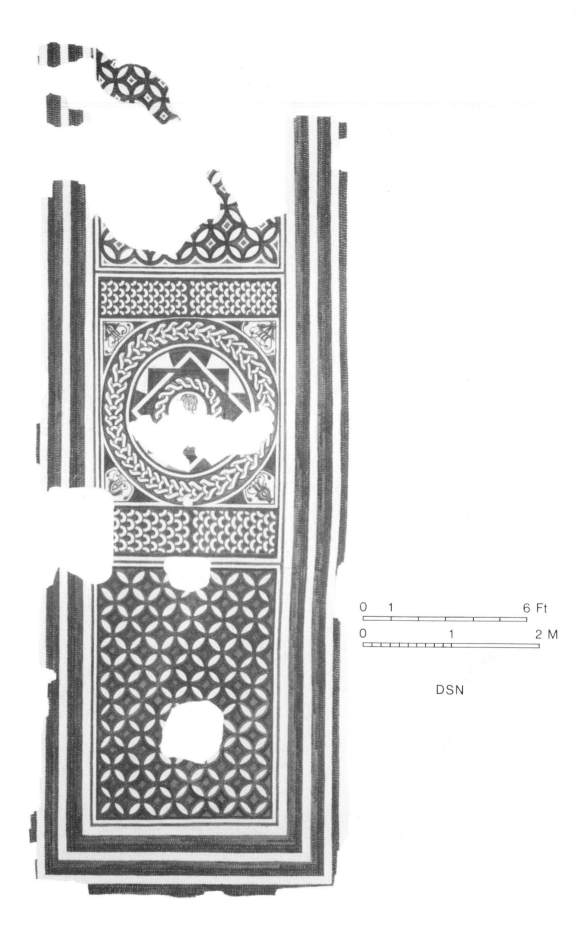

0 1 6 Ft

0 1 2 M

DSN

84   Winterton, S Humberside. Fortuna

DSN

85   Winterton, S Humberside. Providentia

0 1   12 Ins

0   5   50 Cms

86   Winterton, S Humberside. Geometric

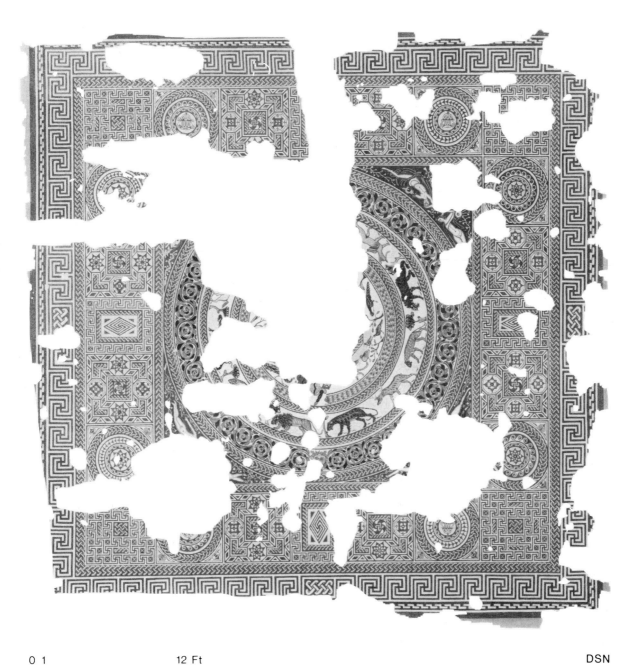

0 1   12 Ft

0   1   4 M

DSN

87a   Woodchester, Glos. The Great Pavement (overall)
(See colour plates between pp. 104-5.)

DSN

87b Woodchester, Glos. The Great Pavement (detail).

0 1   6 Ft

0   1   2 M

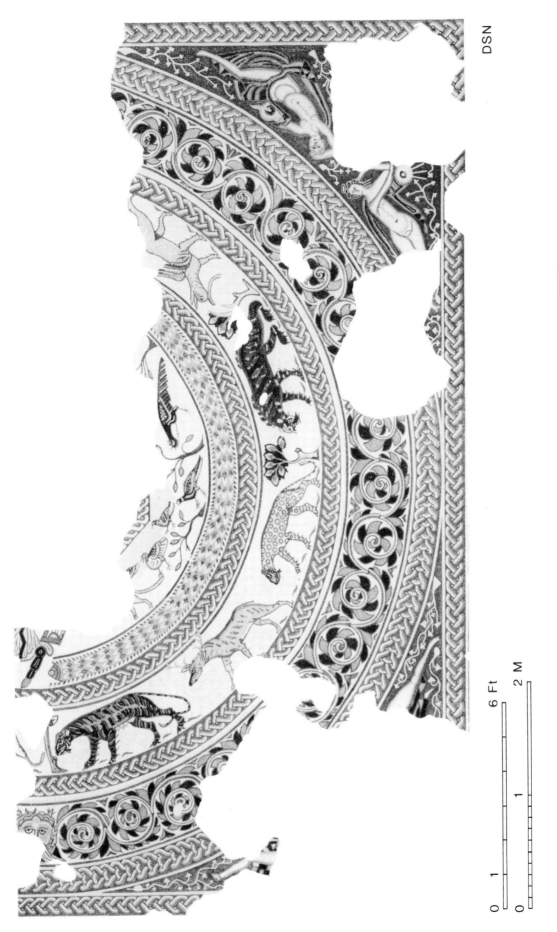

DSN

6 Ft

2 M

0   1

0   1

87c   Woodchester, Glos. The Great Pavement (detail of the animal procession).

0   1   3 Ft

0   1 M

DSN

88   Brantingham, N Humberside. Mosaic discovered in 1941 and stolen in 1948 during lifting operations! Drawing prepared from photographs taken in 1941